IFIP Advances in Information and Communication Technology 311

IFIP – The International Federation for Information Processing

IFIP was founded in 1960 under the auspices of UNESCO, following the First World Computer Congress held in Paris the previous year. An umbrella organization for societies working in information processing, IFIP's aim is two-fold: to support information processing within its member countries and to encourage technology transfer to developing nations. As its mission statement clearly states,

> *IFIP's mission is to be the leading, truly international, apolitical organization which encourages and assists in the development, exploitation and application of information technology for the benefit of all people.*

IFIP is a non-profitmaking organization, run almost solely by 2500 volunteers. It operates through a number of technical committees, which organize events and publications. IFIP's events range from an international congress to local seminars, but the most important are:

- The IFIP World Computer Congress, held every second year;
- Open conferences;
- Working conferences.

The flagship event is the IFIP World Computer Congress, at which both invited and contributed papers are presented. Contributed papers are rigorously refereed and the rejection rate is high.

As with the Congress, participation in the open conferences is open to all and papers may be invited or submitted. Again, submitted papers are stringently refereed.

The working conferences are structured differently. They are usually run by a working group and attendance is small and by invitation only. Their purpose is to create an atmosphere conducive to innovation and development. Refereeing is less rigorous and papers are subjected to extensive group discussion.

Publications arising from IFIP events vary. The papers presented at the IFIP World Computer Congress and at open conferences are published as conference proceedings, while the results of the working conferences are often published as collections of selected and edited papers.

Any national society whose primary activity is in information may apply to become a full member of IFIP, although full membership is restricted to one society per country. Full members are entitled to vote at the annual General Assembly, National societies preferring a less committed involvement may apply for associate or corresponding membership. Associate members enjoy the same benefits as full members, but without voting rights. Corresponding members are not represented in IFIP bodies. Affiliated membership is open to non-national societies, and individual and honorary membership schemes are also offered.

Charles Palmer   Sujeet Shenoi (Eds.)

Critical Infrastructure Protection III

Third Annual IFIP WG 11.10 International Conference
on Critical Infrastructure Protection
Hanover, New Hampshire, USA, March 23-25, 2009
Revised Selected Papers

 Springer

Volume Editors

Charles Palmer
Dartmouth College, I3P
Hanover, NH 03755, USA
E-mail: charles.c.palmer@dartmouth.edu

Sujeet Shenoi
University of Tulsa
Tulsa, OK 74104, USA
E-mail: sujeet@utulsa.edu

CR Subject Classification (1998): B.8, C.4, B.1.3, B.2.3, B.7.3, C.2, I.6

ISSN   1868-4238
ISBN-13   978-3-642-26040-7 Springer Berlin Heidelberg New York

springer.com

© IFIP International Federation for Information Processing 2009
Softcover reprint of the hardcover 1st edition 2009

Typesetting: Camera-ready by author, data conversion by Scientific Publishing Services, Chennai, India
Printed on acid-free paper   SPIN: 12768615   06/3180   5 4 3 2 1 0

Contents

Contributing Authors

Francesco Adinolfi is a Senior Researcher at the Research Center for Information and Communications Technologies (CRIAI), Portici, Italy. His research interests include knowledge management systems, ontologies and knowledge models, grid computing and open-source platforms.

Zaw Zaw Aung is a Ph.D. student of Information Science and Control Engineering at Nagaoka University of Technology, Nagaoka, Japan. His research interests include operational risk management, interdependency analysis and critical infrastructure modeling.

Fabrizio Baiardi is a Professor of Informatics at the University of Pisa, Pisa, Italy. His research interests include critical infrastructure protection, risk management of information and communications systems, and virtualization-based approaches.

Jonathan Butts is a Ph.D. student in Computer Science at the University of Tulsa, Tulsa, Oklahoma. His research interests include network, telecommunications and SCADA systems security.

Andrea Carcano is a Researcher at the University of Insubria, Varese, Italy. His research interests include industrial SCADA protocols and architectures.

Rodrigo Chandia is a Ph.D. student in Computer Science at the University of Tulsa, Tulsa, Oklahoma. His research interests include SCADA security, computer security and open-source software development methodologies.

Stefano De Porcellinis is a Researcher at University Campus Bio-Medico of Rome, Rome, Italy. His research interests include critical infrastructure modeling, simulation environments for complex systems, and fuzzy and nonlinear control techniques.

Giovanni Dipoppa is a Senior Researcher in the Department of Modeling and Simulation at ENEA Casaccia Laboratories, Rome, Italy. His research interests include real-time embedded systems, machine learning and operations research.

Scott Dynes is a Senior Research Fellow at the Center for Digital Strategies, Tuck School of Business, Dartmouth College, Hanover, New Hampshire. His research interests include information risk management and the resilience of critical infrastructures to cyber disruptions.

Samuel East received his M.S. degree in Computer Science from the University of Tulsa, Tulsa, Oklahoma. His research interests include network security and SCADA systems security.

Thoshitha Gamage is a Ph.D. student in Computer Science at the Missouri University of Science and Technology, Rolla, Missouri. His research interests include information assurance, infrastructure protection and formal methods.

Rajni Goel is an Associate Professor of Information Systems and Decision Sciences at Howard University, Washington, DC. Her research interests include information assurance, forensics, control systems security and data mining.

James Graham is the Henry Vogt Professor of Computer Science and Engineering at the University of Louisville, Louisville, Kentucky. His research interests include information security, digital forensics, critical infrastructure protection, high performance computing and intelligent systems.

Dimitris Gritzalis is a Professor of ICT Security and the Director of the Information Security and Critical Infrastructure Protection Research Group at Athens University of Economics and Business, Athens, Greece. His research interests include critical ICT infrastructure protection, security in ubiquitous computing, IT security paradigms, VoIP security and IT security education.

Jian Guan is an Associate Professor of Computer Information Systems in the College of Business and Public Administration at the University of Louisville, Louisville, Kentucky. His research interests include ontological modeling, fault diagnosis and sales force automation systems.

Janne Hagen is a Ph.D. candidate in Computer and Information Science from the Norwegian Defence Research Establishment, who is studying at the University of Oslo, Oslo, Norway. Her research interests include information security, critical infrastructure protection and risk assessment.

Mark Hartong is a Senior Electronics Engineer with the Office of Safety, Federal Railroad Administration, U.S. Department of Transportation, Washington, DC. His research interests include information assurance, digital forensics, network security, control systems security, risk analysis and theoretical computer science.

Jeffrey Hieb is an Assistant Professor of Engineering Fundamentals at the University of Louisville, Louisville, Kentucky. His research interests include information security, honeypots, digital forensics, secure operating systems and engineering education.

Stig Johnsen is a Senior Research Scientist at SINTEF, Trondheim, Norway. His research interests include information security, SCADA systems, integrated oil and gas operations, and plant safety.

Kyoung-Don Kang is an Assistant Professor of Computer Science at the State University of New York at Binghamton, Binghamton, New York. His research interests include real-time data services, wireless sensor networks, and wireless network and embedded system security.

Hugo Kleinhans is a Ph.D. student in Computer Science at the University of Tulsa, Tulsa, Oklahoma. His research interests include distributed systems, critical infrastructure protection, digital forensics and cyber policy.

Panos Kotzanikolaou is a Lecturer of IT Security and Privacy at the University of Piraeus, Piraeus, Greece; and a Senior Member of the Information Security and Critical Infrastructure Protection Research Group at Athens University of Economics and Business, Athens, Greece. His research interests include critical ICT infrastructure protection, mobile code/agent security, intelligent network security and sensor network security.

Marc Laperrouza is a Postdoctoral Fellow in the College of Management at the Swiss Federal Institute of Technology, Lausanne, Switzerland. His research interests include the reform and regulation of network industries.

Marcelo Masera is a Scientific Officer at the Institute for the Protection and Security of the Citizen, Joint Research Center of the European Commission, Ispra, Italy. His research interests include the security of networked systems and systems of systems, risk governance, and control systems and communication systems security.

Vincenzo Masucci is a Senior Researcher at the Research Center for Information and Communications Technologies (CRIAI), Portici, Italy. His research interests include knowledge representation, ontologies and knowledge models, and their applications in the critical infrastructure domain.

Bruce McMillin is a Professor of Computer Science at the Missouri University of Science and Technology, Rolla, Missouri. His research interests include critical infrastructure protection, computer security, formal methods, distributed systems and parallel algorithms.

Igor Nai Fovino is a Scientific Officer at the Institute for the Protection and Security of the Citizen, Joint Research Center of the European Commission, Ispra, Italy; and a Contract Professor of Operating Systems at the University of Insubria, Varese, Italy. His research interests include system survivability, formal methods for security assessment, secure communication protocols and privacy-preserving data mining.

Gabriele Oliva is a Ph.D. student in Computing and Automation at the Third University of Rome, Rome, Italy. His research interests include critical infrastructure protection, interdependency modeling and mobile robots.

Paul Oman is a Professor of Computer Science at the University of Idaho, Moscow, Idaho. His research interests include various aspects of information assurance, especially securing real-time systems used in critical infrastructure assets.

Stefano Panzieri is an Associate Professor of Automatic Control at the Third University of Rome, Rome, Italy. His research interests include sensor and data fusion, infrastructure modeling and analysis, and mobile robots.

Mauricio Papa is an Associate Professor of Computer Science at the University of Tulsa, Tulsa, Oklahoma. His research interests include distributed systems, information assurance, and network and SCADA systems security.

Julian Rrushi is a Postdoctoral Research Associate at the Oak Ridge National Laboratory, Oak Ridge, Tennessee. His research focuses on the application of applied mathematics and statistics to cyber security.

Paolo Servillo is a Junior Researcher at the Research Center for Information and Communications Technologies (CRIAI), Portici, Italy. His research interests include knowledge representation and knowledge management.

Roberto Setola is the Director of the Complex Systems and Security Laboratory at University Campus Bio-Medico of Rome, Rome, Italy. His research interests include critical infrastructure modeling and analysis, critical infrastructure protection, risk assessment and control strategies for complex systems.

Daniele Sgandurra is a Ph.D. student of Informatics at the University of Pisa, Pisa, Italy. His research interests include ICT systems security, intrusion detection systems and virtualization-based approaches.

Sujeet Shenoi, Chair, IFIP Working Group 11.10 on Critical Infrastructure Protection, is the F.P. Walter Professor of Computer Science at the University of Tulsa, Tulsa, Oklahoma. His research interests include information assurance, digital forensics, critical infrastructure protection, reverse engineering and intelligent control.

Torbjorn Skramstad is a Professor of Computer and Information Science at the Norwegian University of Science and Technology, Trondheim, Norway. His research interests include the safety and security of critical IT systems, and information systems design and testing.

Nils Svendsen is an Associate Professor at the Norwegian Information Security Laboratory, Gjovik University College, Gjovik, Norway. His research interests include the modeling and simulation of critical infrastructures, graph theory, cryptography and coding theory.

Claudio Telmon is an ICT Security Consultant in Pisa, Italy. His research areas include systems management and configuration, software development, audit, and the design and implementation of ICT and SCADA systems.

Marianthi Theoharidou is a Ph.D. candidate in ICT Security and a member of the Information Security and Critical Infrastructure Protection Research Group at Athens University of Economics and Business, Athens, Greece. Her research interests include infrastructure protection, risk assessment, the insider threat and IT security education.

Alberto Tofani is a Junior Researcher in the Department of Modeling and Simulation at ENEA Casaccia Laboratories, Rome, Italy. His research interests include complex systems modeling and simulation, critical infrastructure analysis and formal methods.

Alberto Trombetta is an Assistant Professor of Computer Science and Communication at the University of Insubria, Varese, Italy. His research interests include data security and privacy, data integration, query languages, imprecise data management and systems security.

Kenji Watanabe is an Associate Professor in the Graduate School of Management of Technology, Nagaoka University of Technology, Nagaoka, Japan. His research areas include IT risk management, business continuity management and critical infrastructure protection.

Kristopher Watts received his M.S. degree in Computer Science from the University of Idaho, Moscow, Idaho. His research interests include real-time operating systems development, security analysis and penetration testing.

Duminda Wijesekera is an Associate Professor of Information and Software Engineering at George Mason University, Fairfax, Virginia. His research interests include information, network, telecommunications and control systems security.

Stephen Wolthusen is a Professor of Information Security at the Norwegian Information Security Laboratory, Gjovik University College, Gjovik, Norway; and a Reader in Mathematics at Royal Holloway, University of London, London, United Kingdom. His research interests include the modeling and simulation of critical infrastructures using combinatorial and graph-theoretic approaches, and network and distributed systems security.

Preface

The information infrastructure – comprising computers, embedded devices, networks and software systems – is vital to operations in every sector: information technology, telecommunications, energy, banking and finance, transportation systems, chemicals, agriculture and food, defense industrial base, public health and health care, national monuments and icons, drinking water and water treatment systems, commercial facilities, dams, emergency services, commercial nuclear reactors, materials and waste, postal and shipping, and government facilities. Global business and industry, governments, indeed society itself, cannot function if major components of the critical information infrastructure are degraded, disabled or destroyed.

This book, *Critical Infrastructure Protection III*, is the third volume in the annual series produced by IFIP Working Group 11.10 on Critical Infrastructure Protection, an active international community of scientists, engineers, practitioners and policy makers dedicated to advancing research, development and implementation efforts related to critical infrastructure protection. The book presents original research results and innovative applications in the area of infrastructure protection. Also, it highlights the importance of weaving science, technology and policy in crafting sophisticated, yet practical, solutions that will help secure information, computer and network assets in the various critical infrastructure sectors.

This volume contains seventeen edited papers from the Third Annual IFIP Working Group 11.10 International Conference on Critical Infrastructure Protection, held at Dartmouth College, Hanover, New Hampshire, March 23–25, 2009. The papers were refereed by members of IFIP Working Group 11.10 and other internationally-recognized experts in critical infrastructure protection.

The chapters are organized into four sections: risk management, control systems security, infrastructure security, and infrastructure modeling and simulation. The coverage of topics showcases the richness and vitality of the discipline, and offers promising avenues for future research in critical infrastructure protection.

This book is the result of the combined efforts of several individuals and organizations. In particular, we thank Rodrigo Chandia, Jonathan Butts and Nicole Hall Hewett for their tireless work on behalf of IFIP Working Group 11.10. We gratefully acknowledge the Institute for Information Infrastructure

Protection (I3P), managed by Dartmouth College, for nurturing IFIP Working Group 11.10 and sponsoring some of the research efforts whose results are described in this volume. We also thank the Department of Homeland Security and the National Security Agency for their support of IFIP Working Group 11.10 and its activities. Finally, we wish to note that all opinions, findings, conclusions and recommendations in the chapters of this book are those of the authors and do not necessarily reflect the views of their employers or funding agencies.

CHARLES PALMER AND SUJEET SHENOI

I

RISK MANAGEMENT

Chapter 1

INFORMATION RISK MANAGEMENT AND RESILIENCE

Scott Dynes

Abstract   Are the levels of information risk management efforts within and between firms correlated with the resilience of the firms to information
disruptions? This paper examines the question by considering the results of field studies of information risk management practices at organizations and in supply chains. The organizations investigated differ
greatly in the degree of coupling from a general and information risk
management standpoint, as well as in the levels of internal awareness
and activity regarding information risk management. The comparison of
the levels of information risk management in the firms and their actual
or inferred resilience indicates that a formal information risk management approach is not necessary for resilience in certain sectors.

Keywords: Information risk management, resilience, field studies

1.   Introduction

Viewing information security in terms of managing information risk is a
compelling idea [2, 4, 6, 8, 9] and with good reason. For the information security
practitioner, it provides a wealth of tested risk management frameworks and
processes. For a business executive, it relates what is unfamiliar (information
security) to a very familiar process (managing business risks), enabling the
development of a shared vision of the information-security-related business risk
facing a firm.

Is information risk management (IRM) becoming a common information security practice following a lengthy gestation at the concept stage? This would
represent a maturing of information security processes, moving away from the
ad hoc approaches that were commonly used a few years ago [4]. Several processes that support information risk management, such as OCTAVE [1] and
RiskMAP [10], have been developed. While these processes are conceptually
similar, they differ significantly in terms of the resources required. To address

C. Palmer and S. Shenoi (Eds.): Critical Infrastructure Protection III, IFIP AICT 311, pp. 3–17, 2009.

this issue, OCTAVE comes in three "sizes" ranging from a lightweight small business version to a large enterprise-strength implementation.

We describe RiskMAP to provide a flavor of the information risk management approach. The RiskMAP process works at four levels: (i) top-level business objectives, (ii) business processes that support these objectives, (iii) information flows that support each business process, and (iv) IT assets (hardware and networks) that enable information flows. A ranking takes place at the top level so that the importance of various business objectives are codified as ratios. Dependencies between the levels are exposed by clarifying the impact of the unavailability of a subordinate entity on the success of superordinate entities. For example, how would the unavailability of a database server affect the various information flows? Or, what impact would the loss of an entire business process have on a firm's ability to meet its top-level business objectives?

RiskMAP incorporates four impact categories: (i) no impact, (ii) minor disruption with work-around, (iii) major disruption with work-around, and (iv) cannot accomplish task. Each of these impact categories is codified numerically. The result is a set of matrices that together describe the relative importance of business processes, information flows, etc. on the core objectives of a business. By manipulating these matrices, it is possible to rank the most critical IT devices or to determine the level of exposure of the top-level business objectives.

More concretely, a field study of an oil refinery using RiskMAP identified four mission objectives: "Stay Safe," "Supply Customers Well," "Stay in Compliance" and "Stay Profitable." Each objective was assigned a numeric weight of its relative importance that reflected the shared belief of the CISO and the VP of Refining. The next step enumerated the thirteen business processes that were needed to accomplish these objectives, such as "Offload and Store Crude" and "Perform Fractional Distillation." Evaluating the dependencies between the top-level objectives and the supporting processes resulted in a 4 × 13 impact matrix. Similarly, the information flows that support business processes are determined. The same categories are used to express the impact of the loss of each information flow on each process and the impact of the loss of each device that enables the information flow.

When using RiskMAP, it is important to determine the correct level of abstraction – the refinery had hundreds of information flows and thousands of devices, which was clearly unworkable. The process was rendered both feasible and valuable by abstracting the information flow and devices into groupings such as "Distillation Control Information." The RiskMAP process resulted in a set of matrices as well as a shared understanding between business executives and IT executives of how IT risk maps to business risk. As a result of using RiskMAP, the VP of Refining started looking at information security investments in a fundamentally different way – not as a sunk cost, but as an investment in business resilience.

It should be clear that the core activities of information risk management are to understand and clarify the sources of business risk, to determine the dependencies of business processes on IT, and to coordinate the organization's

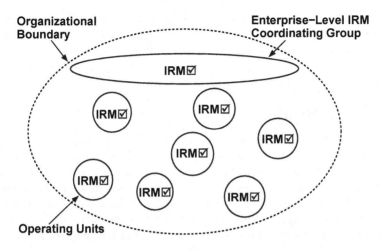

Figure 1. Information risk management process.

response. Clearly, the successful completion of these activities requires a detailed understanding of the firm. In small firms, it is likely that a general manager would have the required breadth and depth of knowledge about the firm. In the case of large firms, individual operating units would have to conduct the information risk management approach internally, and the results would be consolidated at higher organizational levels.

Figure 1 presents a canonical view of information risk management at a firm. Every operating unit conducts an internal information risk management effort; the results are consolidated at higher levels, including the enterprise level. An enterprise-level unit assists individual operating units and manages the information risk management process at the enterprise level, including the enactment of information security and business continuity efforts. Staff in the enterprise-level unit interact with business executives throughout the information risk management process.

This view can be applied to a supply chain as well. In this case, the "operating units" are individual firms that are part of the supply chain network. Unlike the highly integrated nature of an individual firm with its rich set of coordinating mechanisms, supply chain entities generally have few coordinating mechanisms that are primarily related to negotiations for goods and services. Supply chains also lack centralized control. The absence of standardized inter-firm information risk coordination signals and the lack of a central risk management coordinating unit suggest that supply chain networks would be more fragile to information disruptions than individual firms if, in fact, information risk management promotes resilience.

How do actual information risk management processes compare with the canonical model? What can be said about the efficacy of information risk management in promoting firm and sector resilience? This paper examines how closely information security efforts in firms correspond to the canonical information risk management model, and the consequences of various supply disruptions and IT disruptions on the production of goods and services in individual firms and in supply networks. To study these questions, we use data collected from field studies of a health care organization, a pharmaceutical firm, and a grocery store chain and its suppliers.

2.   Field Studies

The field studies consisted of interviews with security, supply chain executives and managers at the participating large firms; only the general manager was interviewed at small firms. The interviews were anonymous and designed to elicit the knowledge and beliefs of the interviewed individuals; audits or assessments beyond the interviews were not part of the study. Interviewees included top-level managers of information security, administration, clinical units and supply chains. Identical questions were asked of interviewees in the same organization to gauge the internal consistency of information provided in the interviews [7]. The interview questions centered on the identification and management of information security risks, and the resilience of the organization to information infrastructure disruptions.

3.   Health Care Field Study

The health care field study focused on an organization comprising a medium-sized hospital and co-located clinics; the organization also operates other hospitals and regional clinics. Several elements of this field study have been presented elsewhere (see, e.g., [3, 5]). The principal hospital houses a data center that runs many applications and databases. Most of the regional clinics depend on the principal hospital for access to the applications and databases, and, in many cases, the Internet.

The hospital uses IT to manage the processes that define the patient experience (e.g., scheduling and billing), the clinician experience (e.g., electronic medical records, documentation, prescriptions, radiological imaging and lab tests), administration (e.g., financial planning and supply management), and the hospital environment (e.g., HVAC). The systems that support these activities are a mix of home-grown systems and commercial off-the-shelf systems located at the data center of the primary hospital; external applications are provided over the Internet.

The hospital has a central information services (IS) department that manages the data center and applications. This department liaises with other departments and units that are heavy users of IT services. Some larger departments have their own small IS units.

3.1   Information Security Practices

Clinical and administrative unit interviewees considered information security as the responsibility of the IS department. Only one interviewee (from among interviewees from eleven units) believed information security to be a responsibility shared between his unit and IS. None of the clinical units had considered or developed contingency plans for information infrastructure disruptions. The unit responsible for supporting surgical patients and procedures, which had spent years developing applications to support its business operations, had never considered the consequences of its systems being infected by a virus. The radiology unit, which is very dependent on technology, had no contingency plans, only a list of phone numbers to call in the event of IT disruptions.

Only the materials acquisition unit had developed contingency plans. These included paper-based backup forms and staffing plans for the unit, and paper-based "favorites" lists that identified the supplies commonly ordered by various organizational units.

3.2 Canonical Model and Resilience

The information security practices uncovered in the health care field study differ greatly from the canonical model. In particular, an information risk management process was utilized in only one of the eleven units interviewed. Moreover, an effective information risk management coordinating group did not exist at the enterprise level. Information risk management was not being practiced by the organization at the time of the field study (November 2005 through February 2006).

As it turned out, the field study permitted the direct investigation of the impact of an information infrastructure disruption on the operations of the health care organization. A few months before the field study (August 2005), the hospital was infected by the Zotob worm [11]. The infection flooded the hospital intranet with network traffic, essentially a denial-of-service attack against the internal servers. Normal access to internal applications and the Internet was affected for approximately three days. However, the IS department was able to make the electronic health record system (widely regarded as the most critical application) available just one hour into the event.

While the worm infection had a significant impact on normal business processes at the hospital, there was little to no impact on the ability of the hospital to provide health care to its patients. The administrative and clinical units were able to provide patient care, with the exception of the radiology unit, which could take images but not deliver them to physicians via the intranet; and the radiation oncology unit, which was not operational. The hospital was resilient to the information infrastructure disruption largely because of the corporate culture. Many interviewees held the view that they simply had to make things happen – not providing patient care was not an option.

4. Pharmaceutical Firm Study

The pharmaceutical field study focused on a mid-size pharmaceutical firm that operates production, and research and development sites in several countries. The field study involved a series of interviews conducted during the first half of 2008.

The pharmaceutical firm is organized into business units along functional and geographic lines; examples include marketing, research and development, enterprise information systems, and U.S. operations. Individual business units have integrative levels of management, and may have local business-unit-specific or function-specific IS organizations. Each business unit has an information officer. At the enterprise level, overarching most business units is a set of enterprise-level information management groups responsible for developing and managing the enterprise architecture, information asset governance policies (e.g., email retention), compliance efforts (e.g., HIPAA and Sarbanes-Oxley) and enterprise-level information risk management. An enterprise-level information infrastructure (EII) group maintains the firm's networks and data centers, and manages enterprise-wide applications such as the enterprise resource planning (ERP) system, which is used across the enterprise. Manufacturing and distribution operations are highly dependent on the ERP system as well as on plant-level applications, including process control systems.

4.1   Information Security Practices

Each business unit has internal information risk management efforts that interact with other business units as necessary. The enterprise-level information risk management group (EIRM) works to understand information risk at the edges of the firm and to manage information risks that exist at the enterprise level.

The enterprise information infrastructure (EII) group views IT risk primarily from a traditional business continuity and disaster recovery perspective. EII approaches IT risk management as a partnership with application owners and users, viewing itself as a supplier of infrastructure but dependent on various application group partners in business units to work with internal users to determine the proper level of disaster recovery and business continuity efforts for each application. EII is responsible for business continuity and disaster recovery for enterprise-wide applications such as email. EII exercises disaster recovery plans twice a year for important IT-backed business processes. EII relies on EIRM for an overall enterprise-level risk assessment and vulnerability management plan; however, EII operationalizes elements of this plan.

In the manufacturing organization, information risk management occurs at the plant and enterprise levels. Internally, the manufacturing IT group sets up and manages information security processes on the applications it owns, whether the applications are located at distant plants (e.g., process automation and control systems) or housed in the corporate data center (e.g., warehouse management systems and portions of the ERP system), where they collaborate with enterprise-level groups (EII and EIRM). EII and EIRM also provide the manufacturing IT group with advice and guidance related to information risk management efforts.

The starting point is to identify applications that are critical to the business processes related to making products, including process control systems and intellectual property management systems. The IT group works with application owners to determine the criticality of the applications and to develop business continuity plans. Business continuity plans for critical applications are exercised at least once a year; plant-level IT managers may exercise certain plans more frequently. Each plant runs a yearly "drawbridge" exercise in which the loss of the connection between the plant and the corporate data center is simulated to provide assurances that the plant can still manufacture product.

The EIRM group arose from the realization that, while every level of the organization should identify and manage information risk, local information risk management efforts were not integrated well at the corporate level. Also, while local initiatives might be effective at managing local risk, it was not clear that they would be effective at managing enterprise-level risk. The EIRM group determines enterprise risk by gathering information risks from across the enterprise and looking for common issues that raise the risks from a local concern to an enterprise-level concern. EIRM finds the common issues by bringing together IT managers who are tasked with canvassing their business units and identifying the risks to critical information processes and assets. Discussion groups are organized in which IT managers identify uncovered risks and share information risk management challenges and best practices. The results are used with other inputs (e.g., results from audits and assessments, other enterprise risk management efforts, external threat trends, and industry and regulatory trends) to generate a list of enterprise information risks. Once the list of risks and recommendations is developed, it is put before a governance board for approval. The approved document is provided to the CIO staff, who use the recommendations in deciding how to manage information risk.

4.2   Canonical Model and Resilience

Based on the interviews, business units at most hierarchical levels in the enterprise are managing information risk. A strong enterprise-level group exists to identify and communicate information risk management issues to the various business units. In general, the firm's information security practices correspond very closely to the canonical model.

How might information disruptions affect the ability of the firm to manufacture and ship product? Unlike the hospital field study, no specific instances of information infrastructure disruptions were mentioned during the interviews. Consequently, resilience is inferred from the interview data.

First, we consider the raw materials used by the firm. The ERP system manages the supply chain operations. Consequently, it is important that the ERP system is functional and that the corporate headquarters and plants can communicate via the Internet. The firm has business continuity plans for its ERP. Also, some plants maintain redundant Internet connections to the corporate data center.

Individual manufacturing plants can function without the ERP system because they operate their process automation and control systems internally. In fact, the manufacturing plants would likely be able to make product for several days without access to the ERP system. The loss of the process automation and control systems internal to plants would have varying levels of impact depending on the type of plant (e.g., manufacturing or distribution). A process control system outage at a manufacturing plant could cause the product to be out of specifications, rendering the entire production batch worthless. As a result, the plant would be shut down until the process control system becomes functional. This is the reason why manufacturing process control networks are segregated from other networks.

Due to the nature of the pharmaceutical business, the firm is keenly aware that an interruption in the supply of certain products would potentially jeopardize human lives; as a result, the firm maintains a safety stock of certain products. The size of this safety stock depends on demand and production timelines. Products that require months to manufacture generally have substantial safety stocks.

It is impossible to accurately assess the resilience of the firm to information disruptions. However, the firm appears to be well-prepared for IT disruptions because the manufacturing side has a strong business continuity process in place, business units have continuity and disaster recovery plans that are exercised (including "drawbridge" exercises), and safety stocks are maintained.

5.   Grocery Field Study

The grocery field study focused on a retail food supply chain stretching from producers of raw ingredients to grocery stores. The results of interviews with individuals from eight firms that play different roles in the food supply chain are presented. The firms include a regional grocery chain with individual grocery stores, providers of fresh produce, canned goods, and a liquid dairy processor with two dairy farms.

5.1   Grocery Store Chain

The grocery chain is a U.S. regional chain with more than one hundred stores and employing tens of thousands of associates. This firm is fairly representative of other grocery store chains from the point of view of data processing, replenishment and supply chain activities.

IT is central to the business activities of the grocery chain. Point-of-sale (PoS) data is used to track the movement of goods at stores; the movement data is used by the grocery chain's distribution centers and direct-to-store vendors to restock most items. Credit card and debit card data are exchanged with banks to complete transactions. IT applications manage the inventories at distribution centers; Internet applications help schedule vendor deliveries to distribution centers and replenishment deliveries to stores.

Most IT systems are located at the data center at the grocery chain's headquarters. No servers are maintained at store locations; PoS and credit card devices connect directly to the grocery chain's data center. The inventory systems used by the distribution centers are also located at the data center. Communications with the grocery chain's vendors are done primarily via electronic data interchange (EDI) transactions or web-based applications. Examples include sending data about the movement of goods to vendors who manage their own inventories at the host's distribution centers, and to trucking firms who make appointments to deliver goods to distribution centers. The grocery chain has invested in a backup data center and each store has redundant connectivity to applications running at the grocery chain's data center.

Information security is handled primarily by an internal business application development group. This group works with business managers to understand the business needs for applications, including the level of redundancy and business continuity plans. The grocery chain's infrastructure group develops the needed infrastructure.

Everything stops when stores cannot communicate with the grocery chain's data center (or its backup). To manage this risk, each store has a leased line to the data center along with a backup modem system as a transparent failover. If both fail, contingency plans include taking PoS data to a sister store and placing orders from that location. When a store cannot send data, managers at headquarters use the store's average order as its replenishment order. Redundant Internet connections exist between the distribution centers and the main data center; the distribution center we visited had multiple electrical power supply sources.

Few, if any, information risk management coordinating signals are exchanged between the grocery chain and its supply network. At the time of the interviews, the chain made no effort to assess information risk management practices at its suppliers. Moreover, no examples of contingency planning between the grocery chain and vendors emerged during the interviews.

The resilience of the grocery chain to IT disruptions was discussed at length. The head of the applications development group spoke of the firm as providing an "essential service." Workers at the grocery chain's headquarters and distribution centers exhibit a high level of dedication to ensuring that food is always on store shelves. If the Internet went down but the grocery chain's internal systems were operational and the stores and distribution centers could access systems at the chain's data center, supply managers believed that they could replicate orders for vendors (who supply goods to the distribution centers) using phone and fax. Ongoing Internet troubles would result in the range of items ordered from vendors to be narrowed over time. The impact of communications outages between the grocery chain headquarters and stores, distribution centers and vendors varies with duration. A one-day outage would affect deliveries to stores, but not have a serious business impact. A two-day outage would impact the replenishment of stores and the restocking of distribution centers. However, when discussing communications outages, grocery managers said they "would wrestle the problem to the ground." One manager said that his distribution center had not missed a store replenishment order in more than 40 years.

From an information risk management perspective, there is no evidence that the grocery chain has information risk management efforts at its edges. However, a central group is in place to coordinate an effective organization-level information risk management effort. Thus, the grocery chain has a poor fit with the canonical model.

5.2   Fresh Produce Vendor

The fresh produce vendor has a multi-region presence covering retail groceries and institutional food settings (e.g., hotels and fast food restaurants). The vendor owns and operates packing plants that clean, mix and bag harvested produce; in addition, it operates several distribution and cross-docking facilities. The vendor has long-term exclusive contracts with fresh produce growers. Most of its orders (including the grocery chain's orders) are received via EDI and are processed by the vendor's order management system. The produce to fill an order is shipped (one day after the order is placed) from a production facility to a cross-docking facility and, from there, to the grocer's distribution center.

Fax or email is used if the vendor is unable to send or receive EDI transmissions. If the Internet is down, the vendor would likely ship an estimated order. The vendor also may have to revert to manually scheduling trucks to ship orders, which would be very challenging and would require additional resources. The resulting slowdown would give rise to delays at the shipping dock. Also, deliveries would be refused because trucks would miss their appointments.

The fresh produce vendor does not have firm-wide information risk management and business continuity planning efforts. It does not fit the canonical model at all.

5.3   Canned Goods Vendor

The canned goods vendor owns production and distribution facilities. Orders from stores are sent via EDI and phone; the firm also has a vendor-managed inventory sales channel. At the time of the interview all supplies were ordered by fax or phone; however, the vendor did plan to move supplier ordering to web-based EDI. EDI orders from customers are entered into the vendor's enterprise resource planning system. For store-based orders, this includes the items and their volumes; for the vendor-managed inventory channel, this includes the inventory and movement of goods at the customer's distribution center. An order is then computed based on the safety stock and other factors. In the case of the vendor-managed inventory, safety stocks range from a little less than a week to two weeks. Once the order (direct or calculated) is in hand, the ERP system places an order for shipping with a third-party trucking vendor, who arranges shipping, makes an appointment at the grocery chain's distribution center and then notifies the canned goods vendor that shipping has been arranged. The canned goods vendor then sends an EDI to its warehouse with the order and shipping arrangements; the order is picked up, loaded and shipped. The order-to-ship cycle is two days.

Customers are expected to fax in their orders if EDI communications were to fail. The vendor could handle the increased volume of faxes for about a week; additional staff would be hired if there is any indication that the EDI outage would last longer. The vendor would communicate with its warehouses via email and send documents via FedEx. Also, the vendor has a comprehensive contingency plan in place with a transportation company to communicate shipping needs via fax. The vendor would be unable to service vendor-managed inventory customers for outages lasting more than one week.

The canned goods vendor has undertaken an enterprise-wide contingency planning effort; this arose from an initiative spearheaded by the vendor's global crisis committee. Portions of the business continuity plan are exercised periodically. These plans were used during a three-day power outage at the order management office, during which time the vendor did not miss a single shipment.

5.4 Dairy Sector

The dairy sector study attempts to examine information risk in the supply chain network of liquid dairy products. The supply chain network includes suppliers to dairy farms, the dairy farms themselves, dairy processors and grocery stores.

Dairy farms revolve around the cows that produce about a hundred pounds of milk in two milkings per day. The production drops considerably when cows miss even a single milking. As a result, dairy farmers take steps to assure a reliable supply of electricity for running the milking machines and for refrigerating the raw milk until it is picked up by the milk processor. Electricity is also needed to run water pumps, lighting and fans.

One small farm that was studied maintains (and periodically tests) two backup generators with six weeks supply of fuel. A larger farm maintains multiple backup generators, each of which uses a different fuel (e.g., gasoline and propane). Dairy farms also require feed mix ingredients, water, drugs and cleaning agents. Safety stocks of feed components at the small farm ranged from one week to a month; the larger farm stored enough feed for one year. Some supplies (e.g., certain feed components and sawdust for bedding) are delivered to the farm automatically; the remaining supplies are ordered by phone.

The amount of information risk at the dairy farms is small, but not zero. Technology is used to track the milk output of cows (for optimizing milk production) and to develop feed rations from various grains, hay, alfalfa, etc. The software programs run on local computers; Internet connectivity does not play a role in core dairy processes. Neither dairy farm had information risk management efforts.

The dairy processor interviewed in the study collects raw milk from several local dairy farms. Upon arriving at the processing plant, the raw milk is tested for bacteria and other impurities. If the raw milk is accepted, it is pasteurized, processed and packaged as various types of milk (e.g., low fat milk) and shipped to stores. Orders from customers are communicated to the processor via an order-processing application hosted at the headquarters of the dairy processor's parent firm. Workers at the dairy processor pick and load the orders onto a truck, which is then dispatched. Orders from stores for liquid dairy products are handled via telephone.

There was no indication of internal information risk management activities or of conversations with headquarters and suppliers of packaging materials on the subject of information risk. The laboratory equipment and control systems for processing raw milk run on a set of computers that have no need for Internet access; a UPS system is available for backup power for twelve hours. In the event of an emergency, a local firm is contracted to deliver a diesel generator within two hours for powering all the plant machinery and refrigeration systems. The dairy processor relies on the Internet to receive shipping orders for stores. The processor maintains three T-1 lines for network communications: one for general networking, one to communicate with the order-processing application, and one spare line. If Internet connectivity is interrupted, requests from the order-processing application would be received by fax. If the order-processing system is down, the dairy processor would send the previous day's order. The evidence suggests that operations would degrade gracefully if the laboratory computers and process control system go down – low fat milk might not be produced, but pasteurized whole milk would be available.

Dairy section managers at four grocery stores belonging to different chains were also interviewed. The four stores have at least two common vendors of liquid dairy products and orders to the vendors are communicated via telephone. The dairy sections have milk products on display and additional stock in reserve. Replenishment orders are computed manually based on the daily movement and remaining stock, or with the assistance of a software application running at the store. Stock and replenishment orders are sized to have just enough product on hand until the next delivery to maintain product freshness and reduce waste. Safety stock ranged from a few cases (with four one-gallon containers per case) to enough product to cover sales for two or three days. The managers said that it was unusual to run out of stock; however, if it did happen, a special delivery order would be placed with the vendor or stock would be obtained from a sister store. The interviews indicated that vendors have never run out of milk.

5.5   Canonical Model and Resilience

The grocery supply network is an ensemble of loosely connected entities. Some of the entities have effective information risk management efforts; however, no network-level body is in place to coordinate or integrate information risk management efforts. Thus, information security efforts in the grocery supply network have a poor fit with the canonical model.

Table 1. Level of information risk management efforts.

Field Study	IRM at Edge	Central Coordination
Health Care	Individual	Low
Pharmaceutical	Systemic	High
Grocery Chain	None	High
Dairy Sector	Individual	None

That said, the sector does seem resilient to short-term IT and communication disruptions. This is because safety stocks are kept in stores and at the main distribution centers, stores and vendors quickly adopt work-arounds or continue to make product and deliveries based on past data, and the entities generally have a "wrestle the problem to the ground" culture.

Prolonged IT disruptions in the grocery sector result in a graceful degradation of functionality. Sugar-free chocolate ice cream cones with sprinkles may not be on the shelves after a weeklong outage, but milk and other staples would be available as usual. It is important to note that the demand may be much higher than normal during outages, possibly due to the perception that the supply chain network has failed. Public awareness campaigns and rationing may be needed in such situations. Also, as noted in several studies, transportation is often the principal challenge during outages.

6. Discussion

Information security efforts at the field study entities ranged from disparate efforts to systematic efforts with strong levels of integration. Table 1 shows the level of information risk management efforts in individual entities and the level of central communication and coordination. An "individual" entry in the table means that individual entities might manage information risk; "systemic" means that information risk management efforts are expected by the firm.

Not one firm interviewed in the field study was of the view that it would cease to function shortly after the onset of an information infrastructure disruption; this includes a disruption to the integrated food supply chain.

Based on the lack of an effective information risk management effort and organizational complexity, the hospital appears to be the least likely to continue to function in the event of a disruption; however, it demonstrated that it could indeed function during a major IT disruption. The pharmaceutical firm has a robust information risk management effort in place; the level of planning and the exercising of contingency plans indicate that IT disruptions would likely not affect the firm's ability to manufacture or distribute products. The grocery chain has also actively investigated its IT-based business risk. The challenge is to devise processes that would allow the stocking of stores; this seems entirely possible given the resilience of the hospital.

The entities in the food supply chain are not well integrated in that they do not exchange a lot of internal process data, only data relating to orders and payments. From a resilience standpoint, it is important to share the orders for replenishing stock and raw materials. All the suppliers indicated that, absent an actual order, they would be able to estimate an order and ship it. As a result, the grocery supply network would likely continue to function in a "ballistic" mode.

The results suggest that three different types of resilience are in play for a firm or sector during information infrastructure disruptions: technical resilience, operational resilience and organizational resilience. Technical resilience results from efforts to reduce the likelihood that IT processes will fail; examples include redundant servers or Internet connectivity. Technical resilience is the result of implicit or explicit information risk management processes applied before a disruption. Examples of technical resilience in the field studies include redundant generators at the dairy farms, redundant Internet connections from the grocery chain's distribution centers and stores to headquarters, and backup data centers at the pharmaceutical firm and grocery chain.

Contingency plans are examples of operational resilience: a planned work-around exists if the standard way of accomplishing a task is not possible due to a system outage. This is also a result of information risk management. Examples include the canned goods vendor requiring workers to work at a backup site to test the effectiveness of procedures and to build "muscle memory" that lessens business disruptions during transitions.

Organizational resilience may or may not be due to prior planning; it arises from the corporate culture and the work ethic and innovation of individual workers. Organizational resilience is what remains when things are not working as planned – it is why the hospital was able to function effectively during the IT disruption.

7.   Conclusions

The field studies suggest that different types of risk might be best managed by focusing on three types of resilience: technical resilience, operational resilience and organizational resilience. For example, IT disruptions (e.g., application failures and network outages) would be best handled by technical and operational resilience if an analysis showed a net benefit. In such cases, the number of likely interruptions should be low, which renders feasible both the analysis and the potential technology investments.

On the other hand, if the number of likely disruptions is high, the enumeration of the disruptions and the analysis of the potential consequences would be very resource intensive. In such a situation, a compelling business case cannot be made for reducing the risk further or for mitigating the consequences. Consequently, the best approach is to develop organizational resilience.

Acknowledgements

This work was partially supported by the Institute for Information Infrastructure Protection (I3P) at Dartmouth College, Hanover, New Hampshire, under Award 2006-CS-001-000001 from the U.S. Department of Homeland Security and Award 60NANB1D0127 from the National Institute of Standards and Technology.

References

[1] C. Alberts and A. Dorofee, *Managing Information Security Risks: The OCTAVE Approach*, Addison-Wesley/Pearson, Boston, Massachusetts, 2003.

[2] L. Bodin, L. Gordon and M. Loeb, Information security and risk management, *Communications of the ACM*, vol. 51(4), pp. 64–68, 2008.

[3] S. Dynes, Information Security and Health Care: A Field Study of a Hospital after a Worm Event, Technical Report, Center for Digital Strategies, Tuck School of Business, Dartmouth College, Hanover, New Hampshire, 2006.

[4] S. Dynes, Information Security Investment Case Study: The Manufacturing Sector, Technical Report, Center for Digital Strategies, Tuck School of Business, Dartmouth College, Hanover, New Hampshire, 2006.

[5] S. Dynes, Emergent risks in critical infrastructures, in *Critical Infrastructure Protection II*, M. Papa and S. Shenoi (Eds.), Springer, Boston, Massachusetts, pp. 3–16, 2008.

[6] D. Geer, Risk management is where the money is, *The Risks Digest*, vol. 20(6) (catless.ncl.ac.uk/risks/20.06.html), 1998.

[7] J. Gubrium and J. Holstein, *Handbook of Interview Research: Context and Method*, Sage Publications, Thousand Oaks, California, 2001.

[8] M. Johnson and E. Goetz, Embedding information security into the organization, *IEEE Security and Privacy*, vol. 5(3), pp. 16–24, 2007.

[9] G. Stoneburner, A. Goguen and A. Feringa, Risk Management Guide for Information Technology Systems: Recommendations of the National Institute of Standards and Technology, Special Publication 800-30, National Institute of Standards and Technology, Gaithersburg, Maryland, 2002.

[10] C. Watters, Analyzing corporate risks with RiskMAP, presented at the *Second Annual I3P Process Control Systems Security Workshop*, 2006.

[11] Wikipedia, Zotob (computer worm) (en.wikipedia.org/wiki/Zotob), 2009.

Chapter 2

DOES THE LIBERALIZATION OF THE EUROPEAN RAILWAY SECTOR INCREASE SYSTEMIC RISK?

Marc Laperrouza

Abstract   Recent large-scale blackouts and other incidents have shown that failures in network industries can have serious economic and social consequences. A large body of literature covers critical infrastructures (and their protection), but most of it is confined to a relatively restricted number of sectors such as electricity and information and communications technology (ICT). In addition, much of the literature discusses systemic risk in complex networks from an engineering perspective with the goal of mitigating risk using quantitative techniques.

The railway sector is a critical infrastructure that shares a number of characteristics with electricity (e.g. interconnection), but it has received little attention when it comes to systemic risk. This paper analyzes the extent to which the liberalization of the railway system increases the sector's systemic risk, a pressing question in the wake of the creation of a single European railway market. The paper also discusses the broader issue of the governance of systemic risk in the railway sector, especially since the mitigation of risk tends to be limited to risk management from a technical perspective while ignoring the institutional dimension.

Keywords: Systemic risk, European railway sector, liberalization

1.   Introduction

Network industries – electricity, transport and communications – are considered to be critical infrastructures: they provide services without which modern society could not function properly. These "systems" or "systems of systems" which, by their nature, are subject to entire system risks are often referred to as "systemic" risks. Broadly, systemic risk refers to "the risk or probability of breakdowns in an entire system, as opposed to breakdowns in individual parts or components, and is evidenced by co-movements (correlation) among all or

C. Palmer and S. Shenoi (Eds.): Critical Infrastructure Protection III, IFIP AICT 311, pp. 19–33, 2009.

most parts" [20]. According to the Organization for Economic Cooperation and Development [29], systemic risk is the risk of failure of vitally important systems, i.e., those on which society depends, such as health, transport, environment and telecommunications.

There are arguments and some evidence that network industries are increasingly vulnerable to systemic failures. These highly complex and interdependent large-scale technical systems are subject to rapid change that poses risks to themselves while also causing disruptions through cascading effects [21, 22]. Similarly, technological change can be disruptive to established steady states, "innovation trajectories" can cascade in unforeseen ways, particularly when technological systems rapidly expand into other systems and areas or life [15].

In the extensive literature on risk in banking and finance, systemic risk is frequently and explicitly addressed and analyzed and is one of the most important concepts in the sector [18, 20]. In contrast, while safety and reliability in the network industries and critical infrastructures are extensively analyzed, systemic risk is only referenced briefly in the literature and has not been subjected to extended analysis [11, 17, 40]. Note also that power grids, telecommunications networks and railway systems face quite different risk situations due to different behaviors (physics) and different topologies. The associated term, "cascading," is used more often and is the subject of intense analysis by the engineering (and physics) community (see [35] for a consideration of small-world properties in the railway sector). However, the analyses tend to be conducted mostly through a technical lens (e.g., reliability engineering).

Because of the increased utilization of the railway infrastructure, the railway system in many countries has become quite vulnerable to disruptions [37, 38]. In most European countries, railway infrastructures are already operating at the limit of their capacity. The expected increase of "priority" trains crossing borders in Europe following the liberalization of the international passenger segment will put additional pressure on railway capacity. The unbundling of the railway sector pushed by the European Commission will add new actors and new functions (e.g., independent slot allocators), further increasing the overall system complexity. These developments, coupled with the political will to increase the share of intermodal freight transport, may put an unduly high pressure on the railway sector without any means (other than technical) to cope with it. On a more positive note, the standardization work conducted by the European Railway Agency (ERA) in the framework of the European Railway Traffic Management System (ERTMS) has forced many of the old and new European railway actors to sit at the same table and to find common answers to increasingly complex problems. However, technical standardization is only one facet of railway interoperability.

The paper argues that traditional studies on risk management in the railway sector (see, e.g., [13, 24]) should be extended to explicitly include the concept of systemic risk. The understanding of systemic risk and the answers it brings – in addition to the prevalent technical perspective – could benefit significantly from a qualitative approach. After discussing the concept of systemic risk, this paper examines its relevance to the railway sector and conducts a broader discussion of the governance of systemic risk in the railway sector.

2.   Systemic Risk

This section reviews the concept of systemic risk. The discussion draws from our previous work related to systemic risk [6].

The concept of risk is not easy to delineate; in modern usage it is closely associated with the notion of hazard. While hazard is the potential to do harm, risk has more to do with "possibilities, chances or likelihoods of events, often as consequences of some activity or policy" [36]. Nevertheless, risk is usually associated with harmful outcomes and is viewed as the likelihood of harm combined in some way with the extent of the harm. Risk therefore involves two elements: (i) the likelihood or probability of a particular event occurring, and (ii) the extent of the harmful consequences of the event. The standard technical definition of risk involves quantification and is the statistical probability of the occurrence of the unwanted event multiplied by its severity [14]. However, there are extended debates on risk and uncertainty in the literature (see, e.g., [5, 7]). The scientific view is that risk is the statistical probability of harm (or uncertainty when probabilities cannot be quantified). The social science view is that risk and uncertainty are difficult to separate in most practical situations, and that the quantification of outcome probabilities is questionable.

Systemic risk refers to breakdowns of entire systems rather than their component parts. Therefore, it can be distinguished from other types of risk primarily because of its widespread and potentially damaging consequences. System breakdown risks are characterized by a break in a causal chain; the threat of system breakdown is a feature of an interconnected world and it exists at many levels ranging from local to global. Some researchers (see, e.g., [39]) further differentiate between system breakdown risks and systemic risks. Nevertheless, definitions of systemic risk often focus on the cause of the harm, the processes involved and the uncertainty in assessing the likely outcomes.

Table 1 presents the systemic risks in the financial sector. The two principal categories are macro risk and micro risk. Kroger [21] proposes a different taxonomy for the potential of triggered events, including cascading events, escalating events, common cause events and confined events.

3.   Complexity and Systemic Change

Moving beyond causation towards process, there are other important distinguishing features of systemic risk associated with the inherent complexity of systems. "Complexity" is a term often used to describe the difficulties of analyzing large systems with many components. Complexity is more than just "complicated" [31]; it is qualitatively more than the difficulty involved in analyzing systems with many components and complicated behavior. Instead, it refers to systems with features that make the prediction of system behavior extremely difficult even when the properties of the component parts are well

Table 1.   Systemic risk in the financial sector (adapted from [20]).

Macro Risk	A single big shock impacts all or most parts of a system – a common cause (e.g., earthquake, hurricane).
Micro Risk (Direct)	A single shock impacts only one part or a small number of parts of a system. The systemic effect is the result of a chain reaction between physically interconnected elements – a domino effect (e.g., power line cascading failures).
Micro Risk (Indirect)	A single shock impacts only one part or a small number of parts of a system. The systemic effect is the result of human interaction with other elements – the result of loss of confidence and herding or contagious behavior.

understood. Schlapfer, *et al.* [34] observe that breakdowns of complex networks are often the result of relatively slow system degradation that escalates into a rapid avalanche of component failures.

The features of complexity include nonlinearities, multiple stable states, hysteresis, contagion and synchrony, which are all features of complex adaptive systems [18]. Complex systems also manifest the characteristics of "chaos" – high sensitivity to initial conditions and outcomes that are practically impossible to predict. Abrupt regime shifts can also occur; in the economy, these can lead to inferior but stable equilibria [18]. Complexity has become a significant feature of modern scientific and technological infrastructures. Whereas scientific and technological developments proceed in an incremental manner, products and processes are added incrementally to the complex whole of science, technology, life, environment, society, politics and the economy. This creates unexpected emergent phenomena that tend to increase the vulnerability of network industries. Vulnerability has two dimensions: physical (i.e., the propensity to suffer damage when subjected to an external stress) and functional (i.e., the propensity of an element to suffer loss in functionality). These vulnerabilities can be extended to include systemic vulnerability, which is the propensity of an element to endure a loss of functionality not only due to a stress on its physical structure, but also because of its connections to other elements [27]. According to Kroger and Dietz [22], interdependencies can be characterized by their types (input, mutual, co-located, shared and exclusive); interaction levels (physical, cyber, geographic and logical); and coupling (order of coupling and tightness of linkage).

4.   Systemic Risk in the Railway Sector

The notion of risk is widely used in the railway sector, but it usually refers to non-systemic types of risks. For example, the Swedish Railway Authority notes that significant risks exist within areas such as new technology for signal sys-

Table 2. Railway sector interactions (adapted from [17]).

	Electricity	ICT	Water
In	Many electrified rail systems have their own power supply but some rely on the general power grid	Disruption of ICT systems that control rail systems and manage reservations and dispatch	
Out	Disruption of coal supply to generators (typically a delayed effect)	Many communication lines follow rail rights-of-way and can be disrupted by rail accidents or attacks	Contamination from hazmat spills due to derailments

tems, EU standardization of the railway infrastructure, price trends for metals and electrical energy, very high utilization of railway capacity in urban areas and the completion of railway projects within time and budget constraints [4]. When it is mentioned, the concept of systemic risk is restricted to safety issues [16, 32, 33].

This is surprising because railway systems are part of the critical infrastructure and an interruption can have immediate and far-reaching consequences. In countries with large metropolitan areas or high population densities, there is often no alternative to railway travel. Nevertheless, the degree of criticality is moderate – the impacts of failures, losses and non-availability will in most cases be limited in scope (local to regional), magnitude (minimal to moderate) and time (hours). At the same time, the rail infrastructure depends on other critical infrastructures to varying degrees, especially energy supply and ICT systems [17]. Also, the energy sector depends on fuel transported by rail and ICT systems use data transmission lines that are often routed along rail rights-of-way. In fact, 51.7% of the electricity in the United States and 30.4% in the European Union is generated by burning coal, which is mostly delivered by rail. Table 2 summarizes the interactions between the railway sector and other key infrastructures. Note that the interactions are presented in terms of the dependence on other infrastructures (In) and the dependence by other infrastructures (Out).

Recent work [26] on critical infrastructure dependencies has revealed that most cascades originate in only a limited number of sectors (energy and ICT) and that the interdependencies occur far less often than predicted by theory. Nevertheless, the criticality of the railway sector is especially evident in the (few) cases of complete shutdown of the network. Note also that railways are an attractive territorial target as exemplified by the November 2008 "attacks" on the French TGV tracks that stranded thousands of passengers. Auerswald, *et al.* [2] opine that "in the presence of interdependencies, even if each firm is

Table 3.   Recent rail failures in Switzerland and France.

Country	Date	Downtime	Explanation
Switzerland	6/22/2005	3–4 hours	The shutdown was caused by a power failure at 5:45 p.m. local time on a part of the track in the southern portion of the country. Around 2,000 trains and more than 200,000 passengers were affected. Financial claims amounted to around 5 million Swiss Francs.
Switzerland	2/7/2005	NA	NA
France	8/22/2004	2–3 hours	A local train dragged and broke the cable that provides trains with electricity, requiring all power to the line to be cut off.
Switzerland	1997	40 minutes	Trains were stranded for 40 minutes. Approximately 15,000 passengers were affected.

resilient, the system may still be vulnerable due to lack of coordination among, and communication between, different industry sectors." Currently, the criticality of railways is considered to be medium from the physical, operational and speed of change perspectives [17]. However, this rating should be reconsidered in the light of the fundamental transformations that are occurring in the railway sector.

4.1   Recent Railway System Breakdowns

Recent structural changes in the European railway sector (i.e., unbundling, introduction of competition and increased interoperability) raises the question if the probability of a systemic failure in the network has increased or decreased. Currently, only anecdotal evidence suggests that incidents of a systemic nature are more prevalent now than before. Compared with the extensive reports published after major electricity blackouts, relatively little information is provided by railway operators and infrastructure managers about the causes and consequences of rail breakdowns.

Table 3 lists recent failures in the Swiss and French state-of-the-art railway systems. Switzerland's railway officials blamed licensing procedures and the "not-in-my-back-yard" mentality for blocking new power lines as the underlying cause of the major electrical power outage that affected the national rail network on June 22, 2005. The Swiss power grid design offers limited opportunities to re-route power during a breakdown. The Swiss Railway has attempted to lay back-up transmission cables for three decades, but the progress has been slowed by citizen protests. Meanwhile, feeder lines from Germany are inadequate and the systems of neighboring countries are incompatible. In addition to the complete shutdown of the railway network (as in the June 2005 incident), there are also accidents of a systemic nature with relatively limited incidence (about 100 incidents per day on important lines) according to the Swiss Railway's punctuality statistics. Punctuality is defined as trains arriving at their final destination with less than five minutes delay. In 2005, the punctuality of Swiss freight convoys was 93.6% for national traffic and 74.4% for international traffic.

In our view, one of the important causes of increased vulnerability is that the railway system was designed, built and operated under public ownership in a non-competitive environment, but is suddenly expected to operate very differently in a competitive, albeit regulated, market. Networks were formed geographically at the local, regional and long-distance levels. For example, the main railway companies in Europe still make use of different signaling and electricity systems and different track gauges. Traditionally, these networks were largely separate and were owned and operated by one – often state-owned — company. Recently, larger networks have been formed by linking networks physically (same infrastructure) and organizationally (timetables and ticketing). As a result, the previously isolated railway systems that were constructed in a fairly uncoordinated and inconsistent manner have to interact with each other. The central issue is whether and to what extent these developments place pressure on operating safety margins, the transparency of reporting on safety issues and the capacity of market players and their regulators to render the vast network systems sufficiently resilient to major disruptions [29].

One way to increase reliability is to reduce the propagation of delays due to interdependencies between trains [38]. For example, the interdependencies can be decreased by reducing the running time differences per track section and creating more homogeneous timetables. When investigating railway reliability, it is important to make a distinction between primary and secondary delays. Primary delays are initial delays due to external factors, not because of other trains. These delays are caused by malfunctioning rolling stock, malfunctioning infrastructure, bad weather conditions, excessive alighting and boarding times of passengers, accidents at railroad crossings, and so on. Secondary (or knock-on) delays are train delays caused by delays of other trains; they also arise as a result of shared infrastructures and rolling stock connections. Carey [8] distinguishes between exogenous delays and knock-on delays. Exogenous delays are due to failures of equipment or infrastructure, and delays in passenger boarding or alighting (also known as primary delays). Knock-on delays are caused by exogenous delays and schedule interdependence (also known as secondary delays).

There is a well-established belief that an infrastructure capacity utilization above 75% or 80% reduces punctuality [28]. Capacity utilization above 60% is not recommended (except for rush hour traffic) because it limits railway system recovery. In fact, an exponential relationship exists between adding trains to a congested network and the expected level of network performance [12]. For the time being, the focus is on solving small primary disturbances, mainly because no timetable is robust enough to handle large disruptions without drastic real-time traffic adjustments [38].

4.2   Interoperability and Systemic Risk

It believed that the systemic risk in the railway sector could be mitigated as a result of the European Commission's ERTMS Project whose goal is to achieve interoperability of the European network by 2020. While interoperability may directly reduce a multitude of risks, it could indirectly increase the systemic risk by making the European railway network more interconnected and, therefore, prone to supra-regional disruptions. Table 4 summarizes the systemic risks in the railway sector.

Interoperability is defined as the ability of two or more systems to communicate and work together without any problems. In general, interoperability can be expected to reduce the risks of reduced performance, stability and coherence. However, interoperability needs to be understood at two levels:

- **Technical Interoperability:** This covers the technical issues of linking systems and services. It includes aspects such as infrastructure, traction units and locomotives, energy, passenger carriages and telematics applications for passenger services. Technical interoperability is directed by framing and revising Technical Specifications for Interoperability (TSI). In the railway sector, this task is taken up by the European Railway Agency, which acts as the system authority.

- **Operational Interoperability:** This is concerned with the harmonization of rules and implementations. For example, different implementations in the European rail network produce a variety of degraded situations at border crossings.

Special conditions related to rail system capacity must be considered when operating long-distance rail services. Long-distance trains often have to pass through several bottlenecks that can affect the punctuality of long-distance services as a whole. The risk of delays is greater for regional traffic than for local rail traffic because the times and distances are longer. Increasing rail traffic without increasing capacity renders the existing bottlenecks even more problematic.

5.   Discussion and Analysis

While the understanding of interoperability in railway sector is only now starting to shift from a technical to an operational viewpoint, we argue that a well-performing (and safe) railway sector will require institutional interoperability. This will move the debate from the engineering domain to the political

Table 4. Systemic risks in the railway sector (based on [19]).

Triggering (crisis) event	Natural event (lightning, personnel strike), device failure (power loss), voltage collapse, protection system failure (relay system fault), inadequate right-of-way maintenance
Sector vulnerability	Growth in demand, rise in cross-border traffic, inadequate reinforcement of the power grid (failure to provide sufficient reserves), poor coordination among neighboring slot allocators, hidden failures, lack of investment in infrastructure (within and between countries)
Potential dangers	Integration of smaller systems into larger systems (facilitated by ETCS), which increases complexity and transboundary propagation of disturbances, spillover to other network industries (interdependencies)
Type of systemic risk	Large shock, direct causation and contagion, common shock contagion
Transmission channels	Interconnectedness, similar systems, high level of cross-border traffic
Requirements for contagious systemic risk	Interdependence, coordination failure between operators and slot allocators
Recent changes in systemic risk	Increased interconnection, ERTMS (interoperability), operating at the limit of capacity, market liberalization (unbundling of network elements and price)
Historical evidence of contagious systemic risk	Direct causation (more impact), common shock (less impact)
Corrective policies	Public (domestic and international) regulation

realm where harmonization is much harder to achieve. Indeed, in some European countries, the company that manages the railway infrastructure also provides railway services. In other countries, the railway market is partially or completely deregulated with different stakeholders managing the infrastructure and the railway services. In Sweden, for example, railway traffic management is performed by a neutral authority that governs the overall use of the infrastructure, while various private and public companies operate the trains that carry freight and passenger traffic.

Complexity has become a significant feature of modern technological infrastructures. System analysis shows that this comes with unexpected and unforeseen emergent phenomena that not only pose risks themselves but also cause disruptions that may cascade. Systemic risk is heightened by the fact that there is no longer a single owner, operator or regulator of the infrastructure and that, in the unbundled market paradigm, agents' decisions are based on different logics and incentives. In addition, interoperability itself may have unforeseen consequences.

Proposing techniques for mitigating risk in the railway sector is beyond the scope of this paper. However, an enhanced understanding of the systemic risk in railway systems is the first and necessary step to improve their governance. For example, it is important to avoid confusion between common cause vulnerabilities (e.g., an earthquake causing simultaneous, but unrelated effects in two critical infrastructures) and dependencies [25]. It is also important to recognize the multi-dimensional nature of dependencies. Numerous models and quantitative methodologies have been proposed to minimize cascading failures. We believe that these approaches should be supplemented by an improved qualification of risk.

Some policy recommendations for critical infrastructure protection are focused in this direction. They include upgrading and revising intergovernmental standards for security, quality assurance, education and training in order to cope with more challenging uses of the railway system (higher density of timetables, tighter safety margins) and new threats (transborder transport of dangerous goods and devices); and implementing effective technical, organizational and socio-political measures against malicious attacks that are balanced against social values (e.g., privacy and freedom of expression).

6.   Regulating Systemic Risk

Much of the banking regulation in place today is designed to reduce systemic risk [1]. In many countries, capital regulation in the form of the Basel Agreements is one of the most important measures for reducing systemic risk. If one pushes the comparison with the banking sector, it is interesting to note that in the early 19th century, assuring financial stability was primarily the responsibility of central banks. The Great Depression led the United States to impose many types of banking regulation to prevent systemic risk. The recent events in the financial sector are a powerful reminder that one needs to question whether regulation, as currently implemented, actually increases financial stability. Allen and Gale [1] observe that poorly designed and implemented capital regulation can lead to increases in systemic risk. However, one of the difficulties in crafting policy to reduce systemic risk is the rarity of events and incidents that lead to complete system breakdowns. Note that system breakdown risks are not affected by societal risk perceptions or cultural views; instead, it is the "visible" breakdown risks that have to be addressed and managed.

Mechanisms in place to manage risk vary across countries [39]. Due to the interconnected nature of the risk, a national forum would be insufficient. The ideal response could be a pan-European risk management institution even if there are many factors that might inhibit its creation. Every system invites free riders and a global system that manages and enforces standards could threaten free riding. Similarly, there are always winners when a system collapses, so certain institutions may stand to gain by not participating in or by obstructing a comprehensive response to system breakdown risks.

An idealized societal response to systemic risk could be the formation of cross-disciplinary risk management agencies (possibly even situated within existing institutions). These agencies would be required to link the physical, financial and political (governance) links between the risks. One potential avenue to mitigate systemic risk would be to create a pan-European railway regulator. Currently, the European railway system is regulated at several levels. At the national level, member states have independent regulators as stipulated by Directive 2001/12. In addition, Directive 2001/14 provides that the infrastructure manager publish a network statement that contains information about the (technical) nature and limitations of the network, access conditions to the network and rules on capacity allocation. At the pan-European level, the European Railway Agency (ERA) regulates safety and interoperability. Meanwhile, RailNetEurope (RNE) is making significant progress in establishing, shaping and improving a harmonized timetabling process for international train path requests.

Several analyses that advocate a more socio-political approach suggest a move from risk management to risk governance [11, 17, 21, 31]. Another study [30] posits that complex infrastructure systems should be analyzed as "socio-technical systems" in which technical systems are not only complex but also involve the "variegated and penetrating involvement of human action, which, in all its forms, is able to affect, even critically to affect, the functioning of the system." Understanding and interpreting systems thus requires an analysis of the relationships between human actors and organizations and physical components and systems.

A comparison of the railway and electricity sectors in the context of regulatory reforms over the past two decades suggests that there needs to be a coherence between the "critical institutional arrangements that support the technical functioning of the systems" [23]. The European Union has included the notion of risk in its interoperability directives [9]. However, it is in the hands of the national safety authorities who "define, after consultation with the applicant, the scope and content of the additional information, the risk analyses and the tests requested."

The question thus arises as to whether there is a need for any special forms of governance to address systemic risk in the railway sector. Clearly, the most fundamental aspect of systemic risk is its system-wide nature and this suggests the need for a system-wide or centralized approach to governance. As discussed above, the most important systemic risks may have micro causes – such as a tree falling on a power line or a malicious individual destroying a section of track – that are propagated throughout the system. This implies that some aspects of systemic risk must be managed on a decentralized basis. Overall, the right balance should be struck between centralized and decentralized governance, depending, of course, on the type of risk.

Table 5.   Coordination mechanisms (adapted from [10]).

Coordination Mechanism	Technical Coordination	Institutional Coordination
Centralized	Centralized control: Top-down	Planned economy
Decentralized	Distributed control: Bottom-up	Market economy; Classical contracting
Matricial	Integrated	Combined

In the railway sector, issues of systemic risk and the kinds of risks addressed are generally considered to be localized and bounded, albeit with severe consequences. As a result, the preparation for and coordination of such events are limited. Kunneke and Finger's work on coordination mechanisms [23] could provide a useful framework to discuss coordination with the aim of mitigating systemic risk in the railway sector (Table 5). In their view, liberalization is likely to introduce a certain incoherence between technical coordination and institutional coordination. From a technical point of view, interoperability, capacity management and system management have to be coordinated in a hierarchical manner. However, there is a certain pressure to allocate slots commercially and even to have competition among timetables. In other words, coordination problems are likely to significantly increase as a result of liberalization, which, in turn, will increase the incoherence between technical and institutional coordination.

7.   Conclusions

Methods for dealing with infrastructure interdependencies must capture the complexity and interconnectedness of modern, open systems of systems; human factors; the full spectrum of threats; dynamic, non-linear emergent behavior; and the influence of contextual factors such as markets and operating environments. Systemic risk is a matter of great concern to the financial sector. As in the financial industry, research should focus on the mechanics and channels of shock transmission within and between railway networks. At the same time, more attention should be given to the regulatory nature of systemic risk. The large-scale blackouts in Europe and the United States leave a sense that the rates of occurrence of major incidents are increasing. However, additional research needs to be conducted to establish the prevalence of systemic breakdowns in the railway sector, and the relationships between increased technical interconnections, market liberalization and systemic breakdowns

The following questions should be addressed as part of a research agenda focused on systemic risk in the railway sector: How is systemic risk currently governed at the national and European levels in the railway sector, particularly in relation to technocratic and socio-political forms of management and governance? What are the strengths and weaknesses of current systemic risk governance and how might it be improved? What might governance institutions, structures and processes look like at the national and international levels in the railway sector? Which stakeholders should be involved in systemic risk governance of the railway sector? What sort of involvement should the various stakeholders have? Should the involvement be limited to information sharing or should there be close consultation and co-decision making among the various stakeholders?

References

[1] F. Allen and D. Gale, Systemic Risk and Regulation, Working Paper No. 95-24, Wharton Financial Institutions Center, Wharton School, University of Pennsylvania, Philadelphia, Pennsylvania, 2005.

[2] P. Auerswald, L. Branscomb, T. La Porte and E. Michel-Kerjan, *Seeds of Disaster, Roots of Response: How Private Action Can Reduce Public Vulnerability*, Cambridge University Press, New York, 2006.

[3] Banverket, Annual Report 2006, Borlange, Sweden, 2006.

[4] Banverket, Swedish Rail Sector Development, Borlange, Sweden, 2007.

[5] I. Bartle, Risk-based regulation and better regulation in the UK: Towards what model of risk regulation? presented at the *Second Biennial Conference of the ECPR Standing Group on Regulatory Governance*, 2008.

[6] I. Bartle and M. Laperrouza, Systemic risk in the network industries: Is there a governance gap? EPFL-MIR Working Paper, Centre for the Study of Regulated Industries, School of Management, University of Bath, Bath, United Kingdom, 2008.

[7] I. Bartle and P. Vass, Risk and the Regulatory State – A Better Regulation Perspective, Research Report 20, Centre for the Study of Regulated Industries, School of Management, University of Bath, Bath, United Kingdom, 2008.

[8] M. Carey, Optimizing scheduled times, allowing for behavioral response, *Transportation Research, Part B: Methodological*, vol. 32(5), pp. 329–342, 1998.

[9] European Commission, Directive 2008/57/EC of the European Parliament and of the Council of 17 June 2008 on the Interoperability of the Rail System within the Community, Publication L 191, Brussels, Belgium, 2008.

[10] M. Finger and R. Kunneke, Technology matters: The cases of the liberalization of electricity and railways, *Competition and Regulation in Network Industries*, vol. 8(3), pp. 301–333, 2007.

[11] A. Gheorghe, M. Masera, L. De Vries, M. Weijnen and W. Kroger, Critical infrastructures: The need for international risk governance, *International Journal of Critical Infrastructures*, vol. 3(1/2), pp. 3–19, 2007.

[12] S. Gibson, G. Cooper and B. Ball, Developments in transport policy: The evolution of capacity charges on the UK rail network, *Journal of Transport Economics and Policy*, vol. 36(2), pp. 341–354, 2002.

[13] J. Haile, Quantified risk assessment in railway system design and operation, *Quality and Reliability Engineering International*, vol. 11(6), pp. 439–443, 1995.

[14] S. Hansson, Risk, Stanford Encyclopedia of Philosophy, Stanford University, Palo Alto, California (plato.stanford.edu/entries/risk), 2007.

[15] T. Hellstrom, Critical infrastructure and systemic vulnerability: Towards a planning framework, *Safety Science*, vol. 45(3), pp. 415–430, 2007.

[16] B. Hutter, *Regulation and Risk: Occupational Health and Safety on the Railways*, Oxford University Press, Oxford, United Kingdom, 2001.

[17] International Risk Governance Council, Managing and Reducing Social Vulnerabilities from Coupled Critical Infrastructures, IRGC White Paper, Geneva, Switzerland, 2007.

[18] J. Kambhu, S. Weidman and N. Krishnan, *New Directions for Understanding Systemic Risk*, National Academies Press, Washington, DC, 2007.

[19] G. Kaufman, Banking and currency crises and systemic risk: A taxonomy and review, *Financial Markets, Institutions and Instruments*, vol. 9(2), pp. 69–131, 2000.

[20] G. Kaufman and K. Scott, What is systemic risk, and do bank regulators retard or contribute to it? *The Independent Review*, vol. 7(3), pp. 371–391, 2003.

[21] W. Kroger, Critical infrastructures at risk: A need for a new conceptual approach and extended analytical tools, *Reliability Engineering and System Safety*, vol. 93(12), pp. 1781–1787, 2008.

[22] W. Kroger and S. Dietz, Interdependencies among technical systems: The why, what and how, presented at the *European Safety and Reliability Conference*, 2008.

[23] R. Kunneke and M. Finger, The co-evolution between institutions and technology in liberalized infrastructures: The case of network unbundling in electricity and railways, presented at the *Eleventh Annual Conference of the International Society for New Institutional Economics*, 2007.

[24] C. Leighton and C. Dennis, Risk assessment of a new high speed railway, *Quality and Reliability Engineering International*, vol. 11(6), pp. 445–455, 1995.

[25] E. Luiijf, A. Nieuwenhuijs and M. Klaver, Critical infrastructure dependencies 1-0-1, presented at the *International Conference on Infrastructure Systems*, 2008.

[26] E. Luiijf, A. Nieuwenhuijs, M. Klaver, M. van Eeten and E. Cruz, Empirical findings on critical infrastructure dependencies in Europe, presented at the *Third International Workshop on Critical Information Infrastructure Security*, 2008.

[27] R. Minciardi, R. Sacile, A. Taramasso, E. Trasforini and S. Traverso, Modeling the vulnerability of complex territorial systems: An application to hydrological risk, *Environmental Modeling and Software*, vol. 21(7), pp. 949–960, 2006.

[28] N. Olsson and H. Haugland, Influencing factors on train punctuality – Results from some Norwegian studies, *Transport Policy*, vol. 11(4), pp. 387–397, 2004.

[29] Organization for Economic Cooperation and Development, *Emerging Systemic Risks in the 21st Century: An Agenda for Action*, OECD Publishing, Paris, France, 2003.

[30] M. Ottens, M. Franssen, P. Kroes and I. van de Poel, Modeling infrastructures as socio-technical systems, *International Journal of Critical Infrastructures*, vol. 2(2/3), pp. 133–145, 2006.

[31] M. Sajeva and M. Masera, A strategic approach to risk governance of critical infrastructures, *International Journal of Critical Infrastructures*, vol. 2(4), pp. 379–395, 2006.

[32] J. Santos-Reyes and A. Beard, A systemic analysis of the Edge Hill railway accident, to appear in *Accident Analysis and Prevention*.

[33] J. Santos-Reyes, A. Beard and R. Smith, A systemic analysis of railway accidents, *Proceedings of the Institution of Mechanical Engineers, Part F: Journal of Rail and Rapid Transit*, vol. 219(2), pp. 47–65, 2005.

[34] M. Schlapfer, S. Dietz and M. Kaegi, Stress induced degradation dynamics in complex networks, presented at the *International Conference on Infrastructure Systems*, 2008.

[35] P. Sen, S. Dasgupta, A. Chatterjee, P. Sreeram, G. Mukherjee and S. Manna, Small-world properties of the Indian railway network, *Physical Review E*, vol. 67(3), pp. 036106-1–5, 2003.

[36] P. Taylor-Gooby and J. Zinn, *Risk in Social Science*, Oxford University Press, Oxford, United Kingdom, 2006.

[37] J. Tornquist, Railway traffic disturbance management – An experimental analysis of disturbance complexity, management objectives and limitations in planning horizon, *Transportation Research, Part A: Policy and Practice*, vol. 41(3), pp. 249–266, 2007.

[38] M. Vromans, R. Dekker and L. Kroon, Reliability and heterogeneity of railway services, *European Journal of Operational Research*, vol. 172(2), pp. 647–665, 2006.

[39] A. Wilkinson, S. Elahi and E. Eidinow (Eds.), Section 3: Expert interviews, *Journal of Risk Research*, vol. 6(4), pp. 403–575, 2003.

[40] R. Zimmerman and C. Restrepo, The next step: Quantifying infrastructure interdependencies to improve security, *International Journal of Critical Infrastructures*, vol. 2(2/3), pp. 215–230, 2006.

Chapter 3

RISK-BASED CRITICALITY ANALYSIS

Marianthi Theoharidou, Panayiotis Kotzanikolaou and Dimitris Gritzalis

Abstract   Critical infrastructure protection requires the evaluation of the criticality of infrastructures and the prioritization of critical assets. However,
criticality analysis is not yet standardized. This paper examines the
relation between risk and criticality. It analyzes the similarities and
differences in terms of scope, aims, impact, threats and vulnerabilities;
and proposes a generic risk-based criticality analysis methodology. The
paper also presents a detailed list of impact criteria for assessing the criticality level of infrastructures. Emphasis is placed on impact types that
are society-centric and/or sector-centric, unlike traditional risk analysis
methodologies that mainly consider the organization-centric impact.

Keywords: Risk analysis, criticality, impact

1.   Introduction

A critical infrastructure (CI) is a "service, facility or a group of services or facilities, the loss of which will have severe adverse effects on the physical, social,
economic or environmental well-being or safety of the community" [6]. CIs incorporate material and information assets, networks, services and installations
[4]. All CIs use information and communications technology (ICT) systems
and depend strongly on these systems [3].

The importance of assessing the criticality of CIs, prioritizing them and
implementing adequate security controls has been emphasized by the European
Commission [8], U.S. Government [26] and other governments [6, 22]. Clearly,
there is a close correlation between the protection of CIs and the mitigation of
security risks faced by CIs. However, the "criticality" of a CI is a term that has
not been formally defined. Unlike ICT risk analysis methodologies, criticality
analysis methodologies are relatively obscure and *ad hoc* in nature. In fact,
no specific standards exist for critical infrastructure protection itself, although
certain security and safety standards are being used as auxiliary standards
[3]. Standard CIP-002-1 (Critical Asset Identification) created by the North

C. Palmer and S. Shenoi (Eds.): Critical Infrastructure Protection III, IFIP AICT 311, pp. 35–49, 2009.
© IFIP International Federation for Information Processing 2009

American Electric Reliability Corporation [20] requires a risk-based assessment methodology to identify critical assets. However, it neither suggests a specific method nor provides detailed requirements for a suitable method. There is an urgent need to clarify how existing risk analysis methodologies can be properly utilized to assess, categorize, prioritize and protect CIs.

This paper compares risk and criticality in terms of their scope, aims, impact, threats and vulnerabilities to clarify how risk analysis methodologies can be applied to critical infrastructure protection. It defines "criticality analysis" as a special-purpose, society-centric risk analysis process applied to large-scale interdependent systems and infrastructures. The primary contributions of this paper are a generic risk-based criticality analysis methodology and a detailed list of impact criteria for assessing the criticality of infrastructures.

2.   Criticality

The most common approach used to characterize an infrastructure as critical is to assess the impact level in the presence of security-related threats. Most methods focus on the consequences of an event, i.e., the "outcome of a situation or event expressed qualitatively or quantitatively as being a loss, injury, disadvantage or gain" [6]. Impact factors, or critical asset factors, are criteria used to prioritize assets and infrastructures. Impact is usually evaluated with respect to three primary characteristics [6–8, 17]: (i) scope or spatial distribution – the geographic area that could be affected by the loss or unavailability of a critical infrastructure; (ii) severity or intensity or magnitude – the consequences of the disruption or destruction of a particular critical infrastructure; and (iii) effects of time or temporal distribution – the point that the loss of an element could have a serious impact (immediate, one to two days, one week).

Intensity is usually analyzed using detailed qualitative and quantitative criteria. For example, the European Commission [7, 8] defines a minimum set of criteria that member states should consider in their critical infrastructure assessments: (i) public effect – population affected, loss of life, medical illness, serious injury, evacuation; (ii) economic effect – GDP effect, significance of economic loss and/or degradation of products or services; (iii) environmental effect – effect on the public and the surrounding environment; (iv) interdependency – interdependencies between critical infrastructure elements; (v) political effects – confidence in the government; and (vi) psychological effects – psychological effects on the population. These criteria are evaluated in terms of scope (local, regional, national and international) and time (during and after the incident).

Similarly, the U.S. National Infrastructure Protection Plan [26] lists criteria for evaluating consequences: (i) public health and safety – effect on human life and physical well-being; (ii) economic – direct and indirect economic losses; (iii) psychological – effect on public morale and confidence in economic and political institutions; and (iv) governance/mission – effect on the ability of the government or industry to maintain order, deliver essential services, ensure public health and safety, and carry out national security-related missions.

Table 1. Criticality approaches (impact factors).

Impact Criteria	Approach
Public Health and Safety	[7, 8, 17, 26]
Economic	[7, 8, 17, 22, 26]
Environment	[7, 8, 17]
Political/Governance/Mission	[7, 8, 17, 26]
Psychological/Social/Public Confidence	[7, 8, 17, 22, 26]
Interdependency	[7, 8, 13, 16, 22]
Complexity	[13]
Vulnerability	[13]
Market Environment	[13]
Concentration of People and Assets	[22]
Scope/Range	[7, 8, 17, 22]
Service Delivery/Recovery Time	[7, 8, 16, 17, 22]
National/Territorial Security	[17, 26]

Other proposed factors are [13]: (i) complexity; (ii) dependence on other infrastructures, by other infrastructures, by intra-infrastructure components and on information and communications technology; (iii) vulnerability, including external impact (natural hazards, construction mishap), technical/human failure, cyber attacks and terrorism; and (iv) market environment, especially the degree of liberalization, adequacy of control and speed of change.

The Canadian approach [22] is different in that the criteria are accompanied by impact scales: (i) concentration of people and assets; (ii) economic; (iii) critical infrastructure sector (international, national, provincial or regional); (iv) interdependency (physical, geographic or logical); (v) service delivery (acceptable downtime, availability of substitutes, time and cost required for recovery); (vi) public confidence (in the ability of a state to preserve public health and safety, and provide economic security and essential services).

The Dutch approach [16] uses the notion of "vitality." Indirect vitality is the degree to which other products and services contribute to the dependability of a product or service. Direct vitality is the contribution that a product or service delivers to society. The approach also engages backward and forward dependencies, the failure vs. recovery criterion (time required for minimum recovery and for full recovery) and the point of time when the major impact occurs. The Dutch risk assessment method for CIs [17] evaluates impact based on: (i) territorial security; (ii) physical safety; (iii) economic security; (iv) ecological security; (v) social and political stability; and (vi) social and psychological impact. All the criteria are evaluated in terms of range and duration.

Several terms are used in the literature to express the degree to which an infrastructure is critical. As discussed above, the principal terms are criticality [7, 8, 13, 22], vitality [16] and risk (impact or consequences) [17, 26]. Table 1 presents the impact criteria used by various approaches in the literature.

Interdependencies may be characterized as: (i) physical; (ii) cyber; (iii) geographic; and (iv) logical [23]. Another categorization of interdependencies is: (i) physical (e.g., a fallen tree causes a power outage); (ii) informational (e.g., loss of a SCADA system that monitors and controls the electrical power grid); (iii) geospatial (e.g., a flood damages key telecommunications assets); (iv) policy/procedural (e.g., a safety hazard in one subway station halts transportation throughout the subway system); and (v) societal (e.g., erosion of public confidence after the September 11, 2001 terrorist attacks) [21].

3.   Security Risk and Criticality

Most of the criteria used to assess criticality are impact factors that are commonly used in risk analysis methodologies. Obviously, there is a correlation between the criticality level of a CI and the security impacts and associated security risk levels. We examine this correlation in order to define the criticality level of an infrastructure in relation to its risk level.

Criticality as a Subset of Risk.   Several critical infrastructure protection impact criteria (e.g., health and safety, national security, financial loss, service loss and public confidence loss) are used in risk analysis methodologies. However, some of the more prominent risk analysis methodologies (e.g., CRAMM [9] and OCTAVE [2]) consider additional impact factors. These include competitive disadvantage (due to commercial and economic interests), legal or regulatory sanctions (due to law enforcement or non-compliance with legal or regulatory obligations), and system operation malfunctions (due to flawed management or business operations).

During a typical risk analysis, risk is assessed based on impact factors, threats and vulnerabilities. Thus, the criticality of the system is also evaluated (at least partially) as a side-effect. Indeed, the evaluated risks associated with the criticality-related impact factors include the criticality-related risks. Note that during risk analysis, some of the evaluated risks are based on impact types that are not associated with the criticality level of a system. In this sense, criticality can be considered to be a subset of the risk.

Risk as a Subset of Criticality.   Certain criticality factors are not used as impact criteria in traditional risk analysis methodologies. Examples include scope, economic impact, environmental effects and dependency effects. As a result, a risk analysis conducted for a single organization (or multiple organizations in the same sector) does not evaluate risks associated with external impacts (e.g., social and/or sector-oriented consequences). For example, a criticality analysis may assess the societal impact of an incident that affects the banking sector. Such an impact may not be considered in a risk analysis conducted for an individual bank. In fact, if a risk analysis for an individual bank were to examine the impact of an event that affects the availability of the entire banking sector, it would result in a lower risk level compared with an event that only affects the availability of services at that particular bank. This is because the bank in question would not lose its competitive disadvantage or face legal/regulatory consequences. Thus, certain criticality factors are not considered as typical risks, and risk can be viewed as a subset of criticality.

Risk vs. Criticality. Impact is the basic connecting element between risk and criticality. However, other issues should also be considered in order to clarify how risk analysis can be used when evaluating CIs.

- **Interdependency of CIs:** Risk analysis methods mainly focus on information systems, which they treat as isolated entities. Thus, they fail to capture the complexity of CI interconnections, cross-sector impacts, dependencies with other systems or CIs and cascading effects within a sector or across sectors. Therefore, the integration of key critical infrastructure protection models with risk analysis methodologies is important. Examples include critical infrastructure protection layers, the implications of dependencies between layers, and the multi-dimensional nature of the impact of an incident [1]. Approaches for interdependency identification, modeling, visualization and simulation should be embedded in risk analysis methodologies [5, 11, 19, 23, 24].

- **Impact Scope:** Risk analysis mainly evaluates internal impacts. However, criticality analysis also considers impacts external to the examined CI such as societal impacts, sector impacts and impacts to citizens that are not directly related to the examined CI (e.g., users, customers, candidate customers and contracted third parties). As a consequence, risk analysis only evaluates the factors that relate to internal impacts, while criticality analysis mainly focuses on the security risks related to external impacts (societal/sector-based impacts).

- **Impact Scale:** Since external and cascading impacts must be taken into account, the evaluated impacts tend to be higher than the internal impacts. New impact scales related to criticality factors must be defined and evaluated; these should differentiate between impact types as well as impact levels.

- **Objectives:** Although critical infrastructure protection objectives may appear to be similar to information assurance objectives (e.g., confidentiality, integrity and availability), achieving the objectives is much more complex for a CI. This is due to the global dimension of CIs, the complexity due to inter- and intra-dependencies, new threats, and dependability and survivability issues [3]. Also, attacks can be the result of structural threats (e.g., natural disasters, accidents, strikes, epidemics, technical failures, human error and supply shortages) or intentional attacks, which may be executed by actors ranging from disgruntled employees to terrorists and nation states. These issues are generally not considered in traditional risk analysis [4].

Table 2.   Risk analysis vs. criticality analysis.

	Risk Analysis	Criticality Analysis
Aim	Organization	Society
Scope	Internal assets	Internal assets and interdependencies
Impact Type	Organization-centric	Society-centric
Threats	System	CI and interdependencies
Vulnerabilities	System	CI and interdependencies
Impact Scale	Variable	Higher

Table 2 compares and contrasts risk analysis and criticality analysis. Based on this summary, we provide two definitions:

DEFINITION 1 (Criticality): Criticality is the: (i) level of contribution of an infrastructure to society in maintaining a minimum level of national and international law and order, public safety, economy, public health and environment, or (ii) impact level to citizens or to the government from the loss or disruption of the infrastructure [16].

DEFINITION 2 (Criticality Analysis): Criticality analysis is the process of assessing the criticality level of an infrastructure. It is a special-purpose, society-centric risk analysis process that attempts to protect infrastructures that are vital to society. Criticality analysis mainly considers the societal impacts instead of the organizational impacts. The scope of the analysis is extended to cover interdependent infrastructures and, thus, possible threats and vulnerabilities. Criticality analysis is performed on large-scale CIs that provide services to large numbers of users/citizens and, thus, it usually involves higher impact scales.

The results of a risk analysis of a CI and/or its interdependent CIs may be used as input when assessing the criticality level of the CI. Since there are common impacts, threats and vulnerabilities in both processes, risk analysis can provide preliminary metrics, especially those obtained by examining the security risks based on commonly-used impacts, threats and vulnerabilities.

4.   Generic Criticality Analysis Methodology

This section describes a generic criticality analysis methodology based on the preceding discussion of security risk and criticality. The methodology has six steps, which are described below.

- **Step 1: Identify Critical Assets.** As in risk analysis, the assets of the CI under consideration are documented (facilities, services, hardware, software, information, human resources, etc.). This task may be performed with the assistance of infrastructure asset owners.

- **Step 2: Define Interconnections and Dependencies.** Interconnected CIs should be defined. These may be categorized as dependent CIs (i.e., infrastructures that depend on the examined CI) and requisite CIs (i.e., CIs that are required by the examined CI for its operation). Although this process has similarities with the definition of third parties during risk analysis, it serves a different purpose. In risk analysis, third parties are only considered if they pose security risks to the examined system/organization (e.g., service providers, software/hardware suppliers and customers). In criticality analysis, the interconnected CIs that imply a general societal risk should be considered even if they do not imply any risk for the CI. Defining the interconnections and dependencies ensures that the criticality impacts consider more than just the organization/system-oriented impacts; in particular, it helps evaluate the global threats and common vulnerabilities within the interconnected CIs.

- **Step 3: Evaluate Criticality Impact.** After the interconnections and dependencies have been identified, the criticality impact factors are examined. As explained in Section 3, the impact factors have an extended scope and focus on societal rather than internal impacts (e.g., public safety, public services and economy). The assessment of impact is based on scope, severity and time. The analysis may take into account several scenarios where a critical asset or service is unavailable or where the confidentiality or integrity of information is affected.

- **Step 4: Define Threats.** Since criticality depends on the interconnected CIs, an extended list of threats must be created. Examples of threats include masquerading as authorized users, unauthorized use of resources, introduction of malware, interception or manipulation of communications, communication failures, technical failures, power failures, software failures, operational errors, maintenance errors, user errors, fire, water damage, natural disasters, staff shortages, theft, willful damage, terrorism and espionage [9].

- **Step 5: Evaluate Threat and Vulnerability Levels.** Possible threats are evaluated for each CI asset. The threat levels should consider the possibility of realizing a threat within the examined CI as well within the scope of CI interconnections and dependencies. The likelihood of a threat can be based on the history of previous incidents, existing literature and interviews with experts. The threats that affect a CI are a superset of those used in traditional risk analysis. The vulnerabilities that lead to incidents must also be identified and evaluated; this is by no means a trivial task because vulnerabilities can be inherited by other CIs.

- **Step 6: Evaluate Associated Criticality Risk Factors.** As in typical risk analysis, risk is quantified by taking into account all possible combinations of threats, vulnerabilities and criticality impacts for each asset, i.e., risk = threat × vulnerability × criticality impact.

Table 3. Scope impact factors.

Impact Factor	Very High	High	Medium	Low
Population Affected	>10,000	1,000–10,000	100–1,000	<100
Concentration (persons/km^2)	>750	500–750	250–500	<250
Range	International	National	Regional	Local

5.   Criticality Impact Assessment

We compiled a set of criteria based on our review of critical infrastructure protection approaches (described in Section 2), and proceeded to enrich them using generic risk methodologies [9]. The criteria were categorized in terms of scope, severity and time. A criticality impact assessment was conducted using a survey of experts. The survey respondents were asked to specify their levels of agreement with various statements using a Likert four-item psychometric scale [14]. Note that the numerical scales used in practice vary considerably; to our knowledge, no standardized or widely accepted ranges for these scales exist. The following tables present indicative examples of the scales we use for criticality impact assessment. Our intent is to demonstrate the characteristics of each impact factor and how the scales may differ from traditional risk analysis.

The scope of an incident may be expressed using three factors: population affected, population concentration and range. Table 3 shows the three scope impact factors and their scales (based on [22]).

- **Population Affected:** This is the number of people affected by an incident. Note that this factor is not used to evaluate the type of impact.

- **Population Concentration:** A higher concentration implies a higher potential for catastrophic effects. Population density (persons/km^2) is a useful criterion [17]; Table 3 presents an adjusted scale for this criterion.

- **Range:** This criterion evaluates the geographical scope of an event (e.g., <100 km^2, 100–1,000 km^2, 1,000–10,000 km^2, >10,000 km^2 [17]; or international, national, regional, local [22]).

The three criteria evaluate scope in different ways. The first criterion quantifies the number of affected individuals. The other two criteria do not evaluate scope in absolute terms: concentration expresses the density of population while range provides an abstract representation of the geographical effect.

A number of criteria may be used to quantify the severity of incidents. Table 4 presents several severity impact factors. Note that the scales can be adjusted according to national policy and currency.

- **Economic Impact:** This criterion measures the direct economic impact of an incident. It includes the losses to the CI itself from service degrada-

Table 4. Severity impact factors.

Impact Factor	Very High	High	Medium	Low
Economic Impact	>$100 million	$10–$100 million	$1–$10 million	<$1 million
Interdependency	Debilitating impact on other CIs or sectors	Significant impact on other CIs or sectors	Moderate impact on other CIs or sectors	Minor impact on other CIs or sectors
Public Confidence (Perception)	High risk and ability to control in doubt internationally	High risk and ability to control in doubt nationally	Moderate risk and ability to control risk	Low risk and ability to control risk
International Relations	Seriously damage international relations	Raise international tension	Materially damage diplomatic relations	Adversely affect diplomatic relations
Public Order	Direct threat to internal stability	Widespread industrial action	Demonstrations; lobbying	Localized protest
Policy and Operations of Public Service	Shut down or substantially disrupt national operations	Seriously impede the development or operation of government policies	Impede the development or operation of government policies	Undermine management or operation of a public sector organization
Safety	Widespread loss of lives	Severe injuries; chronic illnesses; potential casualties	Severe injuries; chronic illnesses	Minor injuries
Defense	Grave damage to the security of allied forces	Grave damage to the security of a nation	Minor damage to the security of a nation	n/a

tion or loss of assets and information, recovery costs, and the estimated loss due to cascading effects. The GDP can be used to estimate the economic impact. Possible scales are >$1 billion, $100 million to $1 billion, $10 to $100 million, <$10 million [22]; and <€50 million, <€500 million, <€5 billion, <€50 billion, >€50 billion [17]. Note that the scales are significantly higher than those used in traditional risk assessment methods (which may have a maximum level of £1 million [9]). The scales vary according to the scope of the analysis and the value of critical assets. Furthermore, they should be adjustable as in the case of risk methods [9].

- **Interdependency:** This criterion assesses the likelihood of a cascading effect within the sector and across sectors. Interdependencies may be physical, cyber, geographic and logical [23].

- **Public Confidence:** This criterion assesses the impact on public confidence or on the ability of the government to provide public services, maintain health and safety, etc. [26]. The scale used in Table 4 is based on [22].

Next, we describe five additional criteria that are used in risk analysis [9] as well as in critical infrastructure protection. These impacts, which are primarily societal in nature, are assigned relatively high assessments by [9] (7 to 10 on a ten-point scale) and are generally not applicable to commercial organizations.

- **International Relations:** This criterion evaluates the impact of an incident on diplomatic relationships [9, 17]. The effects include demonstrations or threats against a country or its embassies, negative publicity and diplomatic actions (e.g., expulsion of diplomats, termination of diplomatic relations, cancellation of visits by foreign representatives, cancellation of trade agreements and treaties) [17].

- **Public Order:** This criterion estimates the impact on public order. The impact on public order could be due to the disclosure of confidential information or the unavailability of critical public services (e.g., electricity or water supply). The scaling [9] has been adjusted to fit a four-item scale.

- **Public Policy and Operations:** This criterion assesses the ability of the government to implement its policies and operations. It is different from the public confidence criterion because it does not consider psychological effects, but the actual ability of the government to function. The scaling [9] has been adjusted to fit a four-item scale.

- **Public Safety:** This criterion relates to the welfare of individuals; it includes injuries, chronic illnesses and fatalities. It also encompasses pain, suffering and grief [17]. Unlike the scope criteria, it does not consider the number of people affected or the percentage of the population affected.

- **Defense:** This criterion considers the ability of a government to protect its population from hostile attacks [9] either due to the unavailability of CIs or through the modification or disclosure of critical information. Because of its nature, this criterion does not have a low value; thus, the scale ranges from medium to very high.

Table 5. Time-related impact factors.

Impact Factor	Very High	High	Medium	Low
Recovery Time	Years	Months	Days	Hours
Duration	Years	Months	Days	Hours

Two criteria are used to assess the temporal aspects of incidents (Table 5):

- **Recovery Time:** This criterion measures the time needed for recovery. It is affected by the availability of substitutes and the cost incurred before an asset or service is restored.

- **Impact Duration:** This criterion is different from the recovery time because, although some services may become functional, the long-term effects of the incident may still affect the CI and its environment (e.g., public confidence or economic impact). Possible ways to represent time factors are 2–6 days, 1–4 weeks, 1–6 months, 6 months or longer [17]; and years, months–year, days–weeks, hours–days [22]. Traditional risk analysis methods often use shorter time frames, e.g., <15 mins, 1 hour, 3 hours, 12 hours, 1 day, 2 days, 1 week, etc. [9]. Our scale ranges from hours to years.

Table 6. Critical points of time.

Impact Factor	Points of Time			
Impact Peak	Immediate	Within hours	Within days	Within months
Critical Frames	Time periods that indicate variations in criticality			

The following criteria deal with "time-critical moments" for a CI (Table 6):

- **Impact Peak:** This is the point of time when an incident produces its most severe effect (e.g., immediate, one to two days, one week, etc.).

- **Critical Time Frames:** These refer to moments/periods that demonstrate variations in criticality (e.g., the difference in criticality of telecommunications during normal operation and during a crisis situation).

In order to assess the overall criticality, the applicable scope, severity and time criteria have to be assessed for an incident or threat. It is also essential to define the expected impact peak and the critical time frames for a CI when a particular incident may have a greater impact. Clearly, different impact levels are expected for these critical points of time. We recommend applying a "worst-case" approach instead of calculating the average impact. For each scenario,

Table 7.   Applicable criteria.

Criteria	Impact Factor	Normal Traffic	Rush Hour
Scope	Population Affected	Low	Medium
Severity	Economic Impact	Low	Medium
	Interdependency	Medium	Medium
	Public Confidence	High	High
	Safety	High	Very High
Time	Recovery Time	High	High
	Duration	Low	Low

the impact is evaluated for each time point/frame; the worst-case impacts are combined to obtain the overall impact.

6.   Illustrative Example

This section illustrates the criticality assessment methodology using a metro system (transportation sector) as an example. The metro system transports up to 975,000 commuters a day, and is interconnected with other transportation sector components (buses and trams). In the example, we evaluate the critical asset "Central Station" with respect to the "Fire" threat.

We use a worst-case scenario to assess the impact of the fire scenario on the metro station. We identify two critical points of time – normal traffic and rush hour – and proceed to perform a separate assessment for each time frame. The rush hour time frame differs from the normal traffic period in terms of the number of people affected and the economic impact (e.g., transportation assets at the station). Also, due to the number of the people at the station, rescue and evacuation would present difficulties, which may lead to a higher safety impact.

Interdependent CIs would be affected due to the presence of connecting stops inside or close to the station. Also, passengers would require other means of transportation during the recovery period, giving rise to congestion elsewhere in the transportation system. Thus, the impact on the interconnected CIs is expected to be moderate. Due to the presence of fire control assets at the station and the proximity of the fire department, the duration is estimated to be a few hours. However, the recovery time is expected to be 1.5 months. The impact peak is estimated to be within one hour for both time frames. The impact on public confidence is anticipated to be high with regard to metro system safety and rescue team efficiency. Based on a worst-case impact assessment, the overall criticality is assessed to be high for normal traffic and very high during the rush hour (Table 7).

In order to assess the associated criticality risk factors, it is necessary to estimate the possibility of a fire occurring in the central station based on statistics of previous incidents (this information would be available from the fire department). Also, the enabling vulnerabilities have to be identified. Examples include the presence of flammable materials, poor maintenance of circuits and cabling, etc. Although the impact is assessed as being high, the overall risk could be low, especially if the threat level and vulnerability level are both low.

7. Conclusions

Current approaches for evaluating and prioritizing CIs are mainly based on criticality impact factors; in particular, they do not exploit the results of well-defined risk analysis methodologies. The resulting CI categorizations and prioritizations are often inherently biased due to their reliance on organization-oriented impacts and security risk factors. The risk-based criticality analysis methodology presented in this paper addresses this deficiency by considering societal and sector-based impact factors as well as CI interdependencies. Our future work will focus on the definition of criticality-oriented threats and vulnerabilities, interdependency modeling and numerical assessments of risk in CIs.

References

[1] E. Adar and A. Wuchner, Risk management for critical infrastructure protection challenges: Best practices and tools, *Proceedings of the First IEEE International Workshop on Critical Infrastructure Protection*, 2005.

[2] C. Alberts and A. Dorofee, *Managing Information Security Risks: The OCTAVE Approach*, Addison-Wesley/Pearson, Boston, Massachusetts, 2003.

[3] A. Bialas, Information security systems vs. critical information infrastructure protection systems – Similarities and differences, *Proceedings of the International Conference on the Dependability of Computer Systems*, pp. 60–67, 2006.

[4] E. Brunner and M. Suter, *International CIIP Handbook 2008/2009: An Inventory of 25 National and 7 International Critical Infrastructure Protection Policies*, Center for Security Studies, ETH Zurich, Zurich, Switzerland, 2008.

[5] E. Casalicchio and E. Galli, Metrics for quantifying interdependencies, in *Critical Infrastructure Protection II*, M. Papa and S. Shenoi (Eds.), Springer, Boston, Massachusetts, pp. 215–227, 2008.

[6] Emergency Management Australia, Critical Infrastructure Emergency Risk Management and Assurance Handbook, Mount Macedon, Australia, 2003.

[7] European Commission, Communication from the Commission of 12 December 2006 on a European Programme for Critical Infrastructure Protection, COM (2006)786 Final, Brussels, Belgium, 2006.

[8] European Commission, Proposal for a Directive of the Council on the Identification and Designation of European Critical Infrastructure and the Assessment of the Need to Improve Their Protection, COM(2006)787 Final, Brussels, Belgium, 2006.

[9] Insight Consulting, CRAMM User Guide, Issue 5.1, Walton-on-Thames, United Kingdom, 2005.

[10] International Organization for Standardization, ISO/IEC Guide 73:2002: Risk Management – Vocabulary – Guidelines for Use in Standards, Geneva, Switzerland, 2002.

[11] J. Kopylec, A. D'Amico and J. Goodall, Visualizing cascading failures in critical cyber infrastructures, in *Critical Infrastructure Protection*, E. Goetz and S. Shenoi (Eds.), Springer, Boston, Massachusetts, pp. 351–364, 2007.

[12] KPMG Peat Marwick, Vulnerability Assessment Framework 1.1, U.S. Critical Infrastructure Assurance Office, Washington, DC, 1998.

[13] W. Kroger, Critical infrastructures at risk: A need for a new conceptual approach and extended analytical tools, *Reliability Engineering and System Safety*, vol. 93(12), pp. 1781–1787, 2008.

[14] R. Likert, A technique for the measurement of attitudes, *Archives of Psychology*, vol. 140(22), pp. 1–55, 1932.

[15] E. Luiijf, Threat Taxonomy for Critical Infrastructures and Critical Infrastructure Risk Aspects at the EU-Level, Version 1.04, Deliverable D1.2, Technical Report VITA PASR-2004-004400, TNO Defence, Security and Safety, The Hague, The Netherlands, 2006.

[16] E. Luiijf, H. Burger and M. Klaver, Critical infrastructure protection in the Netherlands: A quick-scan, *Proceedings of the EICAR Conference*, 2003.

[17] Ministry of the Interior and Kingdom Relations, National Risk Assessment Method Guide 2008, The Hague, The Netherlands, 2008.

[18] J. Moteff, Risk Management and Critical Infrastructure Protection: Assessing, Integrating and Managing Threats, Vulnerabilities and Consequences, CRS Report for Congress, Document RL32561, Congressional Research Service, Library of Congress, Washington, DC, 2005.

[19] A. Nieuwenhuijs, E. Luiijf and M. Klaver, Modeling dependencies in critical infrastructures, in *Critical Infrastructure Protection II*, M. Papa and S. Shenoi (Eds.), Springer, Boston, Massachusetts, pp. 205–213, 2008.

[20] North American Electric Reliability Corporation, Standard CIP-002-1, Cyber Security – Critical Asset Identification, Washington, DC, 2006.

[21] P. Pederson, D. Dudenhoeffer, S. Hartley and M. Permann, Critical Infrastructure Interdependency Modeling: A Survey of U.S. and International Research, Technical Report INL/EXT-06-11464, Idaho National Laboratory, Idaho Falls, Idaho, 2006.

[22] Public Safety and Emergency Preparedness Canada, Selection Criteria to Identify and Rank Critical Infrastructure Assets, Ottawa, Canada, 2004.

[23] S. Rinaldi, J. Peerenboom and T. Kelly, Identifying, understanding and analyzing critical infrastructure interdependencies, *IEEE Control Systems*, vol. 21(6), pp. 11–25, 2001.

[24] R. Setola, S. Bologna, E. Casalicchio and V. Masucci, An integrated approach for simulating interdependencies, in *Critical Infrastructure Protection II*, M. Papa and S. Shenoi, (Eds.), Springer, Boston, Massachusetts, pp. 229–239, 2008.

[25] G. Stoneburner, A. Goguen and A. Feringa, Risk Management Guide for Information Technology Systems: Recommendations of the National Institute of Standards and Technology, Special Publication 800-30, National Institute of Standards and Technology, Gaithersburg, Maryland, 2002.

[26] U.S. Department of Homeland Security, National Infrastructure Protection Plan 2009, Washington, DC, 2009.

Chapter 4

MODELING AND MANAGING RISK IN BILLING INFRASTRUCTURES

Fabrizio Baiardi, Claudio Telmon and Daniele Sgandurra

Abstract   This paper discusses risk modeling and risk management in information and communications technology (ICT) systems for which the attack impact distribution is heavy tailed (e.g., power law distribution) and the average risk is unbounded. Systems with these properties include billing infrastructures used to charge customers for services they access. Attacks against billing infrastructures can be classified as peripheral attacks and backbone attacks. The goal of a peripheral attack is to tamper with user bills; a backbone attack seeks to seize control of the billing infrastructure. The probability distribution of the overall impact of an attack on a billing infrastructure also has a heavy-tailed curve. This implies that the probability of a massive impact cannot be ignored and that the average impact may be unbounded – thus, even the most expensive countermeasures would be cost effective. Consequently, the only strategy for managing risk is to increase the resilience of the infrastructure by employing redundant components.

Keywords: Risk modeling, risk management, billing infrastructures

1.   Introduction

This paper describes the modeling and management of risk in an information and communications technology (ICT) infrastructure where the average impact of an attack is unbounded. A mathematical model is developed to express the impact of attacks and is then applied to a billing infrastructure. A billing infrastructure is an ICT infrastructure that is designed, constructed and managed to bill a large set of customers for services they access or consume. Such an infrastructure comprises a set of peripheral nodes and an intelligent backbone [2]. An example is a metering infrastructure in which the peripheral nodes measure the amount of a good (e.g., water or electricity) distributed to customers, and the backbone records, delivers and updates customer bills [9]. In general, the inner structure of a peripheral node depends on the service

C. Palmer and S. Shenoi (Eds.): Critical Infrastructure Protection III, IFIP AICT 311, pp. 51–64, 2009.
© IFIP International Federation for Information Processing 2009

that is offered and billed. The intelligent backbone connects the peripheral nodes and includes additional computing nodes that manage and update the information shared by the peripheral and backbone nodes.

The impact of an attack against a peripheral node in a billing infrastructure is bounded. However, the impact of an attack against the intelligent backbone cannot be bounded because it depends on the infrastructure cost and/or the value of the business processes that use the infrastructure. Mathematical models for estimating the overall impact of attacks on peripheral nodes and on the backbone may be defined as the sum of two random processes described by a normal distribution and a power law distribution, respectively [5, 12–14, 17]. This paper discusses the models and their implications on risk management for the overall infrastructure. In particular, it considers the problem that arises when the average impact of an attack is unbounded, and demonstrates that, in such a case, it is difficult to predict the impact of attacks even when historical attack data is available. The paper also discusses how this result influences the selection of countermeasures [22, 23].

2.   Billing Infrastructures

This section briefly describes a billing infrastructure, which corresponds to an abstract model of an ICT infrastructure [1, 2, 15]. A billing infrastructure is characterized by the types of attacks and their impact on the infrastructure rather than the specific ICT components used in the infrastructure. The section also presents some real-world infrastructures that match the abstract billing infrastructure [9].

2.1   Infrastructure Overview

A billing infrastructure charges customers for a service that they receive. The service is supplied by the same infrastructure or by a different infrastructure; the service provider is also the infrastructure owner. The infrastructure consists of a set of peripheral nodes, one for each customer (in general), along with an intelligent backbone. Peripheral nodes may be distributed across a large region (e.g., a country); each node stores, manages and updates information about the quantity of service received by a user. The backbone interconnects the peripheral nodes and other computing nodes. The computing nodes store information about the peripheral nodes in order to manage the overall service distribution and to bill users.

As example is a content distribution service, where the billing infrastructure charges each user for the content that has been accessed; the content may be distributed by another infrastructure as in the case of pay-per-view movies. Another example is a metering infrastructure, where each peripheral node is connected to a meter that measures the quantity of some good (e.g., water, gas or electricity) that is distributed to a customer. In this type of infrastructure, each peripheral node computes and transmits to the backbone the amount of good consumed by each user and the corresponding bill.

An infrastructure can terminate the distribution of a good when a condition related to the quantity of the good consumed and/or consumer status is met. For example, the infrastructure may prevent a customer who has not paid his bill from further resource usage. In an advanced metering infrastructure, a peripheral node can also program the behavior of other devices to optimize the overall amount of the resource that is consumed or to optimize a combination of parameters such as the overall amount of the consumed resource and the customer bill. This can happen, for example, if a peripheral node schedules multiple devices in a home to minimize the overall amount of electricity that is consumed.

From our point of view, the internal behavior of peripheral nodes and the backbone are not fundamental because the important properties of the two subsystems are related to the attack impact. In particular, we are interested in billing infrastructures where the impact of an attack against a peripheral node is bounded whereas the impact of an attack on the backbone is unbounded (e.g., if the attacker seeks to control the overall infrastructure). In practice, the impact may be bounded by the cost of the overall business process that uses the infrastructure. However, because this cost depends on the infrastructure that is considered, no bound may exist in the general case. Furthermore, the overall impact may also depend on other infrastructures that are connected to the infrastructure under consideration. This problem is discussed below in the context of developing a mathematical model for attack impacts.

Note that the two types of attacks considered in this paper are distinguished by the goal of the attacker instead of the subsystems that are involved. Thus, an attack that targets a peripheral node as the first step of an attack against the backbone is considered to be an attack against the backbone.

2.2 Threat Model

The threat model considers two types of attacks against the infrastructure: (i) peripheral attacks that attempt to reduce user bills by attacking peripheral nodes; and (ii) backbone attacks that seek to control the infrastructure.

A peripheral attack that attempts to reduce a customer's bill is typically executed by an unethical costumer. We assume that general statistics about the customer population are available, which implies that the percentage of customers who may behave in an unethical manner is also known.

A backbone attack may seek to reduce the bills of a large number of customers, access confidential information about a set of customers, or control the use of a resource or service. Such an attack may be executed by a competitor, organized crime group or terrorist entity.

For both types of attacks, we distinguish between an attack that requires skill and knowledge that cannot be encapsulated in a tool that automates the attack, and an attack that can be fully automated so that its execution does not require any knowledge about the implementation of the infrastructure and nodes, only the availability of an attack tool. The two cases correspond to distinct pools of attackers because if an attack cannot be automated, then only a customer/attacker with the requisite skill and knowledge who is willing to act in an unethical manner can execute the attack. If a tool that implements the attack is available (e.g., downloadable from the Internet), then any unethical customer can launch the attack. For both types of attacks, the impact of a peripheral attack is bounded by the customer bill plus the cost to replace the peripheral node.

In the case of backbone attacks, we also distinguish between automated attacks and non-automated attacks. However, the impact is not related to customer bills because the goal of the attack may be to control the entire infrastructure or distinct systems connected to the infrastructure and managed by the owner. As described below, the notion of an average impact is questionable when modeling backbone attacks because the average impact of distinct sets of backbone attacks may converge to distinct values. Another difference between the two classes of attacks is related to the discovery of a vulnerability after the infrastructure has been deployed. If a newly-discovered vulnerability only enables peripheral attacks, then it increases the probability of one of these attacks but not the largest impact, which is always bounded by the customer bill. On the other hand, a vulnerability that enables a backbone attack may increase the probability of a successful attack and, thus, increase the overall impact or the overall value at risk.

3.   Modeling Attacks and Attack Impact

This section discusses the modeling of peripheral attacks and backbone attacks, and the impact of these attacks on the billing infrastructure. The attack impact is modeled by considering a time interval and attempting to predict all the impacts of interest in this interval and the information needed for prediction.

3.1   Peripheral Attacks

If an attack can only be executed manually (i.e., it cannot be automated), then the average number of attacks is proportional to the number of unethical customers who have the knowledge and the skills required to execute the attack. On the other hand, the number of automated attacks is proportional to the number of unethical customers. This also covers the case where unethical customers contract external agents to execute attacks on their behalf.

In the following, Npa denotes the expected number of potential attackers (this is always very large, but is much larger in the case of automated attacks). The impact D_i due to customer C_i is described by a random process with a probability distribution $Imp_i(D)$ specifying the probability that C_i executes an attack that yields an impact of D. $Imp_i(D)$ is larger than zero if $D \in 0..M_i$, where M_i is C_i's largest bill. The shape of Imp_i cannot be easily deduced as it depends on the amount of resources and skill C_i can summon to execute the attack. Hence, the variance of Imp_i is unknown and its rigorous approximation depends on several factors, including: (i) the ability of C_i to implement the attack that, in turn, influences the probability of a successful attack; and (ii) the gap between the time distribution of the attacks of C_i and the resource usage of C_i.

However, the variance of Imp_i can be approximated if a representative sample of peripheral attacks is available. In this case, we can compute the largest customer bill M, which represents the upper bound of the impact. Obviously, M is finite and any error in the approximation of Imp_i is bounded because the distance between impacts is always bounded by M.

The overall impact of a collection of peripheral attacks Ima is a stochastic process that is the union of the processes $D_1, \ldots, D_n$ corresponding to the impacts of the individual attacks by customers. Since $Ima = \Sigma_{i=1..n} D_i$, whenever the number of customers is very large, the shape of Ima can be approximated by assuming that the impacts of distinct customers are independent and applying the central limit theorem. Under these assumptions, Ima is normally distributed with a mean and variance equal to the sums of the means and variances of D_i, respectively. Since each sum can be restricted to Npa unethical customers (the only individuals who can execute attacks), the mean of Ima is bounded by $Npa \times M$ where M is the largest customer bill. By profiling unethical customers, we can replace M by Mun, the largest bill in the group of unethical customers. Similar considerations apply to the estimation of the upper bound for the variance of Ima. Thus, the estimate of the overall impact of peripheral attacks improves if it is possible to profile unethical customers.

Obviously, Npa strongly increases when attacks can be automated. Nevertheless, Ima can always be approximated by a normal distribution when the number of attackers or (from another point of view) the number of unethical customers is so large that the error due to the application of the central limit theorem is acceptable. Note that the independence property of customer attacks is fundamental. We assume that this property holds even if some customers belong to social networks and exchange information about vulnerabilities and attacks. Thus, the relevance of social networks is ignored when computing the overall impact. However, even if social networks are considered, and the number of successful attacks increases and the parameters of the normal distribution change, the overall impact and the approximation error are still bounded.

3.2 Backbone Attacks

The approach adopted for modeling peripheral attacks cannot be used for backbone attacks because it is not possible to approximate the largest impact or the average impact of attacks. In fact, any successful attack against the backbone has an unbounded impact if the appropriate backbone components are controlled as a result of the attack. While some attackers would be interested in achieving as large an impact as possible, other attackers may be interested in a bounded impact in order to achieve their goals (i.e., they execute attacks to control infrastructure components that may cause larger impacts than the attacks that interest them).

In order to model the impact probability distribution, we assume that the backbone is often optimized to minimize its overall cost [6] and that this may result in the adoption of a preferential attachment strategy to define the interconnections among backbone components at distinct implementation levels (ranging from the physical interconnections to the services offered by software components) [1, 16]. In this case, the impact of an attack depends on the component that is the target of the attack, and the impact probability distribution is a power law of the form:

$$\frac{C}{x^{1+a}}$$

where C is a normalizing constant.

In general, the probability distribution of an impact x assumes arbitrary values if x is in the range $0..xmax$, and subsequently follows a power law. If the sum of the values that x assumes before the power law behavior is γ, i.e.,

$$\Sigma_{x \in 0..xmax} p(x) = \gamma,$$

then, for $x \geq xmax + 1$, the distribution has the form:

$$\frac{a \cdot (1 - \gamma)}{(xmax + 1)} \cdot \left(\frac{xmax + 1}{x}\right)^{1+a}$$

This also covers the more interesting case where $x = 0$ is the only impact with a non-null probability in the range $0..xmax$ because every successful backbone attack has an impact larger than $xmax$. It is important to note that the impact probability distribution has power law behavior whenever the parameter to be optimized is the overall cost (or return on investment) even if faults or external attacks are considered. As an example, the high optimized tolerance methodology introduces components into a system to minimize the impact of faults [4, 18]. However, because this methodology optimizes the return on investment, the impact distribution also has power law behavior. Furthermore, any error in the approximation of the fault distribution strongly reduces the effectiveness of the optimization and may give rise to unbounded impacts.

We assume that the overall impact due to a single attacker also has a power law distribution. This implies that the attacker targeting the backbone is interested in executing just one attack, but the most powerful attack he can implement. Obviously, the actual impact would depend on the attacker's motive and knowledge, but this only influences the parameters in the power law equation. Therefore, in the worst case, the probability distribution of the impact x, $Psa_i(x)$, is a heavy-tailed power law [12, 13, 21] given by:

$$Psa_i(x) = \frac{C}{x^{1+a}}$$

where $0 < a < 1$. This is the worst case because the probability of a large impact decreases very slowly.

In the following, we use a power law rather than a heavy-tailed power law. The corresponding results hold for the larger class of probability distribution functions (i.e., subexponential functions [7]), which includes any function that decreases slower than an exponential function. A process X has a subexponential distribution if:

$$limit_{d \to \infty} \frac{Prob\,(X_1 + ...X_n > d)}{Prob\,(max(X_1, ..., X_n) > D)} = 1$$

where any X_i is distributed as X and all the X_i are independent.

This condition implies that the sum is large because of the large contribution provided by only one term of the sum. In a billing infrastructure, the condition implies that an attacker is interested in causing one large impact rather that several average impacts. This is often the case because low impact attacks are of limited interest to several classes of attackers. For example, a terrorist entity or a competitor would be interested in executing one large impact attack that results in considerable publicity (and loss of credibility for the owner of the targeted infrastructure) rather than several low impact attacks that also increase the probability of being detected and apprehended.

The class of subexponential functions strictly includes the class of heavy-tailed functions. The class of heavy-tailed functions includes any distribution of a process X where for any h:

$$limit_{D \to \infty} \frac{Prob\,(X > D + h)}{Prob\,(X > D)} = 1.$$

In other words, as D increases, for any h, the probability that X is larger than D is that same as the probability that X is larger than $D + h$. This implies that an attack that produces an impact D can also produce an impact $D + h$. Note that this class faithfully models the case under consideration because, as D increases, the backbone components that must be attacked to produce an impact D make it possible to achieve an even larger impact.

Alternatively, a process X is deemed to have a heavy-tailed distribution if a value V exists such that, if $X \geq V$, then the ratio:

$$\frac{Prob\,(X > nD)}{Prob\,(X > D)}$$

is independent of D for any $n > 0$. In our case, this again expresses the fact that if the impact of an attack is larger than D, then it may be unbounded. Another reason to describe the impacts of backbone attacks using a power law is that the impacts may be proportional to the overall value of the infrastructure. Additional reasons for using a power law are discussed in [10, 21].

An important consequence of a power law distribution of impacts is that, depending on the exponent, it may be impossible to build a representative sample of backbone attacks. This implies that the central moment estimators (e.g., mean and variance) of finite-sized samples drawn from the impact distribution may not converge to a value when data is accumulated. This is because no moment is defined for the distribution and a key property of a billing infrastructure is that the impact of just one attack may be unbounded. The overall impact of attacks on the infrastructure is the sum of the impacts of all the attacks; the corresponding random process is the union of all the processes corresponding to the individual attacks. Note that the probability distribution of a process created by the union of several processes, each described by a power law, is also a power law whose exponent is equal to the minimum of the exponents of the individual power laws [24]. Informally, the differences between the summands may be so large that the behavior of the sum largely depends on the maximum term and the probability distribution of this term is a power law.

Another implication is that the attack impacts are distributed according to a power law even if only a few attackers are interested in very large impacts because the overall impact mostly depends on these attackers. In other words, a general model of backbone attacks against a billing infrastructure assumes that there are at least two sets of attackers who are interested in finite impacts and unbounded impacts, respectively. The behavior of attackers in the first class is described by a normal distribution that can be handled in a manner similar to that for peripheral attacks. However, a new problem posed by backbone attacks is that attackers are interested in impacts that are distributed according to a power law, which determines the overall impact for the infrastructure owner. It is possible to introduce an upper bound also on the impact of backbone attacks by summing a negative exponential term to the power law to quickly cut off the probability of an impact that is larger than a threshold. However, this solution increases the complexity of the model without increasing its accuracy, especially for a large threshold. Note that in many instances it is almost impossible to determine a proper threshold value.

As an example, consider the case where a billing infrastructure is connected to other infrastructures outside the control of the owner or, even worse, where the existence of such a connection may not be known but cannot be excluded *a priori*. In this case, the impacts on other infrastructures must be considered, but they cannot be estimated easily. Therefore, in the next section, we assume that the probability distribution $Iia(D)$ of the random process that describes the overall impact of backbone attacks follows a power law. Based on historical data about infrastructure attacks, power law behavior may occur only for values larger than a positive threshold, while a distinct distribution models lower impacts. One of the key issues related to adopting a power law is discussed in the following section – it concerns the interpolation of the characteristic parameters of the probability distribution of the overall impact $Iia(D)$.

3.3   Overall Attack Impact

As described above, the overall impact of attacks against a billing infrastructure is a random process $OvImp$ that is the sum of two processes:

- **Imppa:** Impact of peripheral attacks, which has a normal distribution Nld.

- **Impba:** Impact of backbone attacks, which has a power law distribution Pld.

Note that the power law behavior may start at any positive integer value and that the mean of the normal distribution may be strongly shifted towards large positive values when the percentage of unethical customers and the maximum bill of the group of unethical customers are both very large. If we assume that Ima and Iia are mutually independent, then the probability distribution of $OvImp$, $Iia(D)$, is the convolution of Nld and Pld. Unfortunately, the mean and other moments of $Iia(D)$ cannot be computed because these statistics do not exist for Pld.

First, we consider the interpolation of the parameters of $Iia(D)$ and the component distributions, Nld and Pld, using actual attack data. The complexity of the interpolation strongly depends on the amount of information that is available. It has been shown [22] that this problem is extremely complex when only a sequence of outputs of the overall process ($OvImp$, in our case) is available because it is almost impossible to determine which component process (impacts of peripheral and backbone attacks, in our case) generates each output. This occurs when the two process domains overlap in a manner that prevents the pairing of some outputs with the corresponding processes.

Since the outputs are impacts, this means that we can only observe a sequence of impacts, i.e., a decrease in revenue for the owner. Also, the overlap of Pld and Nd may prevent us from recognizing their relative contributions to each observed impact and, thus, from approximating the parameters of each distribution. Moreover, the time frame available for impact data collection may be too short to cover a number of backbone attacks completely, which would make it impossible to deduce the parameters of the corresponding processes [22]. This is an important, but pessimistic, result because it means that the properties of $Iia(D)$ cannot be deduced even when a large sequence of attack impacts is used. The impossibility of forecasting future attacks and their impacts arises not only because of the lack of data about previous attacks but also because the distributions of interest cannot be approximated from the available data.

While the previous considerations hold for the abstract case of stochastic processes and a sequence of impacts, attacks on a billing infrastructure (as with most physical systems) often leave evidence in certain infrastructure components. Furthermore, some infrastructure components may be designed to facilitate the discovery of evidence (e.g., log files that record infrastructure activities and intrusion/anomaly detection systems that analyze the interactions between infrastructure components). This evidence may be used to pair an impact with the corresponding attack and to discover the relative contributions of attacks. From a probability point of view, proper attack classification makes it possible to analyze (separately) the probability distribution of each process and attempt to approximate Nld and Pld instead of using the distribution of the union process $Iia(D)$. In other words, a forensic analysis of attacks can help pair each impact with a successful attack against the infrastructure in order to deduce the properties of each distribution. This implies that the infrastructure should be designed to facilitate the forensic analysis of successful attacks as well as attempted attacks.

## 4.	Risk Management Strategies

This section examines the implications of the attack impact probability distribution on risk management for a billing infrastructure and on the return on security investments.

The primary problem related to managing risk in a billing infrastructure is the evaluation of the cost effectiveness of countermeasures implemented against peripheral and backbone attacks. Since the impact of a single peripheral attack and that of the entire class of peripheral attacks can be bounded, it is possible to determine the conditions that guarantee the cost effectiveness of countermeasures in terms of the impact probability distribution for peripheral attacks, the bounds on attack impacts and the cost of the countermeasures. The cost effectiveness of countermeasures for a single peripheral node depends on the average loss for the node, and the overall impact places a bound on the largest return on investment in security for all the peripheral nodes. Knowledge of the normal probability distribution of the overall impact of peripheral attacks can be used to fine-tune the choice of countermeasures by taking into account the distribution variance and the exponential decrease of the probability of very large impacts. The error in approximating the actual probability distribution as a normal distribution should also be taken into account.

Backbone attacks are more complex because of the power law distribution of their impact. A heavy-tailed distribution makes it almost impossible to evaluate the cost effectiveness of a countermeasure because very little information is available about the expected impacts of the attacks that are foiled by the countermeasure. In particular, a power law distribution implies that even if the probability of an impact is very low, its relative weight that cannot be ignored. Since the relative impact of some attacks cannot be easily bounded, the overall impact strongly depends on these attacks. This results in an unmanageable situation from the point of view of cost effectiveness because the impact justifies extremely expensive countermeasures while the probability of the attacks does not justify such an expense and no information about the average impact is available.

From a mathematical point of view, this situation strongly resembles the St. Petersburg paradox regarding a lottery with an expected unbounded payoff. In our model, if the impact probability distribution is a power law and if a proper condition on the $1 + a$ exponent holds (i.e., $a \in 0..1$), then the average impact of infrastructure attacks is infinite. This implies that we cannot claim that a set of countermeasures is optimal because the overall cost of any set of countermeasures is less than the impact it is intended to prevent.

A problem also arises when attempting to approximate the probability distribution parameters based on the available attack data. We have shown that even if a forensic data collection system has been implemented, a large amount of evidence about attempted and successful attacks and their impacts may be required to approximate the distribution. Moreover, small data errors can produce large differences in the parameters of the impact distribution. Consequently, a risk management strategy based on cost effectiveness of countermeasures cannot be adopted in the majority of scenarios.

The only feasible risk management strategy is to minimize the probability of successful attacks while recognizing that some attacks will be successful and minimize their impact. According to this strategy, in the worst case, a successful attack should cause a graceful degradation of infrastructure performance and functionality, which is measured in terms of the ability of the billing infrastructure to meter service usage and charge customers. In other words, risk management should increase infrastructure resilience in order to minimize the probability of successful attacks and their impact [1, 11, 15].

A fundamental issue is the absence of singularity points of catastrophic failure at any level – from hardware components to the personnel responsible for infrastructure management – because any of these points is an ideal target to maximize the attack impact. In general, an approach that attempts to increase infrastructure resilience cannot be cost effective (based on the simple view of cost effectiveness described above) because it involves the addition of redundant components in the infrastructure. Furthermore, such an approach avoids large optimizations that result in scale-free networks.

Instead of introducing a few components with a large number of connections, a redundancy-based approach would distribute the same number of connections among a larger number of interconnected components, with an increase in the cost of connections and components. In terms of probability, redundancy implies the independence of the random variables used to model the components of interest. Therefore, whenever two random variables used to model infrastructure components are not independent, some dependencies exist among the components so that a successful attack against one component may simplify attacks against another. The adoption of redundancy at the software level may be even more costly than at the hardware level because (as far as reliability is concerned) two instances of the same software module will always be affected by the same faults or vulnerabilities. Hence, the adoption of redundant active software components implies the presence of distinct providers for each copy of a component to guarantee independence of both vulnerabilities and faults. Note also that to prevent the introduction of a single point of catastrophic failure, the redundant components may have to be executed in parallel by different computing resources and they have to be properly synchronized, which increases the execution time. This also contributes to increased overall cost and reduced cost effectiveness.

Consider, for example, a standard implementation of triple-modular redundancy with three components and a voter, where the voter is a point of catastrophic failure [8]. If the threat model assumes erroneous but not malicious behavior of a component and possible voter failure, then a spare replacement for the voter increases the overall redundancy. On the other hand, if the threat model covers both erroneous and malicious behavior, then a distributed implementation of the voter is required where all the consumer components (i.e., components that receive the output of the components that act as producers) need to exchange the received values to compute their correct input [19]. However, a solution that is correct independently of the behavior of each producer can be defined only if at least five consumers exist, so that at least five instances of each module are required to discover malicious behavior in just one producer. This simple example shows that failure independence implies that redundancy is effective only if the failure of each instance is independent of the failure of other instances.

Consider also the case where two copies of a database reside on physical systems maintained at different locations. The databases may be independent with respect to physical threats such as earthquakes or floods, but they can be attacked by the same malware or infected by the same virus and are, therefore, are not independent in general. The incorporation of components to discover attacks and their impact can further reduce the cost effectiveness because they are not required for normal infrastructure operations. Note also that a rigorous approach to risk assessment, security and integrity of an infrastructure may distinguish between the strategies to manage the risk due to unethical customers, a customer that attacks the entire infrastructure, and business continuity. While there are good management reasons for the approach underlying these, or similar, classifications, it is important to recognize that a modular approach to risk management should not ignore the fact that several threats may result in similar impacts, and that it is complex (if not impossible) to assess the probability that one of these threats implements a successful attack.

5.   Conclusions

Attacks that target billing infrastructures have heavy-tailed impact probability distributions, typically power law distributions. This implies that the mean value of the impact of attacks cannot be computed and that the choice of countermeasures cannot be made on the basis of cost effectiveness. As a consequence, the only risk management strategy appropriate for a billing infrastructure is one that introduces redundant components to increase the resilience of the infrastructure and decrease the probability of successful attacks.

References

[1] R. Albert, H. Jeong and A. Barabasi, Error and attack tolerance of complex networks, *Nature*, vol. 406, pp. 378–382, 2002.

[2] F. Baiardi, C. Telmon and D. Sgandurra, Hierarchical, model-based risk management of critical infrastructures, *Reliability Engineering and System Safety*, vol. 94(9), pp. 1403–1415, 2009.

[3] P. Bernstein, *Against the Gods: The Remarkable Story of Risk*, Wiley, New York, 1996.

[4] J. Carlson and J. Doyle, HOT: A mechanism for power laws in designed systems, *Physical Review E*, vol. 60(2), pp. 1412–1427, 1999.

[5] A. Clauset, C. Shalizi and M. Newman, Power-law distributions in empirical data, arXiv:0706.1062v2, arXiv, Cornell University, Ithaca, New York (arxiv.org/PS_cache/arxiv/pdf/0706/0706.1062v2.pdf), 2007.

[6] R. D'Souza, C. Borgs, J. Chayes, N. Berger and R. Kleinberg, Emergence of tempered preferential attachment from optimization, *Proceedings of the National Academy of Sciences*, vol. 104(15), pp. 6112–6117, 2007.

[7] C. Goldie and C. Kluppelberg, Subexponential distributions, in *A Practical Guide to Heavy Tails: Statistical Techniques and Applications*, R. Adler, R. Feldman and M. Taqqu (Eds.), Birkhauser, Boston, Massachusetts, pp. 435–459, 1998.

[8] L. Lamport, R. Shostak and M. Pease, The Byzantine generals problem, *ACM Transactions on Programming Languages and Systems*, vol. 4(3), pp. 382–401, 1982.

[9] L. LeMay, R. Nelli, G. Gross and C. Gunter, An integrated architecture for demand response communication and control, *Proceedings of the Forty-First Annual Hawaii International Conference on System Sciences*, p. 174, 2008.

[10] T. Maillart and D. Sornette, Heavy-tailed distribution of cyber-risks, arXiv:0803.2256v2, arXiv, Cornell University, Ithaca, New York (arxiv.org /PS_cache/arxiv/pdf/0803/0803.2256v2.pdf), 2008.

[11] D. Maluf, Y. Gawdiak and G. Bell, On space exploration and human error: A paper on reliability and safety, *Proceedings of the Thirty-Eighth Annual Hawaii International Conference on System Sciences*, p. 79, 2005.

[12] B. Mandelbrot, *Fractals and Scaling in Finance: Discontinuity, Concentration, Risk*, Springer, New York, 1997.

[13] B. Mandelbrot, New methods of statistical economics revisited: Short versus long tails and Gaussian versus power law distributions, *Complexity*, vol. 14(3), pp. 55–65, 2009.

[14] M. Mitzenmacher, A brief history of generative models for power law and log-normal distributions, *Internet Mathematics*, vol. 1(2), pp. 226–251, 2003.

[15] National Infrastructure Protection Center, Risk Management: An Essential Guide to Protecting Critical Assets, Washington, DC, 2002.

[16] M. Newman, The structure and function of complex networks, *SIAM Review*, vol. 45(2), pp. 167–256, 2003.

[17] M. Newman, Power laws, Pareto distributions and Zipf's law, *Contemporary Physics*, vol. 46, pp. 323–351, 2005.

[18] M. Newman, M. Girvan and J. Doyne Farmer, Optimal design, robustness and risk aversion, *Physical Review Letters*, vol. 89(2), pp. 028301.1–028301.4, 2002.

[19] M. Pease, R. Shostak and L. Lamport, Reaching agreement in the presence of faults, *Journal of the ACM*, vol. 27(2), pp. 228–234, 1980.

[20] S. Resnick, *Heavy-Tail Phenomena: Probabilistic and Statistical Modeling*, Springer, New York, 2007.

[21] D. Sornette, *Critical Phenomena in Natural Sciences: Chaos, Fractals, Self-Organization and Disorder: Concepts and Tools*, Springer, Berlin-Heidelberg, Germany, 2006.

[22] N. Taleb, Black swans and the domains of statistics, *The American Statistician*, vol. 61(3), pp. 1–3, 2007.

[23] N. Taleb, *The Black Swan: The Impact of the Highly Improbable*, Random House, New York, 2007.

[24] C. Wilke, S. Altmeyer and T. Martinetz, Large-scale evolution and extinction in a hierarchically structured environment, *Proceedings of the Sixth International Conference on Artificial Life*, pp. 266–272, 1998.

II

CONTROL SYSTEMS SECURITY

Chapter 5

A TAXONOMY OF ATTACKS ON THE DNP3 PROTOCOL

Samuel East, Jonathan Butts, Mauricio Papa and Sujeet Shenoi

Abstract   Distributed Network Protocol (DNP3) is the predominant SCADA protocol in the energy sector – more than 75% of North American electric utilities currently use DNP3 for industrial control applications. This paper presents a taxonomy of attacks on the protocol. The attacks are classified based on targets (control center, outstation devices and network/communication paths) and threat categories (interception, interruption, modification and fabrication). To facilitate risk analysis and mitigation strategies, the attacks are associated with the specific DNP3 protocol layers they exploit. Also, the operational impact of the attacks is categorized in terms of three key SCADA objectives: process confidentiality, process awareness and process control. The attack taxonomy clarifies the nature and scope of the threats to DNP3 systems, and can provide insights into the relative costs and benefits of implementing mitigation strategies.

Keywords: Distributed Network Protocol (DNP3), attacks, attack taxonomy

1.   Introduction

In September 2007, CNN released dramatic footage of the "Aurora" test involving a cyber attack on an electric generator. The test conducted by Idaho National Laboratory (INL) scientists caused the generator to "shudder, shake, then go up in smoke – destroyed just as effectively as if with a smuggled bomb" [8].

The INL test underscores the vulnerability of the electrical power grid to cyber attack. Of particular concern are supervisory control and data acquisition (SCADA) systems that monitor and control vital equipment throughout the power grid [5, 7]. Attacks on SCADA systems, possibly launched over the Internet, can disrupt electrical power generation and transmission, and even cause physical destruction of key assets as in the Aurora experiment.

C. Palmer and S. Shenoi (Eds.): Critical Infrastructure Protection III, IFIP AICT 311, pp. 67–81, 2009.

This paper focuses on attacks on the Distributed Network Protocol (DNP3), which defines how SCADA devices communicate control commands and data. DNP3 is the primary SCADA protocol used in the electrical power grid. According to EPRI [4], more than 75% of North American electric utilities currently employ DNP3. Meanwhile, DNP3 is also being used in other critical infrastructure sectors, including oil and gas distribution, and water supply [3].

DNP3 attacks fall into three categories: attacks that exploit the DNP3 specifications, attacks that exploit vendor implementations, and attacks that target the underlying infrastructure. We focus on attacks in the first category, which target all SCADA systems that conform with the DNP3 standard.

Our analysis of the DNP3 protocol has identified 28 attacks. The attacks assume the ability to sniff DNP3 traffic and/or craft and inject messages. Each instance or manifestation of an attack is inserted in a taxonomy based on threat category and target. The threat categories considered are interception, interruption, modification and fabrication. The targets are the control center (master unit), outstation devices and network/communication paths. Each attack is associated with the specific DNP3 protocol layer it exploits. Thus, a separate taxonomy is presented for each of the three principal DNP3 protocol layers: data link layer, pseudo-transport layer and application layer.

Because of space constraints, it is not possible to describe all 28 attacks. However, fifteen representative attacks, with effects ranging from obtaining device configuration data to disabling or spoofing the master unit, are discussed. Also, the impact of the attacks is evaluated with respect to the principal SCADA objectives of process confidentiality, process awareness and process control. The attack taxonomy clarifies the nature and scope of the threats to DNP3 systems and, consequently, supports the application of formal risk analysis and threat mitigation strategies.

2.   DNP3 Protocol

DNP3 was developed by Westronic, Inc. (now GE Harris) in the early 1990s. The protocol defines how devices in a SCADA system communicate control commands and process data [15].

DNP3 supports three simple communication modes between a control center (master unit) and outstation devices [1]. In a unicast transaction, the master sends a request message to an addressed outstation device, which responds with a reply message. For example, the master may send a "read" message (e.g., request an amperage reading) or a "write" message to perform a control action (e.g., trip a circuit breaker); the outstation responds with the corresponding message (e.g., the amperage reading, an acknowledgement that the circuit breaker was tripped, or an error message). In a broadcast transaction, the master sends a message to all the outstations in the network (e.g., a "write" message that resets amperage sensors); the outstation devices do not reply to the broadcast message. The third communication mode involves unsolicited responses from outstation devices; these responses are typically used to provide periodic updates or alerts (e.g., an amperage reading exceeds a threshold).

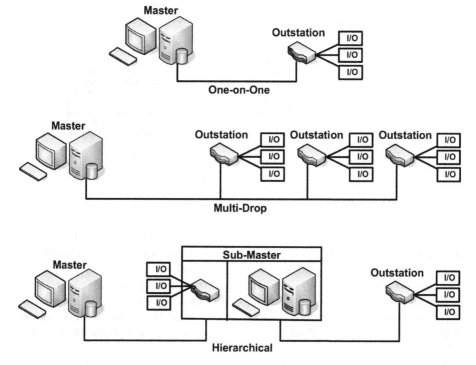

Figure 1. DNP3 network configurations.

The DNP3 protocol supports a variety of network configurations. Three common configurations are shown in Figure 1 [2]. In a "one-on-one" configuration, one master and one outstation device share a dedicated connection such as a dial-up telephone line. The popular "multi-drop" configuration has one master that communicates with multiple outstations. Every outstation receives every request from the master, but each outstation only responds to messages addressed to it. In a "hierarchical" configuration, a device acts as an outstation in one segment and a master in another segment; such a dual-purpose device is called a "sub-master."

Early SCADA architectures often relied on communication circuits that were susceptible to noise and signal distortion. Consequently, DNP3 was designed to incorporate multiple protocol layers. The International Electrotechnical Commission (IEC) initially proposed the IEC 870 standard for telemetry data transmission in SCADA systems based on the Open Systems Interconnection (OSI) model [1]. This three-layer Enhanced Performance Architecture (EPA) was created by eliminating superfluous layers (from the point of view of SCADA systems) from the seven-layer OSI model (Figure 2). However, EPA did not support application layer messages that were larger than the maximum length of a data link frame. DNP3 addressed this issue by incorporating a pseudo-transport layer to allow message fragmentation (Figure 2).

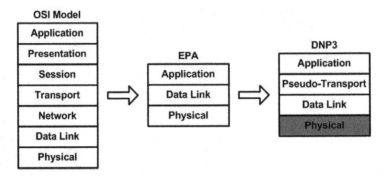

Figure 2.   Design progression from OSI to DNP3.

The DNP3 protocol layers are placed on top of a physical layer, which is responsible for transmitting messages over physical media such as radio, satellite, copper and fiber [15]. The physical layer specification determines the electrical settings, voltage and timing, along with other properties necessary to send signals between devices. The physical layer provides five services: (i) send data, (ii) receive data, (iii) connect, (iv) disconnect, and (v) status update. Note that the physical layer is shaded in Figure 2 because it is not specified in the DNP3 standard.

DNP3 may be transported over a variety of physical media, including old-fashioned serial links. However, modern SCADA systems typically use DNP3 in IP networks. The DNP Users Group has stipulated that the three layers of DNP3 not be modified in IP-based implementations [14]. For this reason, the three DNP3 layers are placed directly above the TCP/IP or UDP/IP layers in the protocol stack.

The attack taxonomy described in this paper is intended to apply to all DNP3 implementations, serial as well as TCP/IP. Consequently, we only consider attacks that exploit the three DNP3 layers common to all implementations – the data link, pseudo-transport and application layers.

2.1   Data Link Layer

The data link layer maintains a reliable logical link between devices to facilitate the transfer of message frames [12]. A data link layer frame has a 10-byte fixed size header and a data or "payload" section containing data passed down from the pseudo-transport and application layers. The maximum length of the data section is 250 bytes (282 bytes including 16-bit CRC fields for every 16 bytes of data). Thus, the maximum length of a data link frame is 292 bytes.

Figure 3 shows the format of a data link header. The Start field always contains the two-byte value 0x0564 to enable the receiver to determine where the frame begins; the Start bytes signal that a DNP3 packet has arrived and must be processed. The Length field provides the number of bytes in the remainder of the frame (not including CRCs).

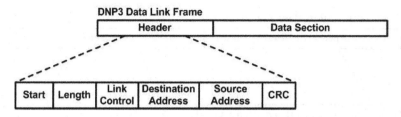

Figure 3. DNP3 data link frame.

The Link Control field in the data link header contains data that controls message flow, provides sequencing and determines the function of the frame. This data helps determine if the device is a master or outstation, identifies the device that initiated the communication, and provides the status of the logical link. The Link Control field also contains a four-bit function code that specifies the purpose of the message. Separate sets of function codes are used in messages originating from a master and in those originating from outstation devices. Examples of master function codes are reset remote link, reset user process, request link status and test function. Outstation device function codes include positive acknowledgement, message not accepted, status of link and no link service. The Link Control field also contains two flags for communication synchronization and flow control. The 16-bit Destination Address in the data link header specifies the intended recipient (which may include a broadcast address of 0xFFFF); the 16-bit Source Address identifies the originator. A 16-bit CRC is also included in the header to verify the integrity of the transmission.

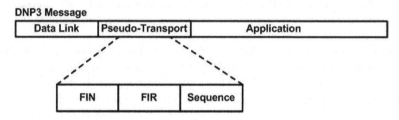

Figure 4. DNP3 pseudo-transport message fields.

2.2 Pseudo-Transport Layer

The DNP3 pseudo-transport layer handles message fragmentation and reassembly [10]. As mentioned above, it enables application messages larger than one data link frame in length to use multiple frames. The pseudo-transport layer adds one byte containing the FIR and FIN flags and a Sequence number (Figure 4). The FIR and FIN flags indicate the first and final frames of a fragmented message, respectively. The Sequence number, which is incremented for each successive frame, is used to reassemble messages for processing by the

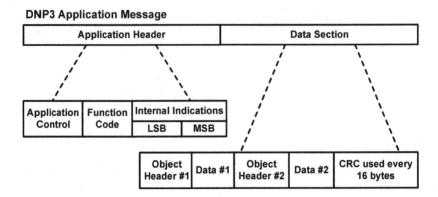

Figure 5. DNP3 application message.

application layer. The sequencing information also facilitates the detection of dropped frames.

2.3   Application Layer

The application layer, which specifies DNP3 request and reply messages [11], defines the roles of the master and outstation devices. A request message from a master directs an outstation device to perform a task, collect and provide data, or synchronize its internal clock. Only a master may send request messages; outstation devices may send solicited or unsolicited messages. The application layer fragments messages that exceed the maximum fragment size (determined by the size of the receiver's buffer). A typical message fragment is between 2048 and 4096 bytes.

Figure 5 shows the format of the application layer header. The Application Control field performs a similar function as the corresponding field in the pseudo-transport layer, but at a higher level. Two flags are included to specify the first or last fragment of a message and the sequence number for ordering and reassembly. An additional flag is included to request confirmation upon receipt of a fragment.

The Function Code field communicates the purpose of a message. This field is used in both requests and replies, but the available functions change with the message type. The 23 defined function codes for request messages are grouped into six categories: (i) transfer functions, (ii) control functions, (iii) freeze functions, (iv) application control functions, (v) configuration functions, and (vi) time synchronization functions.

A reply message can be a: (i) confirmation, (ii) response, or (iii) unsolicited response. Reply message headers incorporate a two-byte Internal Indications (IIN) field that communicates useful information about the outstation unit to the master. Each bit in the IIN field has a specific meaning that is updated in every reply message. Example IIN codes are time synchronization required, device restart, invalid parameters, function code not implemented and requested objects unknown.

Following the header in a DNP3 application layer message are data objects that convey encoded representations of data (Figure 5). Several data objects are defined to enable devices running on different platforms to efficiently communicate data and commands. Examples of data objects are binary inputs, binary outputs, analog inputs, analog outputs and counters.

3.   Attack Taxonomy Development

Attacks on DNP3 systems fall into three categories: (i) attacks that exploit the DNP3 specifications, (ii) attacks that exploit vendor implementations of DNP3, and (iii) attacks that exploit weaknesses in the underlying infrastructure. Attacks on vendor implementations typically exploit configuration errors or code flaws (e.g., via buffer overflows). Attacks on the underlying infrastructure exploit vulnerabilities in information technology, network and telecommunications assets, or weak security policies. We focus on attacks that exploit the protocol specifications, which target all SCADA systems that conform with the DNP3 standard.

Attack identification involves a detailed analysis of the DNP3 protocol. DNP3 was not designed with security in mind. Consequently, security is a major concern for DNP3 implementations that use commodity computing equipment and networking technologies [3]. Protocol analysis helps identify weaknesses and enhance security awareness, enabling vendors and asset owners to design architectures, configure equipment and operate systems in a manner that addresses the identified vulnerabilities.

Our methodology, which was recently used to develop attack taxonomies for the Modbus Serial and TCP protocols [6], involved analyzing the DNP3 protocol specification and identifying weaknesses. Attacks were then formulated to exploit these weaknesses. Each attack was analyzed for its ability to intercept, interrupt, modify and/or fabricate [9] each of the three primary targets: master, outstation devices and network/communication paths. Figure 6 [13] illustrates the four threat categories considered in the DNP3 attack taxonomy.

The identified attacks are classified based on the threat categories and DNP3 targets. Each attack has various manifestations or "instances." For example, the Outstation Data Reset attack reinitializes data objects in an outstation device to values inconsistent with the state of the system, which can affect the operation of the targeted device. Thus, there are two instances of this application layer attack: modifying an outstation and interrupting an outstation.

The attack instances are organized within attack taxonomies for the three layers common to all DNP3 implementations – the data link, pseudo-transport and application layers (Tables 1–3). Classifying attacks within a taxonomy supports formal risk analysis strategies. In particular, a taxonomy can be used to systematically examine mitigation strategies, evaluate attack impact and clarify the magnitude of the threats. Moreover, a taxonomy helps raise awareness about vulnerabilities.

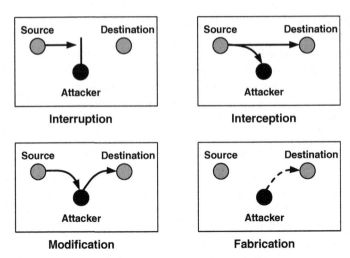

Figure 6. Threat categories [13].

The theorized attacks assume the ability to sniff DNP3 traffic, and/or to craft and inject messages. Note that message modification and fabrication require the appropriate CRC values to be computed and inserted in messages. Principal entry points for attacks include the master, outstation devices and network components. The entry points are, of course, dependent on an attacker's access and intent. The attacks are effective on all SCADA systems that conform with the DNP3 specifications. Of course, if certain aspects (e.g., DNP3 function codes) are not implemented by a vendor, the corresponding attacks (that exploit the unimplemented function codes) would not work.

4.   DNP3 Attack Taxonomy

DNP3 attacks are organized according to the specific protocol layers they exploit. Tables 1, 2 and 3 present the attack taxonomies for the data link layer, pseudo-transport layer and application layer, respectively. The rows of the tables identify the threat categories while the columns list the targeted assets. Attacks that are common (C) to all three layers are designated by Cx; Cx-y denotes the yth instance of the Cx attack. Likewise, attack instances associated only with the data link layer, pseudo-transport layer and application layer are denoted by Dx-y, Px-y and Ax-y, respectively. For example, the Rogue Interloper attack, which is common to all three DNP3 layers, is designated as C3, and its twelve instances are denoted by C3-1 through C3-12.

Because of space constraints it is not possible to describe all 28 attacks. However, several representative attacks are discussed. First, representative attacks common to all three DNP3 layers are presented. Next, representative attacks specific to the data link, pseudo-transport and application layers are described. These attacks and the corresponding taxonomies shed light on the nature and scope of the security threats facing DNP3 systems.

4.1 Common Attacks

As mentioned above, most of the attacks rely on the ability to intercept, modify and/or fabricate DNP3 messages. DNP3 implementations typically do not employ encryption, authentication and authorization; DNP3 devices simply assume that all messages are valid. Three attacks leverage these weaknesses and, because of their flexibility, target all three DNP3 layers. The three common attacks (with 21 attack instances) described below are among the most insidious because they perform reconnaissance and/or execute potentially malicious operations on outstation devices while (possibly) masking their actions.

- **Passive Network Reconnaissance (C1):** An attacker with the appropriate access captures and analyzes DNP3 messages. This attack provides the attacker with information about network topology, device functionality, memory addresses and other data. Tables 1–3 list three instances of this attack: interception of master data (C1-1); interception of outstation device data (C1-2); and interception of network topology information (C1-3).

- **Baseline Response Replay (C2):** An attacker with knowledge of normal DNP3 traffic patterns simulates responses to the master while sending fabricated messages to outstation devices. Tables 1–3 list six instances of this attack: interruption of the master (C2-1) and outstation (C2-2); modification of the master (C2-3) and outstation (C2-4); and fabrication of the master (C2-5) and outstation (C2-6).

- **Rogue Interloper (C3):** An attacker installs a "man-in-the-middle" device between the master and outstations that can read, modify and fabricate DNP3 messages and/or network traffic. Tables 1–3 list twelve instances of this most serious attack: interception of master (C3-1), outstation (C3-2) and network data (C3-3); interruption of the master (C3-4), outstation (C3-5) and network (C3-6); modification of the master (C3-7), outstation (C3-8) and network path (C3-9); and fabrication of the master (C3-10), outstation (C3-11) and network path (C3-12).

4.2 Data Link Layer Attacks

Twelve attacks (including the three common attacks described above) and 54 attack instances (including 21 instances for the three common attacks) were identified for the data link layer (Table 1). Most of the attacks involve intercepting DNP3 messages, modifying message values and sending them to the master or outstation devices. Some of the attacks impact confidentiality by obtaining configuration data and network topology information. Integrity attacks insert erroneous data or reconfigure outstations. Attacks on availability cause outstation devices to lose key functionality or disrupt communications with the master. We discuss five data link layer attacks in more detail.

Table 1. Attack taxonomy for the DNP3 data link layer.

12 Attacks 54 Instances	Master	Outstation	Network
Interception	C1-1 C3-1	C1-2 C3-2	C1-3 C3-3
Interruption	C2-1 C3-4 D1-1 D2-1 D3-1 D7-1 D8-1 D9-1	C2-2 C3-5 D1-2 D2-2 D3-2 D4-1 D5-1 D8-2 D9-2	C3-6 D3-3 D6-1 D8-3 D9-3
Modification	C2-3 C3-7 D2-3 D6-2 D8-4 D9-4	C2-4 C3-8 D2-4 D5-2 D8-5 D9-5	C3-9 D8-6 D9-6
Fabrication	C2-5 C3-10 D8-7 D9-7	C2-6 C3-11 D8-8 D9-8	C3-12 D8-9 D9-9

- **Length Overflow Attack (D2):** This attack inserts an incorrect value in the Length field that affects message processing. The attack can result in data corruption, unexpected actions and device crashes. Table 1 lists four instances of the attack: interruption of the master (D2-1) and outstation (D2-1); and modification of the master (D2-3) and outstation (D2-4).

- **DFC Flag Attack (D4):** The DFC flag is used to indicate that an outstation is busy and that a request should be resent at a later time. This attack sets the DFC flag, which causes an outstation device to appear busy to the master. Table 1 lists the one instance of this attack: interruption of an outstation (D4-1).

- **Reset Function Attack (D5):** This attack sends a DNP3 message with Function Code 1 (reset user process) to the targeted outstation. The attack causes the targeted device to restart, rendering it unavailable for a period of time and possibly restoring it to an inconsistent state. Table 1 lists two instances of this attack: interruption of an outstation (D5-1); and modification of an outstation (D5-2).

- **Unavailable Function Attack (D7):** This attack sends a DNP3 message with Function Code 14 or 15, which indicates that a service is not functioning or is not implemented in an outstation device. The attack causes the master not to send requests to the targeted outstation because it assumes that the service is unavailable. Table 1 lists the one instance of this attack: interruption of the master (D7-1).

- **Destination Address Alteration (D8):** By changing the destination address field, an attacker can reroute requests or replies to other devices causing unexpected results. An attacker can also use the broadcast address 0xFFFF to send erroneous requests to all the outstation devices; this attack is difficult to detect because (by default) no result messages are

Lecture Notes in Computer Science 4439

Commenced Publication in 1973
Founding and Former Series Editors:
Gerhard Goos, Juris Hartmanis, and Jan van Leeuwen

Editorial Board

returned to a broadcast request. Table 1 lists nine instances of this attack: interruption of the master (D8-1), outstation (D8-2) and network (D8-3); modification of the master (D8-4), outstation (D8-5) and network path (D8-6); and fabrication of the master (D8-7), outstation (D8-8) and network path (D8-9).

Table 2. Attack taxonomy for the DNP3 pseudo-transport layer.

5 Attacks 31 Instances	Master	Outstation	Network
Interception	C1-1 C3-1	C1-2 C3-2	C1-3 C3-3
Interruption	C2-1 C3-4 P1-1 P2-1	C2-2 C3-5 P1-2 P2-2	C3-6
Modification	C2-3 C3-7 P2-3	C2-4 C3-8 P2-4	C3-9 P2-5
Fabrication	C2-5 C3-10 P2-6	C2-6 C3-11 P2-7	C3-12 P2-8

4.3   Pseudo-Transport Layer Attacks

The pseudo-transport layer provides less functionality than the other layers; thus, fewer attacks are associated with this layer. The taxonomy in Table 2 lists five attacks (including the three common attacks) and 31 attack instances (including 21 instances for the common attacks). The two attacks associated with the pseudo-transport layer target the fragment flags and sequence number.

- **Fragmented Message Interruption (P1):** The FIR and FIN flags indicate the first and final frames of a fragmented message, respectively. When a message with the FIR flag arrives, all previously-received incomplete fragments are discarded. Inserting a message with the FIR flag set after the beginning of a transmission of a fragmented message causes the reassembly of a valid message to be disrupted. Inserting a message with the FIN flag set terminates message reassembly early, resulting in an error during the processing of the partially-completed message. Table 2 lists two instances of this attack: interruption of the master (P1-1) and outstation (P1-2).

- **Transport Sequence Modification (P2):** The Sequence field is used to ensure in-order delivery of fragmented messages. The sequence number increments with each fragment sent, so predicting the next value is trivial. An attacker who inserts fabricated messages into a sequence of fragments can inject any data and/or cause processing errors. Table 2 lists eight instances of this attack: interruption of the master (P2-1) and outstation (P2-2); modification of the master (P2-3), outstation (P2-4) and network path (P2-5); and fabrication of the master (P2-6), outstation (P2-7) and network path (P2-8).

Table 3. Attack taxonomy for the DNP3 application layer.

17 Attacks 48 Instances	Master	Outstation	Network
Interception	C1-1 C3-1	C1-2 C3-2 A2-1 A14-1	C1-3 C3-3
Interruption	C2-1 C3-4 A10-1 A11-1 A12-1 A13-1	C2-2 C3-5 A1-1 A2-2 A3-1 A4-1 A5-1 A6-1 A7-1 A8-1 A9-1	C3-6
Modification	C2-3 C3-7 A10-2 A11-2 A12-2 A13-2	C2-4 C3-8 A1-2 A3-2 A4-2 A5-2 A6-2 A7-2 A8-2 A9-2	C3-9
Fabrication	C2-5 C3-10	C2-6 C3-11	C3-12

4.4 Application Layer Attacks

The application layer provides the majority of functionality for DNP3 systems; consequently, the largest number of attacks are associated with this layer. The taxonomy in Table 3 lists seventeen attacks (including the three common attacks) and 48 attack instances (including 21 instances for the common attacks). Attacks on confidentiality obtain information about network topology, system configuration and functionality. Integrity attacks modify communication paths, provide bad data to the master and outstation devices, or reconfigure outstation devices. Availability attacks may cause devices to lose key functionality, reboot or crash. We discuss five attacks in more detail.

- **Outstation Write Attack (A3):** This attack sends a DNP3 message with Function Code 2, which writes data objects to an outstation. The attack can corrupt information stored in the outstation's memory, causing an error or overflow. Table 3 lists two instances of this attack: interruption (A3-1) and modification (A3-2) of an outstation.

- **Clear Objects Attack (A4):** This attack sends a DNP3 message with Function Code 9 or 10 to freeze and clear data objects. The attack can clear critical data or cause an outstation device to malfunction or crash. Note that the attack involving Function Code 10 is problematic because a message with this function code does not require an acknowledgement. Table 3 lists two instances of this attack: interruption (A4-1) and modification (A4-2) of an outstation.

- **Outstation Data Reset (A6):** This attack sends a DNP3 message with Function Code 15. The attack causes an outstation device to reinitialize data objects to values inconsistent with the state of the system. Table

3 lists two instances of this attack: interruption (A6-1) and modification (A6-2) of an outstation.

■ **Outstation Application Termination (A7):** This attack sends a DNP3 message with Function Code 18, which is used to terminate applications running on outstations. A message with this function code causes a device to become unresponsive to normal requests from the master. Table 3 lists two instances of this attack: interruption (A7-1) and modification (A7-2) of an outstation.

■ **Configuration Capture Attack (A14):** This attack sends a message with the fifth bit in the second byte of the IIN set, which indicates that the configuration file of the targeted outstation is corrupted. The attack causes the master to transmit a new configuration file, which is intercepted by the attacker. A separate attack is then executed to modify and upload the file to the targeted outstation. Table 3 lists the one instance of this attack: interception of outstation data (A14-1).

Table 4. Impact of attacks on target assets.

28 Attacks 91 Instances	Master	Outstation	Network
Interception	2 Obtain Master Data	4 Obtain Outstation Data	2 Obtain Network Data
Interruption	14 DoS Master	20 DoS Outstation	5 DoS Network
Modification	11 Bad Data in Master	15 Bad Data in Outstation	4 Reconfigure Network Path
Fabrication	5 Control Process	5 Fabricate Outstation	4 Fabricate Network Path

5. Attack Impact

Table 4 summarizes the overall impact of the attacks on control system assets. Eight attack instances intercept device configuration data, process data and network information. Additionally, 39 attack instances result in denial of service (DoS); fourteen instances impact the master, twenty impact outstation devices and five impact network resources. Modification attacks insert erroneous data in devices, which affects the integrity of the control system. Eleven attack instances insert bad data in the master, fifteen in outstation devices, and four affect network paths. Fabrication attacks are particularly dangerous. Five attack instances enable an attacker to spoof outstation devices and four attack instances fabricate network paths. Most alarming are the five attack instances that spoof the master and seize partial or complete control of the process.

Table 5. Impact of attacks on control objectives.

	Data Link Layer	Pseudo-Transport Layer	Application Layer	Common (All Layers)
Loss of Confidentiality	0(0)	0(0)	2(2)	6(2)
Loss of Awareness	33(9)	10(2)	25(13)	15(2)
Loss of Control	29(9)	7(2)	25(13)	13(2)

Table 5 clarifies the impact of the attacks with respect to the principal industrial control system objectives of process confidentiality, process awareness and process control. Loss of confidentiality occurs when important information about device configuration or network topology is obtained by an attacker. Generally, this is the first step of a more serious attack, where reconnaissance is conducted to identify weaknesses and entry points. Loss of awareness occurs when the control center does not have accurate information about system status. For example, an attacker can trip a circuit breaker and prevent an alarm from reaching the operator. Such attacks can lead to serious incidents because their effects may go unnoticed until it is too late. Even more dangerous are the attacks that result in the loss of control – an attacker who usurps control of a SCADA master can potentially wreak havoc. Table 5 lists the numbers of attack instances and distinct attacks (in parentheses) that impact the three control system objectives. For example, two application layer attack instances (two attacks) result in a loss of confidentiality, and thirteen common attack instances (two common attacks) result in loss of control.

6.   Conclusions

Our detailed analysis of the DNP3 protocol layers with respect to threats and targets has identified 28 attacks and 91 attack instances. The effects of the attacks range from obtaining network or device configuration data to corrupting outstation devices and seizing control of the master unit. It is important to note that our analysis, while detailed, is by no means comprehensive. In fact, we believe that many more attacks remain to be discovered. Most surprising is the large proportion of high-impact attacks, especially those involving the interruption, modification and fabrication of control system assets.

We hope that our work will stimulate efforts focused on analyzing SCADA protocols and characterizing cyber attacks on the electrical power grid. The results will contribute to the security of existing critical infrastructure assets as well as the design of next generation SCADA systems that are secure, reliable and resilient.

References

[1] G. Clarke and D. Reynolds, *Practical Modern SCADA Protocols: DNP3, IEC 60870.5 and Related Systems*, Newnes, Oxford, United Kingdom, 2004.

[2] K. Curtis, A DNP3 Protocol Primer (Revision A), DNP3 Users Group, Calgary, Canada (www.dnp.org/About/DNP3%20Primer%20Rev%20A .pdf), 2005.

[3] DNP Users Group, Pasadena, California (www.dnp.org), 2008.

[4] Electric Power Research Institute, DNP Security Development, Evaluation and Testing Project Opportunity, Palo Alto, California (mydocs.epri.com/docs/public/000000000001016988.pdf), 2008.

[5] P. Huber and M. Mills, Brawn and brains, *Forbes*, September 15, 2003.

[6] P. Huitsing, R. Chandia, M. Papa and S. Shenoi, Attack taxonomies for the Modbus protocols, *International Journal of Critical Infrastructure Protection*, vol. 1, pp. 37–44, 2008.

[7] Institute for Security Technology Studies, Cyber Security of the Electric Power Industry, Dartmouth College, Hanover, New Hampshire (www.ists .dartmouth.edu/library/218.pdf), 2002.

[8] J. Meserve, Mouse click could plunge city into darkness, experts say, *CNN.com* (www.cnn.com/2007/US/09/27/power.at.risk/index.html), September 27, 2007.

[9] C. Pfleeger and S. Lawrence-Pfleeger, *Security in Computing*, Prentice Hall, Upper Saddle River, New Jersey, 2007.

[10] M. Smith, DNP V3.00 Transport Functions, DNP Users Group, Pasadena, California, 1992.

[11] M. Smith and J. McFadyen, DNP V3.00 Application Layer Protocol Description, DNP Users Group, Pasadena, California, 1991.

[12] M. Smith and J. McFadyen, DNP V3.00 Data Link Layer Protocol Description, DNP Users Group, Pasadena, California, 2000.

[13] Sun Microsystems, Secure Enterprise Computing with the Solaris 8 Operating Environment, Palo Alto, California (www.sun.com/software/white papers/wp-s8security/wp-s8security.pdf), 2000.

[14] M. Thesing, DNP3 Specification Volume 7: IP Networking, DNP Users Group, Pasadena, California, 1998.

[15] Triangle MicroWorks, DNP3 Overview, Raleigh, North Carolina (www. trianglemicroworks.com /documents/DNP3_Overview.pdf), 2002.

Chapter 6

DESIGN AND IMPLEMENTATION OF A SECURE MODBUS PROTOCOL

Igor Nai Fovino, Andrea Carcano, Marcelo Masera and Alberto Trombetta

Abstract   The interconnectivity of modern and legacy supervisory control and data acquisition (SCADA) systems with corporate networks and the Internet has significantly increased the threats to critical infrastructure assets. Meanwhile, traditional IT security solutions such as firewalls, intrusion detection systems and antivirus software are relatively ineffective against attacks that specifically target vulnerabilities in SCADA protocols. This paper describes a secure version of the Modbus SCADA protocol that incorporates integrity, authentication, non-repudiation and anti-replay mechanisms. Experimental results using a power plant testbed indicate that the augmented protocol provides good security functionality without significant overhead.

Keywords: SCADA systems, Modbus, secure protocol

1.   Introduction

Information and communications technology (ICT) systems are prone to vulnerabilities that can be exploited by malicious software and agents. Modern critical infrastructure assets (e.g., power plants, refineries and water supply systems) use ICT systems to provide reliable services and offer new features. Many maintenance and management operations at these installations involve the use of supervisory control and data acquisition (SCADA) systems, and are conducted remotely using public networks, including the Internet. While the automation and interconnectivity contribute to increased efficiency and reduced costs, they expose critical installations to new threats.

Several studies (see, e.g., [7, 15]) have discussed the threats to critical infrastructure assets. According to Carcano, *et al.* [4], critical infrastructures are exposed to serious *ad hoc* attacks that can interfere with – or even seize control of – process control networks at industrial installations. When one considers

C. Palmer and S. Shenoi (Eds.): Critical Infrastructure Protection III, IFIP AICT 311, pp. 83–96, 2009.

the criticality of the activities performed by a process control network (e.g., gas turbine operation or refinery control), an attack could have devastating consequences to the installation itself as well as other infrastructures due to cascading effects.

The use of traditional ICT security techniques (e.g., firewalls, intrusion detection systems and antivirus software) are effective at dealing with vulnerabilities in corporate networks [15]. However, they do not address attacks that specifically target process control networks. A major concern is the intrinsic weakness of communication protocols used in the SCADA systems that monitor and control field devices in critical infrastructure installations.

SCADA protocols such as Modbus, DNP3 and PROFIBUS were designed decades ago for serial communications between SCADA devices (masters and slaves). Because of network isolation and low threat levels, security features such as authentication, integrity and confidentiality were not considered in SCADA protocol design and implementation. However, with the advent of the Internet era, SCADA vendors began to port SCADA protocols over TCP/IP, offering flexible, economical solutions that also provided interoperability with legacy SCADA implementations. As a result, SCADA networks are highly vulnerable to attacks that would be considered obsolete in the ICT context. For example, as Carcano, et al. [4] have demonstrated, the lack of authentication, integrity and non-repudiation mechanisms in SCADA protocols makes it possible to create ad hoc viruses that compromise master devices and cause them to send potentially destructive messages to sensors and actuators.

This paper describes the design and implementation of a "secure" Modbus protocol that satisfies the basic security requirements of modern ICT protocols. Experiments with the new protocol demonstrate that it is feasible to augment existing SCADA protocols with security mechanisms without incurring significant real-time performance penalties.

2.   Related Work

Most critical infrastructure components adopt network architectures that are tailor-made to the specific systems being operated. These systems also use dedicated SCADA architectures and protocols whose vulnerabilities and attack patterns are different from traditional ICT systems and networks.

Creery and Byres [6] present a detailed analysis of the threats affecting a power plant. In particular, they categorize the devices used in the plant and discuss intrinsic vulnerabilities in the devices and how they relate to the overall power plant architecture. Chandia, et al. [5] describe several strategies for securing SCADA networks; their strategies are designed to reduce overhead and to accommodate legacy SCADA systems.

Other researchers have focused on securing SCADA communication protocols. For example, Majdalawieh, et al. [13] present an extension of the DNP3 protocol (DNPSec) that attempts to address some of the well-known security problems of master-slave control protocols such as device authentication, message integrity and message non-repudiation. A similar approach has been adopted by Heo, *et al.* [8]. On the other hand, Mander, *et al.* [14] present a proxy filtering solution that attempts to identify and mitigate anomalous control traffic. The BACnet protocol [2] implements several security features; however, its authentication mechanism is vulnerable to man-in-the-middle attacks, parallel interleaving attacks and replay attacks [9]. Wright, *et al.* [19] present a low latency encryption protocol for SCADA link protection based on CRC. This protocol is very effective for serial SCADA communications; however, no updates related to this research effort have been released since 2006.

3. SCADA Systems

This section discusses the main concepts related to information assurance and SCADA security.

First, we clarify the concepts of "threat," "vulnerability" and "attack." As defined in [11], a "threat" is the potential for a violation of security; it exists when there is a circumstance, capability, action or event that could breach security and cause harm. A "vulnerability" is a weakness in the architecture, design or implementation of an application or service [1, 3]. An "attack" occurs when a threat agent exploits a system by targeting one or more vulnerabilities.

SCADA systems are widely used to control process systems in industrial plants. They rely on sensors to gather data and actuators to perform control actions. A SCADA system typically involves the following actors/components:

- **Operator:** A human operator monitors the SCADA system and performs supervisory control functions over plant operations.

- **Human-Machine Interface (HMI):** This system presents process data to the human operator and enables the operator to control the process. The SCADA system gathers information from PLCs and other controllers over a network using dedicated application layer protocols. An HMI can also be connected to a database, which records trends, diagnostic data and management information (scheduled maintenance procedures, logistic information, etc.).

- **Master Terminal Unit (MTU):** This master device gathers data from remote PLCs and actuators, presents the data to the operator via the HMI and transmits control signals. It contains the high-level control logic for the system.

- **Remote Terminal Unit (RTU):** This device acts as a slave in the master/slave architecture. It sends control signals to the device under control, acquires data from devices, receives commands from the MTU and transmits the data gathered to the MTU. An RTU could be a PLC.

Securing SCADA systems is an important problem (see, e.g., [15]). However, while the majority of research efforts have concentrated on addressing traditional ICT system vulnerabilities, we focus our efforts on the SCADA communication protocols that are used by MTUs to send commands and receive data from RTUs. Several SCADA protocols, e.g., Modbus, DNP3 and PROFIBUS, have been developed for industrial control applications. We focus on Modbus, the predominant protocol in the oil and gas sector. The security flaws of Modbus are well established (see, e.g., [10]).

4.   Modbus Protocol

Modbus is an application layer protocol that provides client/server communications between devices connected on different buses or networks. Modbus communications are of two types: (i) query/response (communications between a master and a slave), or (ii) broadcast (a master sends a command to all the slaves). A Modbus transaction comprises a single query or response frame, or a single broadcast frame. A Modbus frame message contains the address of the intended receiver, the command the receiver must execute and the data needed to execute the command. Modbus TCP basically embeds a Modbus frame into a TCP frame [16]. The Modbus protocol defines several function codes, each of which corresponds to a specific command. Example function codes are:

- **Read Coils (0x01):** This function code is used to read the status of the coils in a remote device. The request specifies the starting address (address of the first coil) and the number of coils. The coils in the response message are packed as one coil per bit in the data field. Status is indicated as 1 = ON and 0 = OFF.

- **Write Single Coil (0x05):** This function code is used to write a single output in a remote device to ON or OFF. The requested ON/OFF state is specified by a constant in the request data field. A value of 0xFF00 requests that the output be ON; 0x0000 requests that it be OFF. All other values are illegal and do not affect the output.

- **Write Multiple Coils (0x0F):** This function code is used to force each coil in a sequence of coils in a remote device to the status of ON or OFF. The normal response returns the function code, starting address and quantity of coils forced.

Most SCADA protocols in use today were designed decades ago, when the technological infrastructure and threat landscape were quite different from how they are today. For example, Modbus was originally published in 1979 for a multidrop network with a master/slave architecture. Because Modbus networks were isolated and free from security threats, key aspects such as integrity, authentication and non-repudiation were not taken into consideration in the design of the protocol. The next section discusses Modbus vulnerabilities and how the vulnerabilities could be exploited by an attacker.

5. Modbus Vulnerabilities

The transportation of Modbus messages using TCP introduces new levels of complexity with regard to managing the reliable delivery of control packets in a process control environment with strong real-time constraints. In addition, it provides attackers with new avenues to target industrial systems.

Modbus TCP lacks mechanisms for protecting confidentiality and for verifying the integrity of messages sent between a master and slaves (i.e., it is not possible to discover if the original message contents have been modified by an attacker). Modbus TCP does not authenticate the master and slaves (i.e., a compromised device could claim to be the master and send commands to the slaves). Moreover, the protocol does not incorporate any anti-repudiation or anti-replay mechanisms.

The security limitations of Modbus can be exploited by attackers to wreak havoc on industrial control systems. Some key attacks are:

- **Unauthorized Command Execution:** The lack of authentication of the master and slaves means that an attacker can send forged Modbus messages to a pool of slaves. In order to execute this attack, the attacker must be able to access the network that hosts the SCADA servers or the field network that hosts the slaves. Carcano, *et al.* [4] show that the attack can be launched by creating malware that infects the network and causes malicious messages to be sent automatically to the slaves.

- **Modbus Denial-of-Service Attacks:** An example attack involves impersonating the master and sending meaningless messages to RTUs that cause them to expend processing resources.

- **Man-in-the-Middle Attacks:** The lack of integrity checks enables an attacker who has access to the production network to modify legitimate messages or fabricate messages and send them to slave devices.

- **Replay Attacks:** The lack of security mechanisms enables an attacker to reuse legitimate Modbus messages sent to or from slave devices.

Firewalls and intrusion/anomaly detection systems can defend against *ad hoc* exploits that target Modbus vulnerabilities. However, it is always possible to circumvent these security controls. The best way to address the security threats is to solve them at their origin – by attempting to "repair" the security holes in the Modbus protocol. But such a solution is difficult to implement because it requires significant changes to the control system architecture and configuration. Instead, we adopt a practical approach in which a small number of security mechanisms are introduced into the protocol to protect against the attacks described above.

6. Secure Modbus Protocol

A communications protocol is generally considered to be "secure" if it satisfies traditional security requirements such as confidentiality, integrity and non-

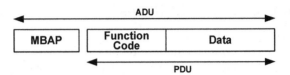

Figure 1.   Modbus application data unit.

repudiation [3]. In other words, a "secure" Modbus protocol should guarantee that:

- No unauthorized entity is allowed to access the content of a message.

- No unauthorized entity is allowed to modify the content of a message.

- No entity is allowed to impersonate another entity.

- No entity is allowed to negate a performed action.

- No entity is allowed to reuse a captured message to perform an unauthorized action.

In this work, we do not consider the confidentiality requirement for Modbus messages for two reasons. First, enforcing confidentiality does not mitigate any of the attack scenarios presented above. Second, confidentiality is generally implemented using encryption, which is expensive and introduces considerable overhead that can impact real-time performance.

The original Modbus Serial protocol defines a simple protocol data unit (PDU), which is independent of the underlying communication layer (Figure 1). The mapping of Modbus messages to specific buses or networks introduces additional fields in an application data unit (ADU).

The Modbus TCP protocol introduces a dedicated Modbus application protocol (MBAP) header. The Slave Address field in a Modbus Serial message is replaced by a one-byte Unit Identifier in the MBAP Header. Also, the error checking field is removed and additional length information is stored in the MBAP header to enable the recipient to identify message boundaries when a message is split into multiple packets for transmission. All Modbus requests and responses are designed so that the recipient can verify that the complete message is received. This is accomplished by simply referring to the function code for function codes whose Modbus PDUs have fixed lengths. Request and response messages with function codes that can carry variable amounts of data incorporate a field containing the byte count.

The proposed Secure Modbus protocol is intended to satisfy the following security requirements:

- **Integrity:** The integrity of a Secure Modbus packet is guaranteed using a secure hashing function. The well-known SHA2 hash function is used to compute a secure digest of the packet, which is transmitted along with

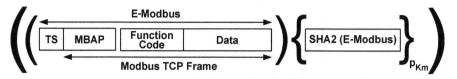

Figure 2. Secure Modbus application data unit.

the packet. The integrity of the received packet is verified by the receiver who computes the SHA2 value of the received packet and compares it with the received digest.

- **Authentication:** The integrity mechanism described above does not prevent an attacker from creating a malicious Modbus packet, computing its SHA2 digest, and sending the malicious packet and the digest to the receiver. To address this issue, the Secure Modbus protocol employs an RSA-based signature scheme [17]. Specifically, the originator of the Secure Modbus packet computes the SHA2 digest, signs the digest with its RSA private key, and sends the packet and the signed digest to the receiver. The receiver verifies the authenticity of the digest (and the packet) using the sender's public key. Thus, the receiver can ensure that the Secure Modbus packet was created by the purported sender and was not modified en route.

- **Non-Repudiation:** The RSA-based signature scheme also provides a non-repudiation mechanism – only the owner of the RSA private key could have sent the Secure Modbus packet.

- **Replay Protection:** The SHA2 hashing and RSA signature schemes do not prevent an attacker from re-using a "sniffed" Modbus packet signed by an authorized sender. Thus, the Secure Modbus protocol needs a mechanism that enables the receiver to discriminate between a "new packet" and a "used packet." This is accomplished by incorporating a time stamp (TS) in the Secure Modbus application data unit (Figure 2). The time stamp is used by the receiver in combination with an internal "time window" to check the "freshness" of the received packet. Our initial solution employed a simple two-byte sequence number and provided all Modbus devices with time windows of limited size to verify freshness. However, this solution was neither elegant nor completely secure. Consequently, our current implementation uses NTP time stamps that facilitate the evaluation of freshness with high precision. Of course, employing NTP time stamps requires an NTP server in the SCADA architecture to provide a reliable clock for all communicating devices.

The Secure Modbus protocol satisfies the minimum requirements of a "secure" protocol. However, it is just as important to ensure that the protocol can be implemented efficiently in real-world SCADA environments. Secure Modbus can be readily deployed in SCADA systems with adequate computing re-

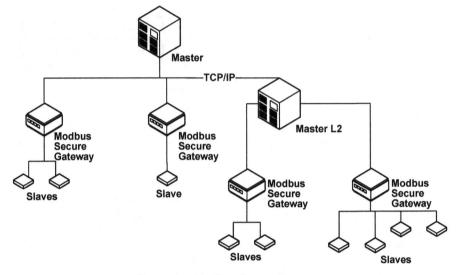

Figure 3. Modbus Secure Gateway.

sources, network bandwidth and modern, upgradeable slave devices. However, many critical infrastructure assets employ decades-old equipment; therefore, it is important to ensure that legacy systems can be retrofitted (at low cost) to support Secure Modbus.

We designed the Modbus Secure Gateway to facilitate the deployment of Secure Modbus in legacy SCADA environments. Figure 3 presents a schematic diagram of the Modbus Secure Gateway. It is a dedicated multi-homed gateway that hosts a TCP/IP interface connected to the process network and a set of point-to-point TCP or serial links connected to legacy slaves. The Modbus Secure Gateway operates as follows:

- When the Modbus Secure Gateway receives a packet on the process network interface:

  - It accepts only authenticated Secure Modbus TCP traffic from allowed masters.

  - It extracts the Modbus packet from the Secure Modbus packet.

  - It forwards the packet to the appropriate slave using the related point-to-point (serial or TCP) link.

- When the Modbus Secure Gateway receives a packet on one of the point-to-point links connected with a slave:

  - It creates a Secure Modbus packet containing the received original Modbus packet.

  - It signs the packet digest with the private key associated with the slave.

– It forwards the new packet to the appropriate master through its process network interface.

The Modbus Secure Gateway constitutes a single point of failure in the SCADA architecture. Therefore, it should be installed only when the "pure" Secure Modbus implementation is not feasible.

Next, we summarize the steps involved in sending and verifying a Secure Modbus request message:

- The master creates a valid Modbus request (M_{req}) with a time stamp and the serial slave address.

- The master computes the digest of the Modbus request, encrypts the digest with its private key (p_{K_m}) and sends the request along with the encrypted digest to a slave or to the Modbus Secure Gateway:

$$C = [TS|Modbus]\{SHA2(TS|Modbus)\}p_{K_m} \qquad (1)$$

- The slave or the Modbus Secure Gateway verifies that the Modbus request is genuine using the master's public key (s_{K_m}):

$$M_{req} = \{C\}s_{K_m} \qquad (2)$$

Note that after verifying that the request is genuine, the Modbus Secure Gateway reads the unit identifier in the MBAP header and sends the Modbus request to the addressed slave.

Similar steps are involved when a slave sends a response to the master.

7. Secure Modbus Implementation

The basic communication layer between the operating system and a Secure Modbus device is implemented using sockets (Level 1). All Secure Modbus protocol communications send and receive data via sockets. The TCP/IP library only provides stream sockets using TCP and a connection-based communication service. Consequently, sockets are created using the socket() function, which returns a number that is used by the creator to access the socket.

Figure 4 presents the architecture of the Secure Modbus module that implements socket-based communications. The TCP/IP level manages the establishment and termination of connections, and the data flow in an established connection. The TCP Stream Builder sets up the connection parameters according to the following constraints:

- KEEP-ALIVE: Client-server applications use the KEEP-ALIVE time to detect inactivity in order to close a connection or to identify a communication problem. Using a short KEEP-ALIVE time can cause good connections to be dropped.

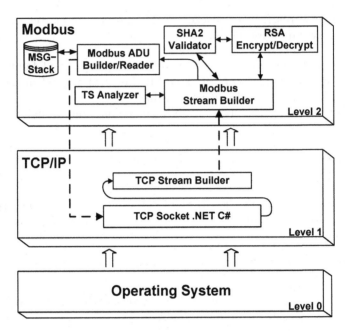

Figure 4.   Secure Modbus module.

- TCP-NODELAY: The TCP-NODELAY parameter is used for real-time systems.

- TIME OUT CONNECTIONS: By default, a TCP connection is timed out after 75 seconds. The default value may be adjusted according to the real-time constraints imposed by the system.

The Secure Modbus module has four main components:

- **Modbus Stream Builder:** This component extracts the Secure Modbus packet contained in the TCP payload and sends it to the RSA Encryption/Decryption Unit that verifies the authenticity of the SHA2 digest. The Modbus Stream Builder then sends the digest to the SHA2 Validator to verify packet integrity. Finally, it sends the time stamp to the Time Stamp Analyzer to verify the freshness of the data. If all these conditions are satisfied, the Modbus Stream Builder sends the Modbus packet to the appropriate application.

- **RSA Encryption/Decryption Unit:** This unit uses the public key of the sender to verify the authenticity of the digest and the private key of the sender to sign the hash message.

- **SHA2 Validator:** This component calculates and validates the hash values of Secure Modbus request and response messages.

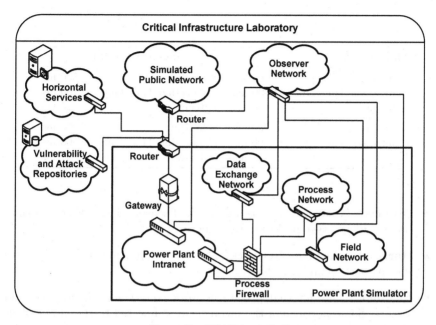

Figure 5. SCADA testbed.

- **Modbus ADU Builder/Reader:** This unit constructs and manages Secure Modbus application data units (ADUs). Also, it communicates with the SHA2 Validator and the RSA Encryption/Decryption Unit to authenticate packets.

- **Time Stamp Analyzer:** This component verifies the validity of time stamps using time windows or an NTP service.

The prototype was written in C# (MS.NET Framework version 2.0) under Microsoft Windows, and was then ported to a standard Linux environment (Ubuntu 10.0).

8. Experimental Results

The Secure Modbus protocol was tested using an experimental power plant testbed. Figure 5 shows the components of the SCADA testbed. The principal components are:

- **Field Network:** This network interconnects the sensors and actuators that interact with electromechanical devices in the power plant.

- **Process Network:** This network hosts all the SCADA systems. Plant operators use these systems to manage the power plant, send commands to sensors and actuators in the field network, and gather plant data and status information.

Table 1.　Comparison of communication latency.

Modbus TCP		Secure Modbus	
Scan Rate	500 ms	Scan Rate	500 ms
Connection Time Out	1,200 ms	Connection Time Out	1,200 ms
Latency	26 ms	Latency	27 ms
Scan Rate	200 ms	Scan Rate	200 ms
Connection Time Out	500 ms	Connection Time Out	500 ms
Latency	29 ms	Latency	31 ms

- **Observer Network:** This is a network of sensors that gathers information about the system during the experiments.

- **Horizontal Services Network:** This network provides support features such as backup and disaster recovery.

- **Intranet:** This internal private network connects company PCs and servers. Some portions of the intranet are connected to the power plant via the process network.

- **Data Exchange Network:** This network hosts data exchange servers that receive data from the process network and make it available to operators who use the corporate intranet.

We conducted two experiments to evaluate the performance of the Secure Modbus protocol. The first experiment examined the latency resulting from the use of the SHA2 hashing and RSA-based signature schemes. The second examined the increased size of Secure Modbus packets for various function codes.

Table 1 compares the communication latency for Modbus TCP and Secure Modbus. The first set of results, corresponding to a master scan rate of 500 ms and a connection timeout of 1,200 ms, show a latency of 26 ms for Modbus and 27 ms for Secure Modbus – a negligible difference. A negligible latency difference of 2 ms (29 ms for Modbus TCP and 31 ms for Secure Modbus) is also observed for a master scan rate of 200 ms and a connection timeout of 500 ms.

Table 2 compares the size of Modbus TCP and Secure Modbus packets for four function codes. Secure Modbus packets are larger than the corresponding Modbus TCP packets. However, the increased size is not a significant issue even for SCADA networks with low bandwidth.

9.　Conclusions

The Secure Modbus protocol offers key security features without introducing significant overhead that can impact real-time performance. The Modbus

Table 2. Comparison of packet size.

Function	Modbus TCP	Secure Modbus	Overhead
Write Coil (0x05)	11 bytes	43 bytes	291%
Write Register (0x06)	12 bytes	44 bytes	267%
Write Multiple Coils (0x0F)	260 bytes	292 bytes	12%
Write Multiple Registers (0x10)	260 bytes	292 bytes	12%

Secure Gateway facilitates the deployment of Secure Modbus in legacy SCADA environments. While the new protocol helps protect against several attacks, it does not address scenarios where an attacker seizes control of a master and sends malicious Modbus messages to slave devices, or where an attacker captures the master unit's private key and forges malicious Modbus messages that are signed with the stolen key. To address the first attack scenario, we are working on a dedicated filtering unit that will identify suspect Modbus messages. Our solution to the second scenario is to use a trusted computing platform to protect key rings. Our future research will also attempt to refine the signature scheme to improve real-time performance.

References

[1] O. Alhazmi, Y. Malaiya and I. Ray, Security vulnerabilities in software systems: A quantitative perspective, in *Data and Applications Security XIX*, S. Jajodia and D. Wijesekera (Eds.), Springer, Berlin-Heidelberg, pp. 281–294, 2005.

[2] American Society of Heating, Refrigerating and Air-Conditioning Engineers (ASHRAE), BACnet, ASHRAE SSPC 135, Atlanta, Georgia (www.bacnet.org).

[3] M. Bishop, *Computer Security: Art and Science*, Addison-Wesley, Reading, Massachusetts, 2002.

[4] A. Carcano, I. Nai Fovino, M. Masera and A. Trombetta, SCADA malware: A proof of concept, presented at the *Third International Workshop on Critical Information Infrastructure Security*, 2008.

[5] R. Chandia, J. Gonzalez, T. Kilpatrick, M. Papa and S. Shenoi, Security strategies for SCADA networks, in *Critical Infrastructure Protection*, E. Goetz and S. Shenoi (Eds.), Springer, Boston, Massachusetts, pp. 117–131, 2007.

[6] A. Creery and E. Byres, Industrial cybersecurity for power system and SCADA networks – Be secure, *IEEE Industry Applications*, vol. 13(4), pp. 49–55, 2007.

[7] G. Dondossola, J. Szanto, M. Masera and I. Nai Fovino, Effects of intentional threats to power substation control systems, *International Journal of Critical Infrastructures*, vol. 4(1/2), pp. 129–143, 2008.

[8] J. Heo, C. Hong, S. Ju, Y. Lim, B. Lee and D. Hyun, A security mechanism for automation control in PLC-based networks, *Proceedings of the IEEE International Symposium on Power Line Communications and its Applications*, pp. 466–470, 2007.

[9] D. Holmberg, BACnet Wide Area Network Security Threat Assessment, NISTIR 7009, National Institute of Standards and Technology, Gaithersburg, Maryland, 2003.

[10] P. Huitsing, R. Chandia, M. Papa and S. Shenoi, Attack taxonomies for the Modbus protocols, *International Journal of Critical Infrastructure Protection*, vol. 1, pp. 37–44, 2008.

[11] A. Jones and D. Ashenden, *Risk Management for Computer Security: Protecting Your Network and Information Assets*, Elsevier, Oxford, United Kingdom, 2005.

[12] R. Leszczyna, I. Nai Fovino and M. Masera, Simulating malware with MAlSim, *Computer Virology*, EICAR 2008 Extended Version, 2008.

[13] M. Majdalawieh, F. Parisi-Presicce and D. Wijesekera, DNPSec: Distributed Network Protocol Version 3 security framework, presented at the *Twenty-First Annual Computer Security Applications Conference (Technology Blitz Session)*, 2005.

[14] T. Mander, F. Nabhani, L. Wang and R. Cheung, Data object based security for DNP3 over TCP/IP for increased utility of commercial aspects of security, *Proceedings of the IEEE Power Engineering Society General Meeting*, pp. 1–8, 2007.

[15] M. Masera, I. Nai Fovino and R. Leszczyna, Security assessment of a turbogas power plant, in *Critical Infrastructure Protection II*, M. Papa and S. Shenoi (Eds.), Springer, Boston, Massachusetts, pp. 31–40, 2008.

[16] Modbus IDA, MODBUS Application Protocol Specification v1.1a, North Grafton, Massachusetts (www.modbus.org/specs.php), 2004.

[17] R. Rivest, A. Shamir and L. Adleman, A method for obtaining digital signatures and public-key cryptosystems, *Communications of the ACM*, vol. 21(2), pp. 120–126, 1978.

[18] M. Wiener, H. Handschuh, P. Pallier, R. Rivest, E. Biham and L. Knudsen, Performance comparison of public-key cryptosystems, smartcard cryptocoprocessors for public-key cryptography, chaffing and winnowing: Confidentiality without encryption, DES, Triple-DES and AES, *CryptoBytes*, vol. 4(1), 1998.

[19] A. Wright, J. Kinast and J. McCarty, Low-latency cryptographic protection for SCADA communications, *Proceedings of the Second International Conference on Applied Security and Network Security*, pp. 263–277, 2004.

Chapter 7

PROVIDING SITUATIONAL AWARENESS FOR PIPELINE CONTROL OPERATIONS

Jonathan Butts, Hugo Kleinhans, Rodrigo Chandia, Mauricio Papa and Sujeet Shenoi

Abstract   A SCADA system for a single 3,000-mile-long strand of oil or gas pipeline may employ several thousand field devices to measure process parameters and operate equipment. Because of the vital tasks performed by these sensors and actuators, pipeline operators need accurate and timely information about their status and integrity. This paper describes a real-time scanner that provides situational awareness about SCADA devices and control operations. The scanner, with the assistance of lightweight, distributed sensors, analyzes SCADA network traffic, verifies the operational status and integrity of field devices, and identifies anomalous activity. Experimental results obtained using real pipeline control traffic demonstrate the utility of the scanner in industrial settings.

Keywords: Pipeline control systems, situational awareness, ROC protocol

1.   Introduction

Imagine flying a modern aircraft with 10% of the instrument panel indicators providing erroneous data. Now imagine controlling a pipeline running from the Texas Gulf Coast to New York City with approximately 100 million pounds of liquids or gas, but with 10% of the field devices either non-operational or of dubious integrity.

Based on our experience, this is sometimes the situation with sensors and actuators in oil and gas pipelines. The sensors measure key process parameters such as pressure, temperature, flow and compositions. The actuators perform vital tasks such as opening and closing valves, operating pumping stations and tripping circuits. Pipeline operators must be able to trust their SCADA devices [14]. Unfortunately, few, if any, tools are available for verifying the status and integrity of SCADA systems.

C. Palmer and S. Shenoi (Eds.): Critical Infrastructure Protection III, IFIP AICT 311, pp. 97–111, 2009.
© IFIP International Federation for Information Processing 2009

This paper describes a SCADA network scanner intended to provide oil and gas pipeline operators with a comprehensive view of network topology along with detailed information about the configuration, status and integrity of SCADA devices and communication links. The scanner architecture incorporates a command module and database located in the control center and sensors positioned within SCADA subnets. The sensors passively monitor traffic and send information to the command module. The command module configures sensors, interacts with the database and provides event updates to operators. The database organizes, correlates and archives data collected by the sensors.

Tests using real pipeline control traffic demonstrate that the scanner can remotely verify the status and integrity of SCADA devices, profile normal SCADA operations and identify anomalous activity. The current implementation is targeted for ROC [3], a popular pipeline control protocol; however, the modular design readily accommodates other SCADA protocols.

2. ROC Protocol

The Remote Operation Controller (ROC) Protocol is used extensively in the oil and gas sector for pipeline operations. ROC is a proprietary protocol maintained by Emerson Process Management [3]. It is used primarily in Emerson products; however, other vendors often implement the ROC protocol to facilitate interoperation with Emerson equipment [11, 12, 16].

The ROC protocol uses a request-response paradigm for message transmission between a master terminal unit (MTU) and remote terminal units (RTUs) [2]. The MTU sends request messages to outlying RTUs to gather monitoring data or to specify control actions. The RTUs collect discrete and analog sensor data and maintain actuator settings specified by the MTU. Response messages are generated by RTUs after direct requests from the MTU. The MTU resends a request when it does not receive a timely response from an RTU. This communication model addresses congestion control and transmission error recovery.

ROC devices maintain control specifications and flow measurements within a database. The data elements, called "points," represent single input or output values [1]. Each database parameter is uniquely identified by a parameter number and point type. A request message from an MTU specifies a function to perform and the associated parameter number and point type. The receiving RTU performs the operation for the specified parameter and sends the desired measurement or a confirmation that the control action was performed. The ROC protocol specifies access mechanisms for the database configuration, real-time clock, event and alarm logs, and historical (archived) data.

Figure 1 shows the structure of a ROC message. A message contains a Destination Address followed by the Source Address. The addresses are split into two components: Unit ID and Group ID. The Unit ID is a unique one-byte address for each host in the system. This address is user configurable, with Unit ID 0 reserved for "broadcast within group" and Unit ID 240 used as the "direct connect address." The Group ID specifies the group to which a device is assigned. This address has a default value of 2, but is user configurable and

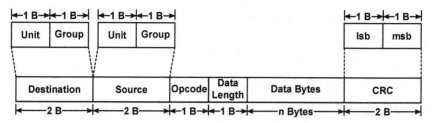

Figure 1. ROC message structure.

can be used to segregate broadcast groups. When a ROC device receives a message, it examines the destination Unit ID and Group ID. The message is accepted and processed if the two destination IDs match the configured device IDs or if the message is a broadcast message with a matching Group ID.

The Opcode field in a ROC message indicates the operation to be performed by the receiving RTU. The operations include configuration modification, retrieval of stored readings and alarms, direct sensor input reading, writing to outputs, acknowledgement of a report by exception, and store-and-forward messaging. An RTU responds to an MTU request with a message containing the original opcode and the results of the operation. When an RTU encounters an error condition (e.g., a request for unavailable data), it responds with Opcode 255 to indicate that the message contained a valid cyclic redundancy check (CRC) but requested invalid parameters.

The Data Length indicates the number of bytes in the Data Bytes field. The Data Bytes field is variable in length and contains the parameters for the operation requested by an MTU or information returned by an RTU. For example, an MTU may use Opcode 167 to request an RTU to measure the Analog Input#6. The RTU responds with Opcode 167 and places the data for the requested point type and parameter number in the Data Bytes field. The ROC protocol specifies the data format and available point types and parameters for each opcode.

The CRC field contains an error detection code to verify message integrity. The standard GPLib CRC routine [4] with the polynomial $x^{16} + x^{15} + x^2 + 1$ is used to compute the 16-bit value. When a device receives a message, it calculates the CRC value and verifies that it matches the value in the CRC field. The message is discarded if the two do not match.

The ROC protocol permits an RTU to generate a "report by exception" message (identified by Opcode 224) when certain conditions occur (e.g., when a sensor value exceeds a predetermined threshold). Upon receiving such a message, the MTU queries the stored alarms and sends a message with Opcode 225 that acknowledges the report by exception message.

3. Scanner Architecture

The SCADA scanner is designed to provide situational awareness for large pipeline systems. Real-time traffic analysis can be very difficult for traditional

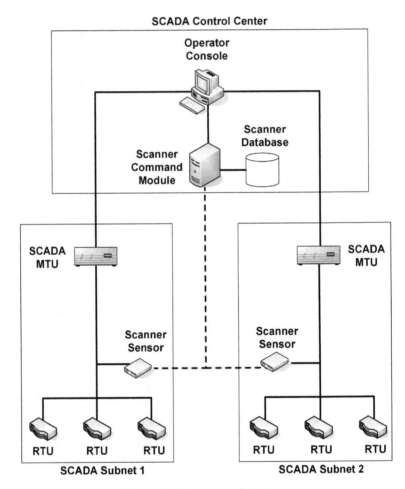

Figure 2.   Scanner architecture.

IP networks, mainly because of high traffic volumes, changing network topologies, the range of protocols and applications that are supported, and the relative unpredictability of network traffic patterns and content [10]. On the other hand, even SCADA systems with thousands of devices have low traffic volumes, static topologies, limited protocols and applications, and highly predictable traffic [8]. These attributes make it feasible to implement a real-time scanner that analyzes SCADA network traffic, verifies the operational status of field devices and identifies anomalous activity.

A SCADA system for pipeline operations is typically organized as multiple subnets, each with a master (MTU) and multiple slaves (RTUs). Operators monitor and control pipeline operations from a control center (Figure 2).

The scanner architecture incorporates a command module and database located in the control center and sensors positioned in the various SCADA subnets (Figure 2). The sensors passively monitor traffic and send information to the command module. The command module configures the sensors, interacts with the database and provides event updates to operators. The database organizes and correlates data collected by the scanner sensors. Ideally, the scanner components are dual-homed and use a dedicated communications network so as not to interfere with SCADA operations. However, if bandwidth is not an issue, the scanner sensors may be configured to use the SCADA network for communications.

Modern SCADA systems often employ TCP/IP for device communications, mainly to leverage the flexibility and cost of commodity LAN and WAN technologies. Consequently, the scanner is designed to operate in an IP-based environment. Because the majority of the scanner functionality resides at the application layer, the scanner can be readily modified for use in different communication environments.

This paper focuses on pipeline operations and the ROC protocol. However, the scanner sensors are designed to be modular and to support "plug and play" operations for other protocols. For example, to support Modbus network scanning, it is only necessary to incorporate a Modbus protocol module in the scanner framework. The following sections describe the scanner sensors, command module and database.

3.1 Sensors

Scanner sensors deployed at field sites operate in the promiscuous mode, enabling them to capture and examine traffic in their subnets. The sensors gather information about device functionality, state and network topology; and identify anomalous traffic (e.g., erroneous and malicious messages and unexpected traffic volumes). The sensors are designed to be implemented using inexpensive embedded devices (e.g., Gumstix [5]).

Each sensor maintains a local table with the attributes of devices in its subnet (address information, device functionality and communication patterns). Sensors "learn" about devices and attributes by examining captured traffic. Initially, the local sensor tables are empty; as the sensors parse traffic, new information is gleaned and stored in their tables. Alternatively, a configuration file with device attributes may be uploaded to each sensor by the command module.

Whenever a new entry is added to a sensor table (e.g., a new device address), an alert is sent to the database, which records information pertaining to the alert. The sensors also send periodic status updates to the database to provide situational awareness.

3.2 Command Module

The command module is accessed by plant personnel via an operator console. It provides facilities for managing alerts, reviewing scanner status, configuring

sensors and storing historical information related to pipeline control operations
in the scanner database.

The command module also serves as the front-end to the database, which
it queries constantly for new alerts and changes to SCADA device state and
configuration. The query results are passed to the operator console. A human
operator processes alerts and examines SCADA device data. Additionally, the
operator can view the status of sensors, e.g., subnet data, alerts generated, time
of last update and status (active/disabled).

Each sensor has a unique configuration file for scanning its subnet. A sensor
may be configured to examine specific device functions and roles, time-out
periods and traffic rates. For example, one of the RTUs in SCADA Subnet 1
(Figure 2) produces minimal traffic and an alert should be generated by the
sensor when the traffic rate exceeds 20 messages/second. On the other hand,
an alert should be generated for the MTU in SCADA Subnet 1 when the traffic
rate exceeds 400 messages/second. Note that the command module can upload
a new configuration file to a sensor or disable a sensor in real time.

3.3   Database

A relational database maintains historical information about SCADA devices, scanner sensors, network traffic and alerts. Figure 3 shows the eight
database tables. The Scanner Traffic table contains the traffic attributes that
generate alerts and/or database updates. The Sensors table holds information
about the scanner sensors. Four device tables (Devices, Device Types, Device
Opcodes and Device Alerts) maintain information about SCADA devices. The
remaining two tables (Alerts and Alert Codes) contain information about the
alerts generated by the scanner.

4.   Scanner Functionality

The ROC scanner provides information about device functionality, device
roles, communication patterns, and anomalous process behavior and SCADA
network activity. This information about the operational status of the SCADA
network and devices provides pipeline operators with vital situational awareness. The ROC scanner generates alerts about anomalous activity by comparing network traffic against normal (profiled) traffic.

4.1   Creating System Profiles

Local tables are maintained by sensors to profile traffic and device operations. Table 1 shows a sample sensor table. When a ROC message is received
by a sensor, it examines the source IP address and source device address to see
if they exist in its table; if not, an entry is added to indicate that a new device
is communicating in the subnet. The sensor also examines the destination IP
address and destination device address in a similar manner.

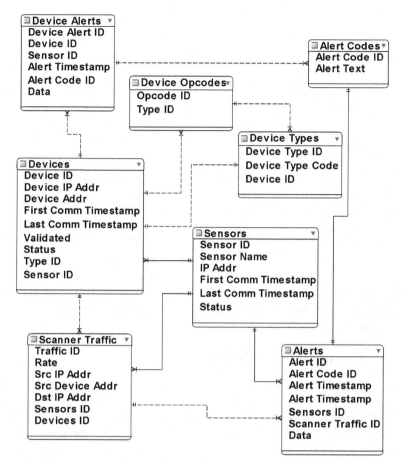

Figure 3. Database relations.

Next, the opcode is examined to determine if the sending device has previously sent a message with the code; the sensor table is updated if the opcode has never been used by the device. The Communication Relations column in the table identifies entities with which devices have communicated. The Opcodes and Communication Relations columns help determine device roles. For example, Device 1 in Table 1 has sent messages to all the devices in the subnet and has used opcodes related to every device in the subnet. Therefore, it can be inferred that Device 1 is an MTU. Devices 2 through 4 use certain opcodes and only communicate with Device 1; thus, these devices are functioning as RTUs.

The Rate column lists the number of messages per second that have been sent or received by a device. This provides an indication of the traffic rate for each device in the subnet. The Last Communication column displays a time stamp and an ordinal date (**ddd**) to identify when the last message originated from the corresponding device.

Table 1. Sensor table data.

Device	IP Addr. Device Addr.	Opcodes	Comm. Assosc.	Rate	Last Comm.
Dev 1	192.168.10.10 0xAB00	0 2 6 8 11 105 166 171	Dev 2 Dev 3 Dev 4	118 msg/sec	23:14:53 244
Dev 2	192.168.10.20 0x4A05	0 2 6 105	Dev 1	33 msg/sec	23:11:14 244
Dev 3	192.168.10.21 0xFC04	0 2 8 166	Dev 1	64 msg/sec	23:13:29 244
Dev 4	192.168.10.22 0xD607	0 105 171	Dev 1	29 msg/sec	23:14:53 244

The table entries provide a profile of the known state of the subnet. This profile identifies the devices, the functions they implement and their roles, and the communication patterns.

4.2   Generating Alerts

This section discusses the steps involved in processing messages and generating alerts (Table 2). The sensor parses a message to analyze the various fields. If new device and IP addresses are observed, an alert is sent to indicate that a new device is communicating in the subnet. If a new device address and an already existing IP address are observed, a possible spoofed IP address or configuration change alert is generated. Similarly, a possible spoofed device address or configuration change alert is sent when an existing device address and a new IP address are encountered.

SCADA devices are configured to use specific TCP communication ports [6]. Therefore, valid traffic should use the designated ROC communication ports and should conform with the ROC protocol. An alert is sent if a non-standard protocol message is received on a ROC port or a ROC message is received on a non-standard port. Note that alerts are not sent for non-ROC messages received on non-standard ports because these messages are ignored by all ROC devices.

The opcodes of ROC messages that use ROC communication ports are then checked to verify control actions and device functionality. An alert is sent when an opcode is encountered that has not been used previously by a device or that has not been configured as a valid code. Note that numerous alerts are generated when the sensors are first turned on. If this is a problem, the number of alerts generated on start-up can be reduced significantly by using a configuration file that contains information about the baseline state of the system.

Table 2. Generated alerts.

Conditions	Alert Message
device address is new==true ip address is new==true	New device
device address is new==true ip address is new==false	Possible spoofed IP address or configuration change
device address is new==false ip address is new==true	Possible spoofed device address or configuration change
roc comm port==false roc msg format==true	ROC message on non-standard port
roc comm port==true roc msg format==false	Non-standard message on ROC port
roc comm port==true roc msg format==true valid control operation==false	Unexpected control operation
exceed rate threshold==true	Traffic rate exceeds threshold
exceed device time-out==true	Device has stopped communicating

Next, traffic rates are computed for the source and destination devices specified in the messages. This is accomplished by maintaining message counts for devices and aggregating the numbers of messages over time. An alert is sent when the traffic rate exceeds the threshold of any of the communicating devices as specified in the configuration file. Finally, a time-out period (in the sensor configuration file) specifies the length of time a SCADA device can go without communication. Each sensor periodically computes the time difference between the current time and last communication time for devices in its local table. An alert is sent when this time difference exceeds the time-out period.

This message processing logic detects several scenarios: (i) an unauthorized system communicating on a subnet; (ii) an attempt to spoof an address or device; (iii) a denial-of-service attack; (iv) a reconnaissance probe performed by an attacker (e.g., port scanning, network mapping, device opcode identification); (v) an attempt to send improper control messages; and (vi) a device performing an unauthorized operation (e.g., a rogue device operating as a master).

5. Experimental Results

This section describes the experimental results obtained for a simulated pipeline control system. The simulation models the control operations of a major gas pipeline company. The experiments, which used real ROC traffic, were designed to evaluate the ability of the scanner to accurately profile system attributes and to identify unauthorized operations (including malicious activity).

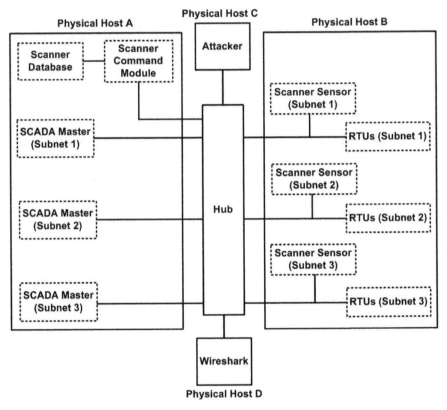

Figure 4. Experimental SCADA testbed.

5.1   Experimental Testbed

Figure 4 illustrates the virtual SCADA testbed used in our experiments. The testbed has three subnets, each with one MTU and ten RTUs; a sensor is positioned in each subnet. The scanner components (control module, database and sensors) and the SCADA system use a common network for communications. SCADA traffic used in the experiments was obtained from an operational pipeline system utilizing Fisher ROC devices.

The boxes with solid lines in Figure 4 denote physical hosts and the dashed boxes indicate virtual machines. Physical Hosts A and B are 2.0 GHZ notebook PCs with 2 GB RAM running Windows XP Service Pack 2. All the virtual machines are VMWare [15] images of SCADA devices and scanner components (three MTUs, three RTUs, three sensors, one command module and one database). The VMWare images for the MTUs, RTUs and scanner sensors use Arch Linux 2.6.22 and are each assigned 256 MB RAM. The database runs MySQL 5.0.51 on Windows XP Service Pack 2 and is assigned 512 MB RAM. The command module also runs on Windows XP Service Pack 2 with 512 MB RAM. The MTUs and RTUs are run on different physical hosts to ensure that

SCADA traffic is visible to the sensors. The IP device addresses are assigned statically as in real-world pipeline operations.

Two additional hosts (Physical Hosts C and D), both 2.0 GHZ notebooks with 2 GB RAM running Windows XP Service Pack 2, are used. Physical Host C sends malicious traffic; it uses the hping2 utility [13] to craft and inject attacks. Physical Host D uses Wireshark [9] to capture network traffic for validation purposes. All the physical hosts are interconnected using Ethernet network interface cards via a 10/100 Ethernet hub.

The local sensor tables are set to empty at the beginning of each test, requiring the sensors to "learn" the SCADA system attributes. Each sensor is configured for a device traffic threshold of 400 messages/second and a time-out period of 1 minute.

5.2 SCADA Network Profiling

Several tests were conducted to evaluate the ability of the scanner to accurately profile SCADA devices and operations. During each test, the sensors examined twenty minutes of pipeline control traffic between the MTU and RTUs in their subnets.

The MTUs and RTUs were identified almost instantly by the sensors and the corresponding new device alerts were generated. After a new device alert was received and correlated with the correct device, the alert was cleared to ensure that the device did not generate additional new device alerts.

Alerts were also generated for new opcodes used by SCADA devices. Practically all the alerts (and sensor table updates) occurred during the first three minutes of sensor operation. A few alerts related to new opcodes were generated during the remaining seventeen minutes of traffic analysis.

The tests were run four times with different traffic. In every case, the scanner accurately identified the SCADA devices and their functionality. Additionally, the device communication relations and device roles were identified correctly.

Table 3 presents the communication patterns identified during SCADA network profiling. The IP addresses have been altered for reasons of sensitivity; however, the addresses presented are representative of the network topology. The network topology and device roles are easily determined using the address information and communication relations. For brevity, some of the devices identified as RTUs are not included in Table 3. Note that Device 1 communicates with Devices 2–11 on the same subnet while Devices 2–11 only communicate with Device 1. Thus, Device 1 (and Devices 12 and 23) appear to be functioning as MTUs while the other devices are RTUs.

5.3 Malicious Activity Detection

Additional experiments were conducted to evaluate the ability of the scanner to accurately identify malicious activity. Traffic corresponding to four attacks was interspersed with regular network traffic. The attacks involved: (i)

Table 3. System profiling results.

Device	IP Address	Comm. Relations	Role
Dev 1	192.168.10.10	Dev 2–Dev 11	MTU Subnet 1
Dev 2	192.168.10.20	Dev 1	RTU Subnet 1
...	...	...	...
Dev 11	192.168.10.29	Dev 1	RTU Subnet 1
Dev 12	192.168.40.10	Dev 13–Dev 22	MTU Subnet 2
Dev 13	192.168.40.20	Dev 12	RTU Subnet 2
...	...	...	...
Dev 22	192.168.40.29	Dev 12	RTU Subnet 2
Dev 23	192.168.70.10	Dev 24–Dev 33	MTU Subnet 3
Dev 24	192.168.70.20	Dev 23	RTU Subnet 3
...	...	...	...
Dev 33	192.168.70.29	Dev 23	RTU Subnet 3

a spoofed device; (ii) network reconnaissance; (iii) a rogue master; and (iv) denial of service.

Two instances of spoofed devices were executed repeatedly with different device addresses. The first involved MTU messages with existing IP addresses (of RTUs) but new device addresses. The second involved MTU messages with new IP addresses but existing RTU device addresses. In every case, the sensors correctly sent alerts indicating the presence of spoofed devices.

Two reconnaissance probes were conducted on the SCADA network. The first attempted to identify the ROC communication ports. This probe involved sending legitimate ROC messages and incrementing the communication port value until a response was received. In every case, an alert was generated that a valid ROC message was sent on a non-standard communication port.

The second reconnaissance probe emulated an nmap scan [7]. ICMP and TCP messages were crafted for host discovery and open port identification. The sensors detected the anomalous messages and raised alerts that non-standard ROC messages were being sent on ROC communication ports. Also, during both the network reconnaissance probes, the machines that generated the messages were correctly identified as new devices.

The rogue master attack involved sending fabricated messages to RTUs. One set of messages requested RTUs to clear their event sequences (Opcode 132). Another requested RTUs to set a new date and time (Opcode 8). The sensors correctly raised alerts about the new master device and anomalous function codes for the associated RTUs.

Table 4. Summary of malicious activity and alerts.

Attack	Details	Alerts Generated
Spoof 1	Rogue device communicates using an existing IP address	Possible spoofed IP address
Spoof 2	Rogue device communicates using an existing device address	Possible spoofed device address
Recon 1	Port scan uses ROC message to determine ROC communication ports	(i) New device (ii) ROC message on non-standard port
Recon 2	Network scan attempts to discover topology and open ports	(i) New device (ii) Non-standard ROC message
Rogue MTU 1	Rogue device functions as an MTU to clear data in an RTU	(i) New device (ii) Unexpected control operation
Rogue MTU 2	Rogue device functions as an MTU to write data to an RTU	(i) New device (ii) Unexpected control operation
DoS 1	Excessive traffic prevents device from functioning properly	(i) New device (ii) Traffic rate exceeds threshold
DoS 2	Device is taken off-line	Device has stopped communicating

The final test involved two denial-of-service attacks. One attack sent large volumes of traffic to an MTU; the other physically took RTUs offline. In the first instance, alerts were generated when traffic rates exceeded the configured thresholds; also, the attacking machine was identified as a new device. In the second instance, an alert that an RTU had stopped communicating was issued when the communication time exceeded the specified time-out period.

Table 4 summarizes the malicious activity and the corresponding alerts generated during the experiments. The correct alerts were generated in a timely manner in all the tests.

6. Conclusions

Oil and gas pipeline operators do not have adequate means to verify the state and integrity of the thousands of widely dispersed SCADA devices used for pipeline control. A lack of situational awareness about the behavior of SCADA systems can complicate – if not degrade – pipeline control operations. Limited situational awareness also makes it more difficult to detect and respond to the effects of unexpected incidents and malicious acts.

Our distributed scanner provides vital situational awareness about SCADA devices and control operations. The scanner can remotely verify the status and integrity of SCADA devices, profile normal SCADA operations and identify anomalous activity. The current implementation is targeted for ROC, a popular pipeline control protocol; however, the design readily accommodates other SCADA protocols via plug-in modules.

Acknowledgements

This work was partially supported by the Institute for Information Infrastructure Protection (I3P) at Dartmouth College, Hanover, New Hampshire, under Award 2006-CS-001-000001 from the U.S. Department of Homeland Security.

References

[1] ArWest Communications Corporation, Supervisory Control and Data Acquisition (SCADA), San Jose, California (www.arwestcom.com/?s=resources&p=scada), 2008.

[2] Emerson Process Management, ROC Protocol User Manual, Bulletin A4199, Houston, Texas, 2007.

[3] Emerson Process Management, St. Louis, Missouri (www.emersonprocess.com), 2008.

[4] C. Frayn, Genetic Programming Library (GPLib), University of Birmingham, Birmingham, United Kingdom (www.cs.bham.ac.uk/~cmf/GPLib/index.html), 2006.

[5] Gumstix, Portola Valley, California (www.gumstix.com), 2008.

[6] Information Sciences Institute, RFC793: Transmission Control Protocol, University of Southern California, Marina del Rey, California (www.faqs.org/rfcs/rfc793.html), 1981.

[7] Insecure.org, Nmap Reference Guide, Palo Alto, California (nmap.org/book/man.html), 2005.

[8] T. Kilpatrick, J. Gonzalez, R. Chandia, M. Papa and S. Shenoi, Forensic analysis of SCADA systems and networks, *International Journal of Security and Networks*, vol. 3(2), pp. 95–102, 2008.

[9] U. Lamping, R. Sharpe and E. Warnicke, Wireshark User's Guide: 27121 for Wireshark 1.0.0 (www.wireshark.org/download/docs/user-guide-us.pdf), 2008.

[10] S. Northcutt and J. Novak, *Network Intrusion Detection*, New Riders, Indianapolis, Indiana, 2003.

[11] OPC Foundation, Matrikon OPC Server for Fisher ROC Plus, Scottsdale, Arizona (www.opcfoundation.org/Products/ProductDetails.aspx?CM=1&RI=8538&CU=1), 2008.

[12] ProSoft Technology, Fisher ROC Communications Module (3150-ROC), Bakersfield, California (www.prosoft-technology.com/prosoft/products/fo r_rockwell_automation/protocol/custom/fisher_roc/3150_roc), 2008.

[13] S. Sanfilippo, **hping2** (www.hping.org), 2006.

[14] R. Shayto, B. Porter, R. Chandia, M. Papa and S. Shenoi, Assessing the integrity of field devices in Modbus networks, in *Critical Infrastructure Protection II*, M. Papa and S. Shenoi (Eds.), Springer, Boston, Massachusetts, pp. 115–128, 2008.

[15] VMWare, VMWare Server Virtual User's Guide (VMware Server 2.0), Palo Alto, California (www.vmware.com/pdf/vmserver2.pdf), 2008.

[16] Wonderware West, Wonderware Universal Server, League City, Texas (www.standard automation.com/products/universal-server), 2008.

Chapter 8

ENHANCING THE SAFETY, SECURITY AND RESILIENCE OF ICT AND SCADA SYSTEMS USING ACTION RESEARCH

Stig Johnsen, Torbjorn Skramstad and Janne Hagen

Abstract   This paper discusses the results of a questionnaire-based survey used to assess the safety, security and resilience of information and communications technology (ICT) and supervisory control and data acquisition (SCADA) systems used in the Norwegian oil and gas industry. The survey identifies several challenges, including the involvement of professionals with different backgrounds and expertise, lack of common risk perceptions, inadequate testing and integration of ICT and SCADA systems, poor information sharing related to undesirable incidents and lack of resilience in the design of technical systems. Action research is proposed as a process for addressing these challenges in a systematic manner and helping enhance the safety, security and resilience of ICT and SCADA systems used in oil and gas operations.

Keywords: Oil and gas sector, ICT/SCADA systems, action research

1.   Introduction

Process management systems used to control oil and gas production incorporate traditional information and communications technology (ICT) systems and supervisory control and data acquisition (SCADA) systems. SCADA systems are often integrated with safety instrumented systems (SISs). Real-time production data is shared between these systems to conduct vital operations at oil and gas facilities.

Process management systems used in oil and gas operations leverage several technologies. The ICT infrastructure consists of networking equipment, production systems (e.g., enterprise resource planning systems), maintenance systems, telephone support systems, radar and video systems (e.g., closed-circuit television and VHF radio systems). Process control systems used in production

C. Palmer and S. Shenoi (Eds.): Critical Infrastructure Protection III, IFIP AICT 311, pp. 113–123, 2009.
© IFIP International Federation for Information Processing 2009

include various field devices, including sensors and actuators. SISs are used for emergency shutdowns and to prevent fire and gas emissions.

Over the years, SCADA systems have evolved from proprietary stand-alone systems to commodity networked workstations that are frequently connected to the Internet. The use of personal computing technology and the interconnectivity of production systems and the ICT infrastructure lead to increased vulnerabilities and threats. Meanwhile, dependencies between the various systems and technologies are increasing. The operating environment is also becoming more complex, involving a multitude of highly-specialized professionals from different organizations and located at widely-dispersed sites.

The consequences of an accident at an oil and gas facility can be catastrophic. However, due to the complex infrastructure and operational environment, it may be impossible to foresee what may go wrong [20]. Consequently, ICT and SCADA systems should be resilient in the face of undesirable incidents. Barriers should be established between systems to protect against common failures. Safety guidelines and information security best practices should be implemented to the maximum extent.

ICT and SCADA systems should be safe, secure and resilient. Safety is the "freedom from unacceptable risks" [6]. Information security involves the protection of information assets from unauthorized access, use, disclosure, disruption, modification and destruction by providing high levels of confidentiality, integrity and availability. Resilience is "the intrinsic ability of a system to adjust its functioning prior to or following changes and disturbances, so that it can sustain operations even after a major mishap or in the presence of continuous stress" [6]. Resilience must be designed into technical systems, the organization and in the workforce.

Two pressing questions in the oil and gas sector are: What is the status of safety, security and resilience of ICT and SCADA systems used in oil and gas operations? How can vulnerabilities be mitigated in order to improve safety, security and resilience?

We conducted a survey of personnel at 46 Norwegian offshore oil and gas installations to assess the levels of safety, security and resilience in ICT and SCADA systems. The survey was mainly based on epidemiological accident models. We assumed that accidents have complex linear dependencies and occur as a result of unsafe acts in combination with weak defenses (i.e., accidents are caused by the lack of barriers or by holes in barriers [6, 15, 16]). The barriers include human factors, technical factors and organizational factors. Defenses and barriers are important aspects of any security model; they reduce the likelihood of undesirable incidents and reduce their consequences. In addition, we attempted to assess system complexity and identify tight couplings based on systemic models (with complex, non-linear relationships). A key objective was to gather data related to "normal accidents" as described by [14], and to identify the likelihood of occurrence and the overall risk in oil and gas facilities.

2.   Oil and Gas Industry Survey

Before designing the questionnaire, we conducted a series of workshops and interviews to identify some of the key vulnerabilities introduced by the use of commodity computing and network resources in oil and gas facilities [10]. Some vulnerabilities were identified, including the susceptibility to virus infections and denial-of-service (DoS) attacks. Our earlier work [10] indicated that the key issues to explore were the use of personal computing technology in SCADA systems; the degree of networking between Internet, ICT systems, SCADA systems and SISs; common failures; risk perceptions; and the lack of awareness about vulnerabilities.

The survey questionnaire was designed to identify the types of ICT and SCADA systems used along with their vulnerabilities. The questionnaire covered four areas: (i) general information; (ii) the connections between systems; (iii) the common infrastructure and the possibility of common failures; and (iv) the level of established risk assessments and the barriers to mitigating the risks. The questions could be answered using Yes/No responses. In addition, the respondents were encouraged to provide free-form comments.

Questionnaires were distributed to 46 installations and were mostly completed by operators; typically, individuals responsible for the SCADA systems at the installations and who worked closely with suppliers. All 46 questionnaires were completed. However, only a qualitative assessment of the results can be provided because Yes/No answers were rarely given; in most cases, the respondents provided comments along with qualifying statements.

Additional information was solicited from the respondents after the survey to clarify several issues that arose when analyzing their responses. In retrospect, the questionnaire and terminology could have been more precise. Also, due to differences in the background and expertise of the respondents and the ICT/SCADA infrastructure at their installations, working group meetings and interviews should have been conducted first. The original questionnaire should then have been adjusted based on the respondents' comments, and a more precise questionnaire should have been distributed later.

The survey and the subsequent discussions yielded several key results:

- **Poor Risk Awareness:** Only five of the 46 installations had performed risk analyses related to the integration of ICT and SCADA systems. ICT professionals and SCADA professionals collaborated on risk analysis efforts at only eight of the 46 installations. ICT and SCADA professionals used different standards and procedures to assess risk. In particular, ICT professionals employed standards such as ISO/IEC 27002 while SCADA professionals used safety standards such as IEC 61508.

- **Lack of Consistent Safety/Security Guidelines:** Three installations did not apply safety and/or security guidelines for ICT/SCADA systems. In twenty cases, various guidelines were referenced; however, we were unable to find even one concise guideline that contained all the relevant material.

- **Absence of Systematic Knowledge Sharing:** Information about undesirable incidents had not been shared among the relevant actors. Two installations had no procedures for reporting ICT/SCADA incidents. One organization used three different reporting systems.

- **Poor Scenario Training and Emergency Preparedness:** A set of undesirable incidents that could be explored as the basis for emergency training had not been identified. Emergency preparedness plans to handle ICT/SCADA infrastructure failures had not been developed nor had scenario-based training been performed. Also, systematic awareness training had not been performed.

- **Lack of System Certification:** SCADA systems were not certified as being resistant to DoS attacks involving large volumes of ICT network traffic (e.g., using Achilles from Wurldtech Security or ISA certifications [8]). However, surveillance and testing of network traffic was conducted at seventeen installations.

- **Common Components and Failures:** SCADA systems and SISs often had common power supplies, operator stations and network components, which significantly increased the probability of common failures. Furthermore, SCADA systems and SISs from the same vendor were closely related and had many common components. While no failures of SISs have been reported (e.g., in the Industrial Security Incident Database (ISID) [19]), stress tests have uncovered vulnerabilities that can influence SIS operation. These vulnerabilities have been prioritized for mitigation by vendors.

- **Lack of Network Barriers:** Few barriers existed between SCADA systems and SISs (e.g., using firewalls or network segmentation). Furthermore, network design best practices (e.g., [7]) were not employed. Poor network design can affect resilience; malfunctions and DoS attacks can impact SCADA systems and SISs.

- **Poor Standardization:** Standardization across companies was lacking and different solutions had been established within the same company. This created a more demanding operational environment because remote support was more complex. At the same time, different solutions can enhance resilience because the same vulnerability is not necessarily present in all the solutions. However, most of the installations used Windows platforms with Ethernet (TCP/IP) for communications.

- **Inadequate Deployment of Patches:** Patches should be deployed immediately after they are made available to address vulnerabilities, protect against attacks and enhance resilience. In general, the ICT infrastructure and applications were centrally administered and patched. However, the SCADA systems were administered and patched locally. The deployment of patches in SCADA systems varied: some SCADA systems were not patched systematically while some systems were not patched at all.

■ **Inadequate Review of Firewall Logs:** In general, firewall logs were not reviewed and analyzed. There were several cases where logs were not inspected due to high workload or other factors.

3. Addressing the Challenges

The survey results indicate that several challenges exist related to safety, security and resilience in oil and gas facilities. To address these challenges, we consider four key phases used in resilience engineering [6]:

■ **Anticipation:** Knowing what to expect (potential).

■ **Attention:** Knowing what to look for (critical).

■ **Response:** Knowing what to do (actual).

■ **Learning:** Knowing what has happened (factual).

According to resilience engineering, an organization that focuses on anticipation, attention, response and learning can mitigate risks and improve safety and security. In the following, we discuss the notions of anticipation and response in the context of the survey results.

3.1 Anticipation

The results of the survey indicate that there is a lack of anticipation about what can go wrong and a lack of attention when something unexpected happens. This is because there is poor risk awareness, no systematic risk assessment and no systematic sharing of information about incidents. Since most organizations do not have safety and/or security guidelines in place, it is difficult to establish anticipation and attention based on formal procedures. Also, the relative absence of formal certification and qualification procedures for ICT/SCADA systems implies that the organizations are uncertain about system resilience and the ability of the systems to handle unanticipated loads and DoS attacks. System tests [11] and actual incidents such as the one at the Browns Ferry nuclear plant [13] demonstrate that ICT/SCADA systems have significant vulnerabilities and are susceptible to DoS attacks.

Common components lead to common failures; however, because risk analyses were not performed at the oil and gas facilities that participated in the survey, there was limited awareness about this issue. Also, networks were not systematically segmented, which can lead to unanticipated problems. Poor standardization often leads to unanticipated results. However, the lack of standardization may, in fact, increase resilience – with different technical solutions at the 46 installations, it would be practically impossible to have a common failure at all the installations. Some of the systems were complex and had tight couplings, which increase the likelihood of "normal accidents." The evaluation of the connections between complex, tightly-coupled systems and incidents is an important topic that deserves further investigation.

3.2   Response

Learning from incidents is perceived to be a challenge because of the lack of systematic information sharing about incidents. The resilience of individual installations with respect to ICT/SCADA incidents is also expected to be poor. Due to the robustness of SISs, an incident would likely result in a production shutdown, but this can be very costly – around \$1 million per stoppage. In the event of a health, safety and environmental incident, an SIS would be expected to shut down the system or, at the very least, move it to a safe state. However, the SIS itself can fail (albeit with very low probability), but the consequences are major [20]. Implementing the correct response to such an incident is a definite challenge because of inadequate scenario training and emergency preparedness. Clearly, it is extremely important to enhance the resilience of ICT/SCADA systems through increased awareness, training and organization.

3.3   Mitigation Actions

Anticipation, attention, response and learning are key to enhancing resilience. The anticipation of undesirable incidents by ICT and SCADA professionals can be improved by having them participate in risk assessment studies where potential scenarios are identified and explored; this helps create common awareness and anticipation. ICT and SCADA personnel should gain a common understanding of risks and mitigating actions and, ideally, have ownership of the mitigating actions.

To improve the ability of personnel to learn from and to respond to incidents, it is important that relevant scenarios are discussed and explored. ICT and SCADA professionals have different knowledge, experience and perspectives. By collaborating on learning and scenario analysis, they can obtain better assessments of the risk and identify appropriate risk reduction measures from a combined ICT and SCADA perspective.

Several other actions should be performed after a risk assessment is completed. These include conducting scenario training and establishing emergency response plans; performing systematic qualification and certification processes on key systems; and implementing barriers between process control systems and SISs using firewalls and network segmentation. Also, systems should be systematically hardened based on the results of the risk assessment (e.g., by installing operating system and application upgrades, security patches and anti-malware updates). Furthermore, firewall logs should be analyzed carefully to increase the understanding of incidents and the awareness of possible threats.

Our analysis indicates that professionals in different units have different expertise and levels of risk awareness; thus, there is a great need to increase risk communication. In particular, all four resilience engineering phases – antici-pation, attention, response and learning – must be improved. Participation, communication, action and ownership can improve operational safety and se-curity. These issues suggest the need for a participatory process based on action research. Action research has been used to improve safety and security in complex organizations. Smith, *et al.* [18] describe how an action research program conducted across the entire New South Wales (Australia) Government contributed to better compliance, increased understanding and knowledge, im-proved policies, and effective business continuity plans. Similar results have been obtained in the Australian health care industry [3, 9].

4. Action Research

Action research is an established method for implementing changes based on reflection and participatory problem solving in team settings. Action research varies in form, but it usually involves technological, organizational and human issues in a change process. The underlying philosophy is that complex changes can be best understood and influenced by action [4].

Our hypothesis is that action research improves safety, security and re-silience. The argument is that the process of action research together with the involved actors, sometimes called the "community of practice," identify relevant issues in design and operations, and also identify mitigating actions. The involvement of a community that includes management, ICT and SCADA professionals and workforce members increases the likelihood that the mitigat-ing actions will be implemented successfully. Action research is especially useful in complex settings such as when multiple entities collaborate on safety-critical oil and gas operations.

Westrum [22] suggests that an organization whose workforce is aligned, aware and empowered is better at rooting out underlying problems. Action research can assist this endeavor by enabling "hidden" problems to be identified and highlighted. At the same time, action research can involve different stakeholders (or communities of practice) in a meaningful and positive dialog, fostering understanding and lasting collaboration. All this can ensure that issues related to safety, security and resilience are handled in a sensible matter. Although the work processes are fragmented, the "entire picture" can be analyzed due to the involvement of all the relevant participants.

Our survey of the action research literature reveals that it contributes to safety improvements. Our survey findings are based on a limited data set and, therefore, may be somewhat biased. The key issue is to identify causal relation-ships between the change process used in action research and the development of safety, security and resilience. We are especially interested in identifying ac-tion research activities that influence safety, security and resilience, the involved stakeholders and the application domains.

Van Eynde and Bledsoe [21] describe action research as the "touchstone of most good organizational development practices." The iterative method of action research has been formalized by Davidson, *et al.* [4] as an iterative process model with five canonical action research principles: (i) researcher-client agreement; (ii) cyclical process model; (iii) theory; (iv) change through action; and (v) learning through reflection.

The involvement of stakeholders and the commitment from the "client" are important in relation to ownership, process, results, learning and reflection. Action research is an approach that is well-suited to complex problems. The relevant actors should be involved in the process because development and improvement may involve many stakeholders outside the organization (e.g., suppliers and service providers).

Alteren, *et al.* [1] have documented the improvements in safety and productivity from an action research project conducted at an offshore oil rig. The number of injuries at the rig decreased and the productivity (drill meters per day) increased. Moreover, the number of incidents involving injuries dropped to one-third of the previous number.

Alteren and colleagues highlighted some key issues: building on communities of practice by involving people who formed working communities at the platform, regardless of the company for which they worked; and implementing a "bottom-up" process involving first-line workers to ensure ownership by all the relevant employees regardless of line position. Other key issues include the need to focus on issues and challenges that the involved personnel deem to be most important, and using search conferences [5] as a tool to create understanding and participation among the workforce.

Antonsen, *et al.* [2] have documented similar improvements in safety (and efficiency) related to the use of service vessels in the oil and gas industry. The initiative realized dramatic reductions in injuries and collisions. Injuries on service vessels (per million working hours) were reduced from 13.8 in 2001 to 2.6 in 2006. Service vessel collisions were reduced from twelve in 2000 to an average of one per year from 2001 through 2005.

The key issues highlighted by Antonsen and co-workers include building on communities of practice whose safety is at stake (e.g., crews on service vessels and offshore installations); developing a unified approach to safety in the logistic chain; focusing on an interpretive bottom-up process in addition to "top-down" support of activities and mitigating actions; increasing worker understanding and ownership of challenges and solutions; basing the work on practical experience from the workforce; and implementing safety improvements without having to wait for an accident, which contributes to mitigating actions being perceived as more legitimate by workers. Other issues include using workgroup meetings (search conferences) as a tool for fostering workforce understanding and participation; generating enthusiasm; shifting from a "blame-oriented" to a "learning-oriented" culture with regard to incidents; and focusing on dialog and reflection (i.e., "two-way" communication).

Richter [17] notes that action research on accident prevention caused accident rates at two Danish enterprises to drop to about 25% of the average of the preceding five years. He observed that safety can be improved by building on communities of practice; focusing on an interpretive bottom-up process in addition to top-down support of activities and mitigating actions; increasing worker understanding and ownership of challenges and solutions; and using search conferences as a tool to create understanding and participation by the workforce.

Richter's results could be a manifestation of the so-called "Hawthorne effect" [12], where increased attention to the principal issues is the real reason for safety and productivity improvements. However, the results appear to have a prolonged effect, lasting more than six months. The thesis that "structured" attention has a positive influence on safety and productivity clearly deserves further investigation.

5. Conclusions

Our survey of technical personnel at oil and gas installations has identified several challenges related to the safety, security and resilience of ICT and SCADA systems used in oil and gas production. The organizations and systems are complex and interdependent, and incidents can be potentially catastrophic. It is, therefore, critical to enhance the resilience of systems, organizations and human actors.

An action research program can help address these challenges. In particular, action research should focus on building communities of practice involving ICT and SCADA personnel in addition to members of the workforce whose safety is at stake; using search conferences as a tool to create understanding and participation among the various actors; using bottom-up and top-down processes; increasing worker understanding and ownership of challenges and solutions; exploring actual incidents and establishing best practices proactively rather than reactively; sharing experiences in an open manner to create awareness and understanding; and implementing a learning-oriented approach to accidents and incidents that incorporates dialog and reflection.

Risk assessment should be performed in a group setting involving professionals from the operating entity as well as from service providers. Actual and potential undesirable incidents should be discussed and explored in an open manner in order to create understanding and awareness of what has happened and what can happen. These incidents should be used to establish scenario training and emergency response plans. Systematic certification of critical equipment should be performed. Systems should be resilient because of their complexity, tight couplings and the possibility of common failures and other vulnerabilities. Therefore, a resilience engineering perspective should be incorporated when performing risk assessments of these systems.

The implementation of mitigating actions should be measured and evaluated. The overall level of resilience should be examined. Finally, key actors should be surveyed periodically to understand the relationship between risk anticipation, risk attention and responses during successful interventions as well as during accidents and undesirable incidents.

References

[1] B. Alteren, J. Sveen, G. Guttormsen, B. Madsen, R. Klev and O. Helgesen, Smarter together in offshore drilling – A successful action research project? *Proceedings of the Seventh International Conference on Probabilistic Safety Assessment and Management*, pp. 1302–1308, 2004.

[2] S. Antonsen, L. Ramstad and T. Kongsvik, Unlocking the organization: Action research as a means of improving organizational safety, *Safety Science Monitor*, vol. 11(1), 2007.

[3] H. Armstrong, Managing information security in healthcare – An action research experience, in *Information Security for Global Information Infrastructures*, S. Qing and J. Eloff (Eds.), Kluwer, Boston, Massachusetts, pp. 19–28, 2000.

[4] R. Davison, M. Martinsons and N. Kock, Principles of canonical action research, *Information Systems Journal*, vol. 14(1), pp. 65–86, 2004.

[5] D. Greenwood and M. Levin, *Introduction to Action Research: Social Research for Social Change*, Sage Publications, Thousand Oaks, California, 2007.

[6] E. Hollnagel, D. Woods and N. Leveson, *Resilience Engineering*, Ashgate, Aldershot, United Kingdom, 2006.

[7] International Society for Automation, ISA Security Compliance Institute, Research Triangle Park, North Carolina (www.isa.org/Content/Naviga tionMenu/TechnicalInformation/ASCI/ISCI/ISCI.htm).

[8] International Society for Automation, Security for Industrial Automation and Control Systems: Establishing an Industrial Automation and Control Systems Security Program, ANSI/ISA-99.02.01-2009, Research Triangle Park, North Carolina, 2009.

[9] H. James, Managing information systems security: A soft approach, *Proceedings of the Information Systems Conference of New Zealand*, pp. 10–20, 1996.

[10] S. Johnsen, R. Ask and R. Roisli, Reducing risk in oil and gas production operations, in *Critical Infrastructure Protection*, E. Goetz and S. Shenoi (Eds.), Springer, Boston, Massachusetts, pp. 83–95, 2007.

[11] S. Luders, CERN tests reveal security flaws with industrial networked devices, *The Industrial Ethernet Book*, GGH Marketing Communications, Titchfield, United Kingdom, pp. 12–23, November 2006.

[12] E. Mayo, *The Human Problems of an Industrial Civilization*, Macmillan, New York, 1933.

[13] Nuclear Regulatory Commission, The effects of Ethernet-based, non-safety-related controls on the safe and continued operation of nuclear power stations, NRC Information Notice 2007-15, Washington, DC (www.nrc.gov/reading-rm/doc-collections/gen-comm/info-notices/20 07/in200715.pdf), 2007.

[14] C. Perrow, *Normal Accidents: Living with High Risk Technologies*, Princeton University Press, Princeton, New Jersey, 1999.

[15] J. Reason, Too little and too late: A commentary on accident and incident reporting systems, in *Near Miss Reporting as a Safety Tool*, T. van der Schaaf, D. Lucas and A. Hale (Eds.), Butterworth-Heinemann, Oxford, United Kingdom, pp. 9–26, 1991.

[16] J. Reason, *Managing the Risks of Organizational Accidents*, Ashgate, Aldershot, United Kingdom, 1997.

[17] A. Richter, New ways of managing prevention: A cultural and participative approach, *Safety Science Monitor*, vol. 7(1), 2003.

[18] S. Smith, R. Jamieson and D. Winchester, An action research program to improve information systems security compliance across government agencies, *Proceedings of the Fortieth Annual Hawaii International Conference on System Sciences*, p. 99, 2007.

[19] K. Stouffer, J. Falco and K. Kent, Guide to Supervisory Control and Data Acquisition (SCADA) and Industrial Control Systems Security, NIST Special Publication 800-82, Initial Public Draft, National Institute of Standards and Technology, Gaithersburg, Maryland, 2006.

[20] N. Taleb, *The Black Swan: The Impact of the Highly Improbable*, Random House, New York, 2007.

[21] D. van Eynde and J. Bledsoe, The changing practice of organizational development, *Leadership and Organizational Development Journal*, vol. 11(2), pp. 25–30, 1990.

[22] R. Westrum, Removing latent pathogens, presented at the *Sixth International Australian Aviation Psychology Conference*, 2003.

Chapter 9

AN ONTOLOGY FOR IDENTIFYING CYBER INTRUSION INDUCED FAULTS IN PROCESS CONTROL SYSTEMS

Jeffrey Hieb, James Graham and Jian Guan

Abstract   This paper presents an ontological framework that permits formal representations of process control systems, including elements of the process being controlled and the control system itself. A fault diagnosis algorithm based on the ontological model is also presented. The algorithm can identify traditional process elements as well as control system elements (e.g., IP network and SCADA protocol) as fault sources. When these elements are identified as a likely fault source, the possibility exists that the process fault is induced by a cyber intrusion. A laboratory-scale distillation column is used to illustrate the model and the algorithm. Coupled with a well-defined statistical process model, this fault diagnosis approach provides cyber security enhanced fault diagnosis information to plant operators and can help identify that a cyber attack is underway before a major process failure is experienced.

Keywords: Process control systems, security, conceptual modeling, ontology

1.   Introduction

Process control systems play a central role in the operation and management of many critical infrastructures, including the electric power grid, water treatment facilities, and chemical and industrial manufacturing plants. In the early days, process control systems were isolated and used proprietary, purpose-built software and hardware. Today, these systems are increasingly connected using Internet technologies, open or semi-open SCADA protocols, and commercial hardware and software. This environment, coupled with the changing landscape of telecommunications and computer networks, introduce the cyber dimension to the security (and safety) of process control systems [1, 10]. While major disasters have thus far been avoided, the recent penetration of a water treatment facility in Harrisburg, Pennsylvania [4] and the Idaho National Lab-

C. Palmer and S. Shenoi (Eds.): Critical Infrastructure Protection III, IFIP AICT 311, pp. 125–138, 2009.

oratory experiment involving the destruction of an electrical power generator [6] indicate that cyber intrusions are a very real threat.

The possibility of cyber intrusions raises several challenges related to control systems security – understanding and assessing risk, integrating cyber security in process control operations, and enforcing a security policy across multiple heterogeneous systems [1, 10]. Another major challenge is fault diagnosis. Fault diagnosis involves the determination of the cause of an identified process fault or abnormal process behavior. Traditionally, fault diagnosis has limited its scope to identifying faulty physical components (e.g., pumps and valves). However, increased network convergence in process control environments means that the detected faults (or abnormalities) in a process could be the result of cyber intrusions instead of component failure.

This paper proposes an ontological model for process control systems. The model supports the formal and explicit representation of a process control system and the process being controlled. A fault diagnosis algorithm is developed based on the ontological model and statistical process models. The algorithm reasons about possible and likely fault sources, including sources that indicate a cyber intrusion. Specifically, it provides cyber security enhanced fault diagnosis information to plant operators, alerting them to a possible cyber intrusion before a process failure is experienced.

The approach is related to the human-assisted intrusion detection technique for process control systems developed by Naedele and Biderbost [12] in that it involves plant operators in security activities. Naedele and Biderbost's approach provides process control operators with visual information generated from network-based intrusion detection metrics, enabling operators to translate their native experience with process monitoring to detect "unhealthy conditions" in the network. The ontological model and fault diagnosis algorithm presented in this paper differ from Naedele and Biderbost's approach by combining traditional process information and process control system information in a formal, precise and semantically-rich manner.

2.   Ontological Modeling

An ontological model defines a set of constructs and rules for modeling a specific domain (e.g., the domain of process control systems) at a high level of abstraction. The model is "an explicit specification of a conceptualization" for the domain [8] and corresponds to a formal and precise definition (specification) of the conceptualization [8, 15]. An ontological model of a process control system allows the sharing of important properties of interconnected control system elements and their interoperability.

Recent research has identified the lack of a sound, comprehensive, theoretical basis for conceptual modeling [15]. Several ontological theories and, in particular, Bunge's ontology [2], have been proposed to provide a theoretical basis. Meanwhile, research on ontologies and conceptual modeling has focused on the evaluation of modeling languages and general modeling issues [3, 5, 14, 15]. Efforts have also been directed at domain ontology construction. It is often

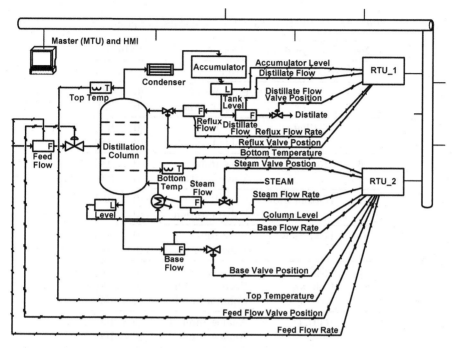

Figure 1. Distillation column system.

impossible to represent even a small part of the world in all its detail. It is more practical to use a limited, essential and relevant number of concepts to describe the static and dynamic aspects of a well-defined part of reality. This set of core concepts forms a conceptualization of that reality. However, such a conceptualization is often informal and ambiguous. A domain ontology is a formal and precise specification of a conceptualization, and is, therefore, concerned with the identification and definition of the essential (static and dynamic) phenomena of the particular domain [16]. A domain ontology for process control systems can help create a common conceptual model for what has become a very heterogeneous mix of technology and systems.

3. Ontological Model for Control Systems

This section presents the constructs used to develop the ontology for process control systems. Bunge's ontological principles [2] form the basis for the constructs. A process control system can be viewed as an information system, possibly embedded in a larger information system. Although Bunge's ontology was not created for information systems, its ontological principles provide a sound theoretical framework for modeling information systems [15].

Figure 1 presents a schematic diagram of a laboratory-scale distillation column and its control system. This distillation column system is used to illustrate the ontological model and fault diagnosis algorithm.

Table 1.   Distillation column components and properties.

No.	Component	Properties	Values
3	Accumulator	Level	$\langle 0 \ldots 100 \rangle$
5	Reflux Flow	Flow Rate	$\langle 0 \ldots 100 \rangle$
		Valve Postiion	$\langle 0 \ldots 100 \rangle$
4	Distillate	Flow Rate	$\langle 0 \ldots 100 \rangle$
	Flow	Valve Position	$\langle 0 \ldots 100 \rangle$
6	Steam Flow	Flow Rate	$\langle 0 \ldots 100 \rangle$
		Valve Position	$\langle 0 \ldots 100 \rangle$
7	Bottom Flow	Flow Rate	$\langle 0 \ldots 100 \rangle$
		Valve Position	$\langle 0 \ldots 100 \rangle$
1	Feed Flow	Flow Rate	$\langle 0 \ldots 100 \rangle$
		Valve Position	$\langle 0 \ldots 100 \rangle$
2	Distillation	Top Temp	$\langle 0 \ldots 100 \rangle$
	Column	Bottom Temp	$\langle 0 \ldots 100 \rangle$
		Column Level	$\langle 0 \ldots 100 \rangle$
8	RTU_1	Analog Input 1	$\langle 0 \ldots 100 \rangle$
		Analog Input 2	$\langle 0 \ldots 100 \rangle$
		Analog Output 1	$\langle 0 \ldots 100 \rangle$
		Analog Output 2	$\langle 0 \ldots 100 \rangle$
		Digital Input 1	$\langle 0 \ldots 100 \rangle$
		Digital Output 1	$\langle 0 \ldots 100 \rangle$
		Digital Input 2	$\langle 0 \ldots 100 \rangle$
		Digital Output 2	$\langle 0 \ldots 100 \rangle$

According to Bunge, the world is made up of substantial individuals or things. Each substantial individual has properties and each property has at least one attribute. Therefore, a process control system can be modeled as a collection of components, each component defined as $X = (x, p(x))$ where x is the component and $p(x)$ denotes the properties of x. A component can be a control system element (e.g., master device, field device or RTU), a conceptual element (e.g., IP network or LAN) that connects control devices, or a SCADA protocol that facilitates communication between devices. Also, a component can be a concept related to the "system under control" (e.g., a flow, temperature or state of a circuit breaker).

Tables 1 and 2 list the components and properties of the distillation column system. The properties of some components (e.g., MTU/HMI) may depend more heavily on the specific system being modeled than others; in such cases, the appropriate properties should be readily identifiable for a given system.

Each component is characterized by a set of state functions, where each state function corresponds to a property of the component. Let X be a component

Table 2. Distillation column components and properties (cont'd.).

No.	Component	Properties	Values
9	RTU_2	Analog Input 1	$\langle 0 \ldots 100 \rangle$
		Analog Input 2	$\langle 0 \ldots 100 \rangle$
		Analog Output 1	$\langle 0 \ldots 100 \rangle$
		Analog Output 2	$\langle 0 \ldots 100 \rangle$
		Digital Input 1	$\langle 0 \ldots 100 \rangle$
		Digital Output 1	$\langle 0 \ldots 100 \rangle$
		Digital Input 2	$\langle 0 \ldots 100 \rangle$
		Digital Output 2	$\langle 0 \ldots 100 \rangle$
10	IP-Network	Source Address	$\{192.168.1.2, 3, 5, 7\}$
		Destination Address	$\{192.168.1.2, 3, 5, 7\}$
11	DNP3	Link Source	$\{0x02, 0x03, 0x05\}$
		Link Destination	$\{0x02, 0x03, 0x05\}$
		Link Direction	$\{0, 1\}$
		Link Function	$\{0x02, 0x03, 0x05\}$
		App Control	$\{0x02, 0x03, 0x05\}$
		App Function Code	$\{0x02, 0x03, 0x05\}$
12	MTU/HMI	Refresh Rate	$\langle 0 \ldots 100 \rangle$
		User Role	$\{Operator, Engineer,$ $Tuner, Sys\_Admin\}$

of a control system. Then, X can be modeled by the functional schema $X_m = \langle M, \tilde{F} \rangle$, where each part of the function $\tilde{F} = \langle F_1, \ldots, F_n \rangle : M \longrightarrow V_1 \otimes \cdots \otimes V_n$ represents a property of X. In this case, M represents the domain of time instances. F_i $(1..n)$ denotes the ith state function of X, $\tilde{F}$ is the total state function of X, and $S(X) = \langle p_i, \ldots, p_n \rangle \in V_1 \otimes \cdots \otimes V_n | p_i = F_i(M)$ is the possible state space of X. Note that the state space of the component Reflux Flow contains all possible combinations of the values of the properties Flow Rate and Valve Position.

Lawful states describe the normal operation of a component; this constrains the values that the properties of a component may take. This construct permits the model to capture and express valid combinations of property values. For example, the DNP3 link layer direction bit (indicating whether a master or outstation sent a particular frame) could be combined with known information about the DNP3 address of the master or outstation, and expressed using laws.

Let $S_L(X) \subseteq S(X)$ be the lawful state space of a component X and let $G_L(X)$ be the set of lawful transformations. Then, a lawful event in X is the ordered pair $\langle s, s \rangle$ where s, $s' \in S_L(X)$ and $s' = g(s)$, $g \in G_L(X)$. For example, for the Distillation Column component, a lawful event resulting from the Feed Flow valve being opened might be: $(\langle 90, 190, 70 \rangle, \langle 85, 150, 88 \rangle)$.

Obviously, an event in one component can affect or act on another component. This relationship is referred to as "coupling," which is defined in terms of the "histories" of the coupled components. The history of a component is simply the set of states that the component has held over time. Let X be a component modeled by a function schema $X_M = \langle M, \tilde{F} \rangle$ and let $t \in M, t > 0$ be a time instant. Then, a history of X is the set of ordered pairs: $h(x) = \langle t, \tilde{F}(t) \rangle$ that can be written as $h(X) = \langle t, (p_1(t), \ldots, p_n(t)) \rangle$. For example the history of the Distillation Column component for two time instances t_0 and t_1 can be expressed as: $h(\text{Distillation Column}) = \langle t_0, (90, 190, 100) \rangle, \langle t_1, (85, 150, 200) \rangle$.

The history notion is used to define when two or more elements interact. A component X acts on component Y if their histories are not independent; this is denoted by $X \triangleright Y$ if $h(Y|X) \neq h(Y)$. Two components X and Y are coupled (written as $B(X,Y)$) if $(X \triangleright Y) \vee (Y \triangleright X)$. For example, Feed Flow and Distillation Column are coupled because a change in Feed Flow affects the bottom temperature property (Bottom Temp) of Distillation Column.

4.   Fault Diagnosis

Fault diagnosis seeks to identify the components that have led to a failure in a process control system or part of a process control system. Diagnosing a fault presents a challenge because it is often the case that when a system fails, the components where the failures are observed are not the failure sources, but the victims of faults that have propagated from other parts of the system [9, 13]. The problem is further complicated by the cyber component of process control systems. A cyber intrusion could cause a fault on its own, requiring plant operators to consider if the fault had a conventional source or was the result of a cyber event. Note that process faults are not necessarily catastrophic; more often than not they simply give rise to abnormal process behavior.

Identifying the source of an observed abnormality helps operators quickly isolate and fix the fault source. In the case of faults induced by a cyber intrusion, identifying that the faults have a common ancestor component that can be targeted by a cyber intrusion could warn operators that a cyber attack may be underway. Thus, operators have more time to react to the problem and, hopefully, direct their efforts appropriately.

Before specifying the fault diagnosis algorithm, we provide some terminology related to fault diagnosis and briefly describe the fault diagnosis process [7].

- **Process Fault:** This manifests itself as a difference between the observed behavior and the desired behavior of a process.

- **Fault Detection:** This involves the determination that abnormal behavior has occurred.

- **Fault Isolation/Diagnosis:** This involves the determination of the cause of a fault.

- **Fault Recovery:** This involves the restoration of the system to its proper operating state.

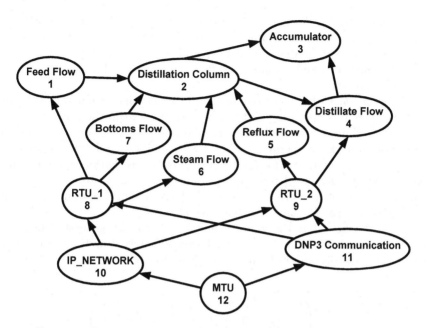

Figure 2. Digraph representation of the distillation column system.

- **Process Monitoring:** This involves the observation of process activity to detect faults and other abnormalities.

Faults must be detected before they can be diagnosed. Every process system has process variables. Manipulated variables are used to control the process; observed variables indicate the status of the process. A mathematical model of the process may be constructed using data gathered from the running system. After the mathematical model is constructed, the values of the current process variables can be compared with the model (process monitoring). Any deviation is considered to be a process fault (fault detection). Readers are referred to [7, 11] for a comprehensive discussion of process monitoring and fault detection.

The ontological constructs defined in the previous section allow the precise and formal representation of key aspects of a process control system. We now demonstrate the utility of the ontological model in fault diagnosis by adapting the Guan-Graham fault diagnosis algorithm [9] to the ontological model for diagnosing faults in a control system.

Let $C = \{X_1, \ldots, X_n\}$ be the set of components in a control system. Then, an impact relation R can be defined on C such that $X_i R X_j$ means that component X_i acts on component X_j, i.e., $X_i \triangleright X_j$. An impact digraph $G = (V, E)$ is then used to represent this relation where $V = \{X_i | X_i \in C\}$ is the vertex set and $E = \{(X_i, X_j) | X_i \triangleright X_j \text{ and } i \neq j\}$ is the edge set. Figure 2 shows the diagraph G for the distillation column example.

Let $A = (a_{ij})$ be the adjacency matrix representing the impact digraph such that $a_{ij} = 1$ if $(X_i, X_j) \in R$ and $a_{ij} = 0$ if $(X_i, X_j) \notin R$. If there is a path in G from X_i to X_j, X_j is said to be reachable from X_i. For completeness, every vertex in G is defined to be reachable from itself by a path of length 0. As defined above, reachability is transitive. For convenience, the components in the distillation column example are numbered from 1 through 12 as shown in Tables 1 and 2.

The history $h(X)$ for each component can be obtained from data gathered when the system is operating and can be used to develop the impact relation R. For the laboratory-scale distillation column system, the impact relation R is based on input from operators familiar with similar distillation columns.

The adjacency matrix A for the laboratory-scale distillation column system is generated by assigning 1 to every a_{ij} if there is an arrow from element i to element j in G; all the other elements in A are assigned a value of 0. The reachability matrix P may be defined as $P = (A + I)^r = (A + I)^{(r-1)} \neq (A + I)^{(r-2)}$ where I is the identity matrix. P can be generated in $O(n^3)$ time using Warshall's algorithm. The adjacency matrix A and the reachability matrix P for the digraph in Figure 2 are given by:

$$A = \begin{pmatrix} 0 & 1 & 0 & 0 & 0 & 0 & 0 & 0 & 0 & 0 & 0 & 0 \\ 0 & 0 & 1 & 0 & 0 & 0 & 0 & 0 & 0 & 0 & 0 & 0 \\ 0 & 0 & 0 & 0 & 0 & 0 & 0 & 0 & 0 & 0 & 0 & 0 \\ 0 & 1 & 1 & 0 & 0 & 0 & 0 & 0 & 0 & 0 & 0 & 0 \\ 0 & 1 & 0 & 0 & 0 & 0 & 0 & 0 & 0 & 0 & 0 & 0 \\ 0 & 1 & 0 & 0 & 0 & 0 & 0 & 0 & 0 & 0 & 0 & 0 \\ 0 & 1 & 0 & 0 & 0 & 0 & 0 & 0 & 0 & 0 & 0 & 0 \\ 1 & 0 & 0 & 0 & 0 & 1 & 1 & 0 & 0 & 0 & 0 & 0 \\ 0 & 0 & 0 & 1 & 1 & 0 & 0 & 0 & 0 & 0 & 0 & 0 \\ 0 & 0 & 0 & 0 & 0 & 0 & 0 & 1 & 1 & 0 & 0 & 0 \\ 0 & 0 & 0 & 0 & 0 & 0 & 0 & 1 & 1 & 0 & 0 & 0 \\ 0 & 0 & 0 & 0 & 0 & 0 & 0 & 0 & 0 & 1 & 1 & 0 \end{pmatrix}$$

$$P = \begin{pmatrix} 1 & 1 & 1 & 1 & 0 & 0 & 0 & 0 & 0 & 0 & 0 & 0 \\ 0 & 1 & 1 & 1 & 0 & 0 & 0 & 0 & 0 & 0 & 0 & 0 \\ 0 & 0 & 1 & 0 & 0 & 0 & 0 & 0 & 0 & 0 & 0 & 0 \\ 0 & 0 & 1 & 1 & 0 & 0 & 0 & 0 & 0 & 0 & 0 & 0 \\ 0 & 1 & 1 & 1 & 1 & 0 & 0 & 0 & 0 & 0 & 0 & 0 \\ 0 & 1 & 1 & 1 & 0 & 1 & 0 & 0 & 0 & 0 & 0 & 0 \\ 0 & 1 & 1 & 1 & 0 & 0 & 1 & 0 & 0 & 0 & 0 & 0 \\ 1 & 1 & 1 & 1 & 0 & 1 & 1 & 1 & 0 & 0 & 0 & 0 \\ 0 & 1 & 1 & 1 & 1 & 0 & 0 & 0 & 1 & 0 & 0 & 0 \\ 1 & 1 & 1 & 1 & 1 & 1 & 1 & 1 & 1 & 1 & 0 & 0 \\ 1 & 1 & 1 & 1 & 1 & 1 & 1 & 1 & 1 & 0 & 1 & 0 \\ 1 & 1 & 1 & 1 & 1 & 1 & 1 & 1 & 1 & 1 & 1 & 1 \end{pmatrix}$$

The reachability matrix can be processed to extract important properties [9, 13]. Two partitions may be defined on the reachability matrix P, the level

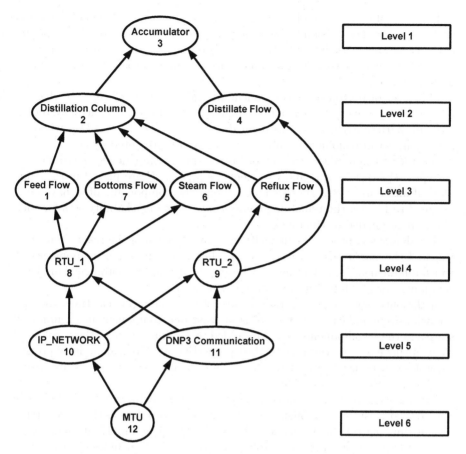

Figure 3. Level partitions for the distillation column.

partition and the separate parts partition. We define the reachability set $R(p_i)$ as the set of vertices reachable from p_i, and the antecedent set $A(p_i)$ as the set of vertices that reach p_i. Then, the level partition $L(P)$ is defined as $L(P) = [L_1, L_2, \ldots, L_l]$ where l is the number of levels. If the 0th level is defined as the empty set, the level partitions of P, $L_0 = \varnothing$, can be found iteratively as follows:

$$L_j = \{p_i \in P - L_0 - L_1 - \cdots - L_{j-1} \mid R_{j-1}(p_i) = R_{j-1}(p_i) \cap A_{j-1}(p_i)\}$$

where $j = 1..l$ and $i = 1..n$.

The levels have three properties: (i) $\cup L_i = V$ for $i = 1..l$, (ii) $L_i \cap L_j = \varnothing$ for $i \neq j$, and (iii) edges leaving vertices in level L_i can only go to vertices in levels L_j such that $i \leq j$. Therefore, there are six levels for the distillation column example and the corresponding level partitions are: $L = (3), (2, 4), (1, 5, 6, 7), (8, 9), (10, 11), (12)$ (Figure 3).

It is possible that some of the components of P constitute a smaller digraph that is separate (i.e., disjoint) from the remainder of the digraph. The separate parts partition is used to identify any disjoint parts of the process control system. A set of bottom-level components is required to define the separate parts partition.

B is a set of bottom-level components if and only if for all $p_i \in B$, $A(p_i) = R(p_i) \cap A(p_i)$. Given the reachability matrix P for a process control system, a separate parts partition $S(P)$ is defined as $S(P) = [D_1; D_2 \ldots; D_m]$ where m is the number of disjoint digraphs in the digraph represented by A.

In order to find $S(P)$, the set of bottom-level components B is found as $B = p_i \in P | R(p_i) \cap A(p_i)$ and two elements $p_i, p_j \in B$ are placed in the same block if and only if $R(p_i) \cap R(p_j) \neq \oslash$. Once the components of B have been assigned to blocks, the remaining components of the reachability sets for each block are appended to the block.

The diagnostic process begins with the computation of the reachability matrix and the partitions described above. Let F be the set of components in which a fault has been identified. Adhering strictly to the ontological model, a component has a fault if it is in an unlawful state.

If the ontological model is used to model the system in real time, then an unlawful event indicates that there is at least one component in an unlawful state and these components would be added to F. Since some of the ontological elements have process variables as their properties, a statistical model of process variables can be used to partition $S(X)$ into lawful and unlawful state spaces $S_L(X)$ and $\overline{(S_L(X)}$, respectively.

Process variable values can be monitored and unlawful events can be easily detected, at least for components that have process variables as their properties. This is similar to the methods described in [7, 11]. The important difference is linking the information to the ontological model, which includes elements that are not in a purely statistical process model. Using this approach, it is not possible to detect all the faulty components in the ontological model because not all components have process variables as properties. Fortunately, this does not prevent the fault source search algorithm (Algorithm 1) from identifying these components as potential fault sources. Approaches for detecting faults in other components are discussed later in this paper.

After the faulty components have been identified, the fault source search algorithm can be used to identify candidate fault sources to be sequentially tested by process operators. The algorithm uses the directed graph G, level partition of G and separate parts partition of G to find the common ancestors of abnormal components and checks the ancestors that are farthest upstream first.

The algorithm starts with all potential error sources. These potential fault sources are the ancestors of the set of components F observed to have failed. According to Step 2, the algorithm terminates when the number of fault source candidates has been reduced to one. If there is more than one ancestor for all the observed faulty components, the testing begins with the ancestor(s)

Algorithm 1 : Fault Source Search Algorithm (adapted from [9]).

Compute the reachability matrix P of G.
Compute the level partition of G.
Compute the separate parts partition of G.

1. Find the set of potential error sources Q where $Q = \cap P(x_i)$ for $x_i \in F$.

2. If $|Q| = 1$, then return Q as the error source.

3. If $|Q| = 0$ or the number of disjoint graphs > 1, multiple sources of error exist. Apply the algorithm to each disjoint digraph that contains at least one observed error.

4. Let $\Sigma = \{v | v \in Q \wedge level(v) = min\{level(v_i) \ \forall v_i \in Q\}\}$.

5. If $|\Sigma| = 1$ and $A(v) = \oslash$ for $v \in \Sigma$, then $Q = \Sigma$ and return Q.

6. If $|\Sigma| = 1$, then $\Sigma = \{immediate \ ancestor(v) | v \in \Sigma\}$ and $Q = Q - \Sigma$; Go to Step 3.

7. Select a node $q \in \Sigma$ and test the component represented by q.

8. If q is normal, then $\Sigma = \Sigma - \{q\}$ and $F = F - \{q\}$.

9. $F = F \cup \{q\}$; Go to Step 1.

---

closest to the observed faulty components or ancestors with the lowest level in the level partition (Step 4). The algorithm also terminates if it reaches a component without any ancestor; in this case, the component is returned as the fault source (Step 5). Steps 6 through 9 attempt to reduce the candidate set Q. Step 7 could be improved by using a heuristic method to decide which component should be tested next.

Past experience often plays a role in determining the likely paths along which faults propagate. This could be included in the model by defining error propagation probabilities for each edge in G. For any component X, an error may have propagated to the component from any of the upstream components (ancestors of X). In some cases, there may be several immediate ancestors of X and the fault could have propagated from any of these ancestors or any of the error propagation paths headed by these ancestors. Obviously, for a given component, a fault is more likely to propagate from some of its ancestors instead of other components. This information can be captured using a propagation probability and added to the digraph G by associating with each edge the probability p_{ij} that a fault will propagate from X_i to X_j. The probability values may be obtained from experienced operators. If the information is not available, equal probability values may be assigned to each p_{ij} and the probability for p_{ij} can be gradually acquired through use of the system [9]. For each element X_j, p_{ij} is defined such that $\sum_{i=1}^{2} p_{ij} = 1$ where n is the in-degree of the vertex corresponding to the component X_j. For example, Figure 4 shows a simple node X_j that has three nodes that could propagate an error to it. The propagation probabilities are used in Step 7 to determine which component to test.

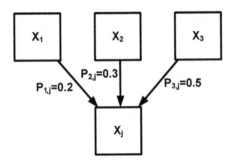

Figure 4.   Fault propagation probability.

The benefits of combining the ontological model with the fault diagnosis algorithm can be clarified using a simple example. Consider a situation where the distillate flow valve is stuck. Process monitoring combined with the ontological model identifies two nodes (Accumulator and Distillate Flow) as entering unlawful states. The fault diagnosis algorithm would identify Distillate Flow as the first component to test, followed by Accumulator.

Now consider a more challenging situation. A hacker penetrates the corporate network and discovers a path through the control gateway that enables him to inject SCADA traffic into the control network. The hacker has no knowledge of the distillation column system, but is able to discover that DNP3 traffic is flowing in the network. To disrupt the process, the hacker injects DNP3 traffic into the control network using different link layer addresses, random sequence numbers and the Direct Operate function code to set Analog Outputs 1, 2 and 3 to their largest possible values (100%). As a result, the reflux flow valve periodically opens to 100% before returning to the target valve position setting, and the steam flow valve periodically opens to 100% and then returns to the target steam valve position setting. This causes the steam flow and reflux flow to become elevated and the bottom temperature to increase, all of which could cause the distillation column to flood. The process monitoring system indicates that Elements 2, 6 and 5 enter unlawful states. The fault diagnosis algorithm identifies the Elements 10 and 11 (IP_Network and DNP3) as the elements to test first. While these elements may not be testable in the same way as a flow valve, the algorithm alerts operators that the process faults may be (in this case are) induced by cyber intrusions, enabling them to take appropriate actions.

5.   Conclusions

Plant operators need sophisticated models for understanding and reasoning about possible cyber intrusions in process control systems. The ontological model described in this paper permits formal and explicit representations of process control systems, including elements of the process being controlled and the process control system itself. The benefits of the ontological model are made apparent by the fault diagnosis algorithm developed using the model. In particular, the fault diagnosis algorithm leverages the ontological model to fuse cyber security relevant components with traditional process control elements to provide plant operators with valuable synthesized information related to process operation and potential cyber intrusions.

Because faults are manifested by anomalous behavior, the fault diagnosis algorithm can be viewed as an anomaly-based intrusion detection system. However, instead of looking for traditional IT anomalies, this intrusion detection system identifies process anomalies and maps them to a traditional fault source or a control system element subject to cyber intrusions.

Several avenues exist for further research. Fault detection is currently limited to process variables. However, the algorithm can be extended because the ontological model is broad enough to include elements that do not have process variables as properties. Another research task is to explore the possibility of extending process monitoring to process control monitoring by adding inputs from traditional IT security appliances such as firewalls and network intrusion detection systems. The ontological model could then be used to aggregate and interpret the heterogeneous information, all of which is relevant to the security (and safety) of a process control system. Finally, it would be interesting to explore the use of forward propagation instead of backward propagation to identify the impact of a cyber intrusion on a specific process control element such as an RTU. This information would be invaluable to risk assessment and risk management efforts.

References

[1] M. Brandle and M. Naedele, Security for process control systems: An overview, *IEEE Security and Privacy*, vol. 6(6), pp. 24–29, 2008.

[2] M. Bunge, *Ontology I: The Furniture of the World; Treatise on Basic Philosophy (Volume 3)*, Reidel, Boston, Massachusetts, 1977.

[3] A. Burton-Jones and P. Meso, Conceptualizing systems for understanding: An empirical test of decomposition principles in object-oriented analysis, *Information Systems Research*, vol. 17(1), pp. 38–60, 2006.

[4] R. Esposito, Hackers penetrate water system computers, ABC News, New York (blogs.abcnews.com/theblotter/2006/10/hackers_penetra.html), October 30, 2006.

[5] J. Evermann and Y. Wand, Toward formalizing domain modeling semantics in language syntax, *IEEE Transactions on Software Engineering*, vol. 31(1), pp. 21–37, 2005.

[6] M. Fickes, Cyber terror, *Government Security*, July 1, 2008.

[7] J. Graham and P. Ralston, Intelligent computer-based monitoring and fault isolation for industrial processes, *International Journal of Computers and Their Applications*, vol. 9(3), pp. 147–157, 2002.

[8] T. Gruber, A translation approach to portable ontology specifications, *Knowledge Acquisition*, vol. 5(2), pp. 199–220, 1993.

[9] J. Guan and J. Graham, Diagnostic reasoning with fault propagation digraph and sequential testing, *IEEE Transactions on Systems, Man and Cybernetics*, vol. 24(10), pp. 1552–1558, 1994.

[10] V. Igure, S. Laughter and R. Williams, Security issues in SCADA networks, *Computers and Security*, vol. 25(7), pp. 498–506, 2006.

[11] R. Isermann, Supervision, fault-detection and fault-diagnosis methods – An introduction, *Control Engineering Practice*, vol. 5(5), pp. 639–652, 1997.

[12] M. Naedele and O. Biderbost, Human-assisted intrusion detection for process control systems, *Proceedings of the Second International Conference on Applied Cryptography and Network Security*, pp. 216–225, 2004.

[13] N. Narayanan and N. Viswanadham, A methodology for knowledge acquisition and reasoning in failure analysis of systems, *IEEE Transactions on Systems, Man and Cybernetics*, vol. 17(2), pp. 274–288, 1987.

[14] A. Opdahl and B. Henderson-Sellers, Ontological evaluation of the UML using the Bunge-Wand-Weber model, *Software and Systems Modeling*, vol. 1(1), pp. 43–67, 2002.

[15] Y. Wand and R. Weber, An ontological model of an information system, *IEEE Transactions on Software Engineering*, vol. 16(11), pp. 1282–1292, 1990.

[16] Y. Wand and R. Weber, Research commentary: Information systems and conceptual modeling – A research agenda, *Information Systems Research*, vol. 13(4), pp. 363–376, 2002.

Chapter 10

USING PHYSICAL MODELS
FOR ANOMALY DETECTION
IN CONTROL SYSTEMS

Nils Svendsen and Stephen Wolthusen

Abstract   Supervisory control and data acquisition (SCADA) systems are increasingly used to operate critical infrastructure assets. However, the inclusion of advanced information technology and communications components and elaborate control strategies in SCADA systems increase the threat surface for external and subversion-type attacks. The problems are exacerbated by site-specific properties of SCADA environments that make subversion detection impractical; and by sensor noise and feedback characteristics that degrade conventional anomaly detection systems. Moreover, potential attack mechanisms are ill-defined and may include both physical and logical aspects.

This paper employs an explicit model of a SCADA system in order to reduce the uncertainty inherent in anomaly detection. Detection is enhanced by incorporating feedback loops in the model. The effectiveness of the approach is demonstrated using a model of a hydroelectric power plant for which several attack vectors are described.

Keywords: SCADA systems, anomaly detection, hydroelectric power plant

1.   Introduction

Most critical infrastructure components rely on supervisory control and data acquisition (SCADA) systems or distributed control systems for operations and maintenance. This situation, in combination with the desire for higher efficiency and centralized operations, have contributed to the increased threat levels encountered in critical infrastructure components from cyber and cyber-physical attacks [19].

The detection of intrusions and subversion attacks is becoming as important for SCADA systems as it has been for traditional computer networks. However, we argue that several properties of SCADA systems, particularly the

C. Palmer and S. Shenoi (Eds.): Critical Infrastructure Protection III, IFIP AICT 311, pp. 139–149, 2009.

uncertainty of measurements and actuator status induced by interactions with the physical environment make signature-based attack detection problematic. In particular, large error margins must be included, which reduce signature specificity. Moreover, the general problem of signature-based systems being able to detect only variations in known or expected attacks is exacerbated by the fact that the configuration of SCADA systems at a given facility is unlikely to be replicated elsewhere. As a result, the creation and replication of signature patterns can be very problematic.

We argue that anomaly detection provides a better match with the constraints found in SCADA environments. While the specificity of anomaly detection techniques can be inadequate, the problem space may be reduced considerably by imposing constraints on the variables based on the knowledge of the modeled system (e.g., minimum and maximum sensor values and gradients), and the margins of error for sensors and actuators; and, especially, by modeling the correlations between components. One area in which an explicit control system model is critical is in the incorporation of feedback loops as these would otherwise result in correlated variables not being detected by most pattern classification and correlation mechanisms.

This paper analyzes selected aspects of the control systems used in a hydroelectric power plant with particular emphasis on the effects induced by the feedback loops that occur at several different time scales. A hydroelectric power plant was chosen for the study because it contains a limited number of well-defined, albeit nested, feedback control loops, and characteristics of feedback itself. In addition, hydroelectric power plants are of particular relevance due to their role as stabilizing (and, in some cases, sustaining) entities for the electric power grid, and also for the potential physical damage that can result from some failure modes. Moreover, the observations and mechanisms described in the context of control systems for hydroelectric power plants are applicable to other control system environments as well.

2.   Hydroelectric Power Plants

Hydroelectric power plants convert hydrological power in a waterfall via mechanical power on a machine shaft to electrical power in a generator. This section briefly describes the structure of a simple hydroelectric power plant without the additions required by pumped storage. The description does not address specific installations or turbine variants that are described in the literature (see, e.g., [12]).

The water intake for a hydroelectric plant is normally constructed with an accumulation dam in a river course. Depending on the formation of the dam, the intake can be of a shallow water or deep water kind. In both cases, a physical rack or sump is installed to protect the intake from debris and biological material. The intake is also equipped with one or more valves that control water flow.

A conduit system channels water from the intake to the turbine. This can be an open channel, tunnel, penstock or pressure shaft, or a combination of these systems. In Norwegian installations, which are frequently constructed as high head power plants, the conduit system consists of a head race tunnel of low inclination where sand traps are installed for sedimentation of suspended particles. A surge chamber system is installed at the downstream end of the head race tunnel to reduce water hammer pressure variations and to keep mass oscillations caused by load changes within acceptable limits. At the same location, there may exist a fine trash rack and a valve that enables the penstock to be emptied upstream of the turbine without having to empty the head race tunnel; this valve also serves as a security feature in case of pipeline rupture. The conduit system often ends with a lined or unlined steel penstock that connects the shaft with the valves in the machine hall.

Turbines convert hydrological power to mechanical power, the most popular being the Pelton, Francis and Kaplan turbines. The type of turbine used depends on the penstock profile and vertical drop. The (usually adjustable) guide vane cascade in a turbine gives the water flow the velocity and direction required for the inlet to the runner. The hydraulic power is then converted to mechanical power on the turbine shaft to which the runner is fixed. The turbine shaft is guided in a radial bearing and an axial bearing that is loaded with the axial force from the runner, which is caused by the water pressure and impulse from the flow and the weight of the rotating parts. The scroll case in the turbine conducts the water flow into the guide vane cascade. The draft tube conducts the water flow from the turbine outlet into the tail race canal.

The mechanical energy from the turbine is transferred to a generator via the generator shaft. The generator produces electrical power by the process of electromagnetic induction. An excitation system provides the DC voltage to the field winding of the generator and modulates this voltage for control purposes (see, e.g., [7, 17]). The excitation power may be provided by a rotating exciter or by controlled rectifiers supplied from the generator terminals. The excitation system includes several subsystems designed to protect the generator and excitation system from excessive duty under abnormal operating conditions.

Hydroelectric power plants are responsive in nature, meaning that they can respond quickly to changes in load demand. These plants can be started and shut down much more quickly and economically than coal-fired plants, let alone nuclear plants. Nevertheless, due to the nature of hydroelectric power plant operations, control systems should be able to implement both long-term and short-term actions. Numerous sensors are positioned to gather data used by automatic control systems to perform the appropriate control actions, and by human operators to run the plant in a safe, reliable, secure and economical manner.

The protection system of a hydroelectric plant has two main elements: (i) an electrical protection system responsible for the major electrical apparatus and auxiliary systems, and (ii) mechanical protection systems for the hydraulic turbine, generator and mechanical systems. Both the elements of the protection system employ large numbers of electronic sensors and actuators. The supervisory process involves comparing plant and equipment operating values against limits, requirements and projections. Typically, the control process monitors hard and soft limits in a hysteresis band and compensates for overshoot, also issuing alarms as control actions. Other activities involve the monitoring of equipment status and the status of sensors and actuators. We only provide a qualitative overview of the control system elements that are relevant to the attack vectors considered in this paper. Readers are referred to [8, 9] for additional details related to the control of hydroelectric power plants.

3.   Attack Vectors

Transient failures of individual power plants are, of course, undesirable, but they do not pose a threat to the overall stability of the electric grid. Therefore, from a critical infrastructure point of view, they are only of limited interest.

Failures resulting in physical damage, however, are relevant to the stability of the power grid. Taking a power plant off the grid for a long period (several months) limits the overall generation capacity and, depending on the demand and grid topology, can weaken the overall grid. Also, inducing coordinated failures across multiple plants, even if they are only transient in nature, can affect the infrastructure as a whole. We concentrate on attack vectors that can lead to either type of failure. Note that these attack vectors are not exhaustive and should not be considered to represent a full attack taxonomy, which is beyond the scope of this paper.

3.1   Components from Dam to Turbine

The geospatial extent of hydroelectric power plants makes it difficult to provide adequate physical security for sensors and actuators located outside the turbine and generation complex (unlike those situated within the reservoir itself or at the penstock). Physical attacks (including manipulations) of these sensors and actuators must be considered along with attacks that target the control networks.

Sensors in or near the reservoir are used to assess the state of the reservoir such as water level and flow rates. Other sensors may monitor hydrological and geological features as well as the dam itself. Of particular interest, however, is the penstock in which a number of valves for normal operation and emergencies must be monitored and operated. Rapid closure of the emergency valves can result in penstock collapse [20]. Operating other valves can result in damage to turbine and generator equipment; control actions based on flow rates that are not measured or reported correctly can induce water hammer or cavitation effects [21]. Likewise, misreported valve settings and flow rates can result in damage to turbine blades or buckets depending on the turbine type and configuration. This can occur during shutdown if the protective closure of guide vanes or needles is not performed within the required time, or in overspeed conditions where bearings could be damaged. Static overspeed conditions and dynamic oscillations can also result in excessive stress on turbine casings and the anchoring of the turbine to its supports.

In addition to the components related to power generation, bypass mechanisms are exist to regulate flow that cannot be handled by the turbine pathways (e.g., during turbine failure or maintenance, or when the influx exceeds capacity). While these mechanisms are not very time-critical and do not have an immediate impact on the generation pathway, manipulations of their sensors and actuators can still result in severe damage, especially if there is a failure to relieve pressure when water levels exceed the designed capacity.

3.2   Generator Components

Attacks on the generator and its components primarily seek to create overload conditions. For the purposes of studying these attacks, the clutches, generator, exciter and governor can be considered together. Voltage and current sensors and the control loops associated with these sensors have tight timing requirements, rendering the introduction of delays into control loops an attractive attack strategy. Moreover, unlike the components discussed in the previous section, these components are not easily inspected visually and require quick feedback from the control system, making manual intervention problematic. In addition, it is possible for attackers to de-synchronize sensors or to misreport sensor readings and actuator feedback, forcing the control system to operate the generator outside its performance envelope while suppressing warnings and fault condition reports to control system operators.

When considering attacks on generator components, it is necessary to view the hydraulic and electrical systems as separate components and as a single system with interacting components. Note that feedback loop and actuator speeds for the hydraulic system are considerably lower than those for the electrical system. Interactions can arise, for example, during electrical system failures that result in load rejection. Also, transients in piezometric heads can cause significant damage that may require an emergency shutdown of a turbine.

3.3   Grid and External Control Elements

Even when the complex case of a pumped storage power plant is disregarded, the generated power is regulated externally based on the utility's load prediction system, state estimators and other factors such as requirements from grid operators. An interference with the delivery of external control messages will not, by itself, force components to operate outside their performance envelopes; however, several types of denial-of-service attacks can be executed. Depending on the security properties of the protocol, the attacks may be limited to message suppression or delay. Replay attacks are possible if freshness tests are not built into the protocol. Inadequate integrity checks can enable malleable ciphertext attacks even if the protocol data units are encrypted.

Other attack vectors can target the transformers that couple the power plant to the power grid. Possible attacks include causing generators and transformers to be out of phase, cycling circuit breakers rapidly and engaging couplers in short succession. These attacks would have to be combined with sensor data suppression to ensure that the damage is effected before alarms can be raised or operators are able to intervene. As with the attack vectors described in the preceding sections, considerable harm can be done by de-synchronizing the internal state control systems with the ground truth, enabling the control system to cause additional damage on its own.

4.   Hydroelectric Plant Control System

This section briefly describes the control system used in a hydroelectric plant.

4.1   Control from Dam to Turbine

The turbine governor is responsible for controlling and adjusting the turbine power output. The governor also evens out deviations between the power and grid load as fast as possible. In particular, the turbine governor keeps the rotational speed stable and constant for the turbine generator unit for any grid load and prevailing conditions in the water conduit. Also, it closes the turbine admission according to the acceptable limits of the rotational speed rise of the unit and the pressure rise in the water conduits using load rejections and emergency stops [12].

The penstocks connect the hydraulic turbine with the intake structure. They are equipped with piezometer taps or pressure flow instrumentation sensors near the connection to the turbine. The flow of water to the turbine is stopped by closing the inlet to the penstocks, by having gates at intermediate points, or by using guards in the penstock just upstream from the generator. The gates are either open or closed; thus, instrumentation and alarms are limited to the fully open and fully closed positions.

4.2   Control of Generating Components

The adjustment of the rotational speed of a turbine depends on the type of turbine. Impulse (Pelton) turbines are controlled by moving the needles into or out of the nozzles. During rapid load changes, water can be channeled using deflectors. Reaction (Francis and Kaplan) turbines are controlled by adjusting wicket gates. The adjustments are monitored by the turbine governor.

The turbine governor uses speed detection, acoustic, differential or Winter-Kennedy taps to measure the rotational speed of the turbine – this is the "speed signal." The speed signal and the speed reference control signal are used to determine whether the turbine is in an overspeed, underspeed or synchronous speed state. The drop/regulation control is used together with set point control to determine if there should be a speed drop or speed regulation. This is accomplished by adjusting the water flow and/or applying air brakes on the turbine shaft. The control decision is made by a PID controller based on the combined speed signals and the gate or power feedback signal. The gate limit further includes the eventual gate limit control signals and start/stop signals to determine the gate set point. 3D blade control is performed on reaction

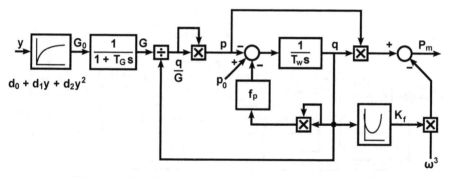

Figure 1. Non-linear model of a hydroelectric turbine [3].

turbines to optimize performance. The adjustments are made based on the gate set point and the head water and tail water levels.

4.3 Control of Grid and External Elements

The power supply to the power distribution network is dependent on numerous generators, all of which must operate in synchrony during normal and disturbance conditions. A power blackout can occur if one or more generators are out of synch. Numerous sources of instability are present in the power distribution network, including short circuits and loss of generation. Interested readers are referred to Grigsby [7] for additional information. Grigsby describes the three main types of stability in the power distribution grid: rotor angle stability, frequency stability and voltage stability; and discusses how stability can be obtained.

5. Control Models of Hydroelectric Turbines

Control system models are frequently used to represent and understand the functionality of industrial processes. This section describes two control models of hydroelectric turbines.

5.1 Non-Linear Model

Figure 1 presents a classical non-linear model of a single turbine and its water supply conduit [3]. The model illustrates the feedback and feed-forward modes involved in the interactions between the hydraulic and mechanical forces.

The valve characteristics G capture the relation between the water flow q and the pressure p in the water column. G can be expressed as a function of the gate position y. Based on experimental data, de Jaeger, *et al.* [3] have identified the function to be a combination of y and a first-order filter. This is one source of non-linearity in the model. The other non-linear component is due to the friction factor K_f, which is a second-order function of the flow q. Readers are referred to [3] for additional details about the non-linear model.

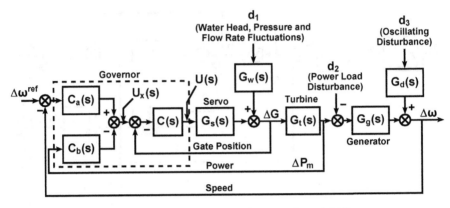

Figure 2. Multi-loop cascade control model [5].

This model can capture some of the attack vectors described above. In particular, deviations in the expected correlations between variables in the model can be used to detect direct manipulations of sensors. However, all the control elements in the model act on the same time scale, which makes it difficult to detect short-term and long-term fluctuations.

5.2   Multi-Loop Cascade Control Model

Hydro governor design has been revisited lately due to the deployment of large generating units, higher transmission voltages, higher power demands and increased complexity in the interactions between generating facilities and the distribution network. This situation is discussed by Eker [5]. Eker also provides a detailed description of a multi-loop cascade control model for hydraulic systems, which is shown in Figure 2.

The advantage of multi-loop cascade control models is that plant parameter uncertainties can be used to investigate stability and robustness. Robustness measures the ability of a plant to realize its full potential in a wide range of operating conditions [5]. The multi-loop cascade control model in Figure 2 shows the relation between the set point of the incremental speed $\Delta\omega^{\text{ref}}$ and the incremental speed $\Delta\omega$. The parameters included in the feedback to the controller in the case of Eker's model are the incremental speed $\Delta\omega$, the incremental power ΔP_m and the incremental gate position ΔG.

Eker's model captures the generator components, the components from dam to turbine, and the effects on multiple time scales. Thus, the model is able to express key aspects of the attack vectors discussed earlier.

5.3   Control System Design Challenges

Control theory provides guidance on adjusting the available degrees of freedom with the goal of achieving acceptable operation of a system (see, e.g., [18]). The task of designing a control system for a hydroelectric power plant involves teams of engineers, the intent being that their common understanding of plant behavior is reflected in the final design.

The control system should also reflect the designers' understanding of relevant threats and disturbances. A traditional reliability approach is likely to be applied where natural exposures to the plant are considered. An essential step in the definition of a control system is the scaling of variables [18], during which time assumptions on parameters such as the largest expected change in disturbance, largest allowed input change, largest allowed control error and largest expected change in reference values are determined. The assigned values have a large impact on system behavior. From a security perspective, this is a challenge because the thresholds are different when the existence of an active adversary is taken into account.

6.   Related Work

Early investigations of the effects of cyber attacks on critical infrastructure assets indicated that physical destruction was a real possibility [13]. However, subsequent research has moderated this view to a large extent.

Gonzalez-Perez and Wollenberg [6] studied interactions of the measurement infrastructure and state estimator accuracy on grid stability; their results indicate a large-scale vulnerability in the case of coordinated attacks. Other researchers have focused specifically on real-time control systems. Oman, *et al.* [15] examined the security and survivability of control systems used in power grid substations. Bigham, *et al.* [1] investigated the applicability of anomaly detection systems in SCADA environments. Oman and Phillips [16] studied intrusion detection and event monitoring in SCADA environments.

Most of the efforts related to intrusion and anomaly detection in SCADA systems have concentrated on the information system component with some exceptions (see, e.g., [10]). The problem of detecting anomalies in noisy SCADA environments has been discussed at a general level [19]. However, we are not aware of research that explicitly includes the control system model and its state prediction mechanisms, especially the consideration of feedback behavior and coupling at different time scales in baseline and anomaly models. Cheung, *et al.* [2] and Valdes and Cheung [22] describe explicit static models as a foundation for anomaly detection, but they concentrate on the control protocols rather than on the underlying system. In some domains, detailed models allow the analysis of specific control-system-dependent infrastructures and their interactions; for example, Nicolet, *et al.* [14] describe a numerical system that can provide predictive abilities beyond those discussed in this paper.

7.   Conclusions

Most research on SCADA security has focused on protecting information and communication systems or the SCADA protocols themselves (see, e.g., [4, 11]). However, analyzing the physical system being controlled is useful for detecting anomalies that might indicate potential intrusions and manipulations of the control system; for examining the implications of shutting down affected components when an attack or successful subversion attempt is detected; and for assessing the potential damage to the physical system in the event of a successful attack.

Control systems in critical infrastructures, such as the hydroelectric power plant considered in this paper, are characterized not only by the potential for direct and indirect damage but also by the delays in feedback control loops. Even if it is known that a system is compromised and can no longer be operated safely, an orderly shutdown may require an extended period of time so as not to cause damage. Delays can lead to non-intuitive behavior in the case of nested feedback loops, where, even after a primary fault has been repaired, secondary effects can lead to cascading failures.

Based on these observations, we have identified the requirements for basing anomaly detection on models of the physical system; otherwise, non-linear dependencies and anomalies are not detectable. Avenues for future research include refining the underlying models, investigating approaches that dynamically derive parameter values for use in anomaly detection, and generating explicit non-linear pattern hypotheses based on control system models.

References

[1] J. Bigham, D. Gamez and N. Lu, Safeguarding SCADA systems with anomaly detection, *Proceedings of the Second International Workshop on Mathematical Methods, Models and Architectures for Computer Network Security*, pp. 171–182, 2003.

[2] S. Cheung, B. Dutertre, M. Fong, U. Lindqvist, K. Skinner and A. Valdes, Using model-based intrusion detection for SCADA networks, *Proceedings of the SCADA Security Scientific Symposium*, 2007.

[3] E. de Jaeger, N. Janssens, B. Malfliet and B. van de Meulebroeke, Hydro turbine model for system dynamics studies, *IEEE Transactions on Power Systems*, vol. 9(4), pp. 1709–1715, 1994.

[4] J. Edmonds, M. Papa and S. Shenoi, Security analysis of multilayer SCADA protocols, in *Critical Infrastructure Protection*, E. Goetz and S. Shenoi (Eds.), Springer, Boston, Massachusetts, pp. 205–221, 2007.

[5] I. Eker, The design of robust multi-loop cascaded hydro governors, *Engineering with Computers*, vol. 20(1), pp. 45–53, 2004.

[6] C. Gonzalez-Perez and B. Wollenberg, Analysis of massive measurement loss in large-scale power system state estimation, *IEEE Transactions on Power Systems*, vol. 16(4), pp. 825–832, 2001.

[7] L. Grigsby (Ed.), *Electric Power Engineering Handbook*, CRC Press, Boca Raton, Florida, 2007.

[8] IEEE, IEEE Standard 1249-1996: IEEE Guide for Computer-Based Control for Hydroelectric Power Plant Automation, Piscataway, New Jersey, 1996.

[9] IEEE, IEEE Standard 1010-2006: IEEE Guide for Control of Hydroelectric Power Plants, Piscataway, New Jersey, 2006.

[10] P. Isasi, J. Molina-Lopez and A. Sanchis de Miguel, Unsupervised neural network for forecasting alarms in a hydroelectric power plant, *Proceedings of the International Conference on Artificial and Natural Neural Networks*, pp. 1298–1306, 1997.

[11] E. Johansson, T. Sommestad and M. Ekstedt, Security issues for SCADA systems within power distribution, *Proceedings of the Nordic Distribution and Asset Management Conference*, 2008.

[12] A. Kjolle, Hydropower in Norway: Mechanical Equipment, Technical Report, Norwegian University of Science and Technology, Trondheim, Norway, 2001.

[13] National Security Telecommunications Advisory Committee, Electric Power Risk Assessment, Technical Report, Washington, DC, 1997.

[14] C. Nicolet, P. Allenbach, J. Simond and F. Avellan, Modeling and numerical simulation of a complete hydroelectric production site, *Proceedings of the IEEE Lausanne Power Tech Conference*, pp. 1044–1048, 2007.

[15] P. Oman, A. Krings, D. Conte de Leon and J. Alves-Foss, Analyzing the security and survivability of real-time control systems, *Proceedings of the Fifth Annual IEEE SMC Information Assurance Workshop*, pp. 342–349, 2004.

[16] P. Oman and M. Phillips, Intrusion detection and event monitoring in SCADA networks, in *Critical Infrastructure Protection*, E. Goetz and S. Shenoi (Eds.), Springer, Boston, Massachusetts, pp. 161–173, 2007.

[17] T. Short, *Electric Power Distribution Handbook*, CRC Press, Boca Raton, Florida, 2004.

[18] S. Skogestad and I. Postlethwaite, *Multivariable Feedback Control: Analysis and Design*, Wiley, Chichester, United Kingdom, 2005.

[19] N. Svendsen and S. Wolthusen, Modeling and detecting anomalies in SCADA systems, in *Critical Infrastructure II*, M. Papa and S. Shenoi (Eds.), Springer, Boston, Massachusetts, pp. 101–113, 2008.

[20] A. Tijsseling, Fluid-structure interaction in liquid-filled pipe systems, *Journal of Fluids and Structures*, vol. 10(2), pp. 109–146, 1996.

[21] A. Tijsseling, Water hammer with fluid-structure interaction in thick-walled pipes, *Computers and Structures*, vol. 85 (11-14), pp. 844–851, 2007.

[22] A. Valdes and S. Cheung, Intrusion monitoring in process control systems, *Proceedings of the Forty-Second Hawaii International Conference on System Sciences*, pp. 1–7, 2009.

Chapter 11

DETECTING ANOMALIES IN PROCESS CONTROL NETWORKS

Julian Rrushi and Kyoung-Don Kang

Abstract   This paper presents the estimation-inspection algorithm, a statistical algorithm for anomaly detection in process control networks. The algorithm determines if the payload of a network packet that is about to be processed by a control system is normal or abnormal based on the effect that the packet will have on a variable stored in control system memory. The estimation part of the algorithm uses logistic regression integrated with maximum likelihood estimation in an inductive machine learning process to estimate a series of statistical parameters; these parameters are used in conjunction with logistic regression formulas to form a probability mass function for each variable stored in control system memory. The inspection part of the algorithm uses the probability mass functions to estimate the normalcy probability of a specific value that a network packet writes to a variable. Experimental results demonstrate that the algorithm is very effective at detecting anomalies in process control networks.

Keywords: Distributed control systems, anomaly detection, applied statistics

1.   Introduction

After decades of research, most of the physical processes underlying a system such as a nuclear power plant are known. If a physical system is operated in a digital (cyber) mode, as is the case of some Generation III, most Generation III+ and all Generation IV nuclear reactors, one can argue that, with the available knowledge in hand, we have a good definition of normalcy about the physical side of such a cyber-physical system. Because several behavior profiles of control systems and networks are induced by physical processes in the physical side, it is intuitively appealing to leverage the knowledge of normalcy in the physical side to obtain an assessment of normal behavior in the cyber side, and, thus, estimate the concept of normalcy for the entire cyber-physical system.

C. Palmer and S. Shenoi (Eds.): Critical Infrastructure Protection III, IFIP AICT 311, pp. 151–165, 2009.
© IFIP International Federation for Information Processing 2009

With this objective in mind, we conducted an observational study on an experimental cyber-physical system formed by a limited number of elements of a distributed control system [20] and simulated components of an advanced boiling water reactor (ABWR) [4]. The study involved the statistical analysis of the contents of random access memory (RAM) of a programmable logic controller (PLC) that contains control logic computation data, input data and output data, which we call "RAM variable memory." We discovered that the evolution of the values of logical and continuous variables stored in RAM variable memory follow specific flows that persist over time. This finding motivated our development of the estimation-inspection algorithm for anomaly detection.

The estimation-inspection algorithm probabilistically estimates the normal flows of values of logical or continuous variables stored in the RAM variable memory of PLCs and determines if a network packet is normal or abnormal by considering the specific evolution of values of a logical or continuous variable caused by the network packet. Experimental results using a simple testbed demonstrate that the algorithm is very effective at detecting anomalies in process control networks.

2.   Related Research

This section discusses related research on intrusion and anomaly detection in process control networks. Cheung, *et al.* [3] have examined protocol-level models for intrusion detection in process control networks. The models employ a definition of normalcy for payloads of byte-oriented protocols such as Modbus [13] and are derived from the protocol specifications and implementation guides. Protocol-level models and the estimation-inspection algorithm both focus on the inspection of network packets. Protocol-level models search for violations related to function codes, exception codes, protocol identifiers and other attributes. They also examine cross-field relationships because a legitimate value of a field may depend on the value of another field. On the other hand, the proposed anomaly detection approach focuses entirely on data fields and uses applied statistics to assess their legitimacy.

Some researchers [17–19] have applied reactor mirage theory (RMT) as a deception-based intrusion detection technique for process control networks in nuclear power plants. RMT, which is based on signal detection theory [8, 12], uses continuous simulation [16] based on genuine control network traffic. The proposed approach differs from RMT in that it addresses situations where attackers target control systems attached to real, operational equipment.

The challenges involved in detecting attacks on control systems have been discussed by Cardenas, *et al.* [1] and by Naess, *et al.* [15]. The approach of Cardenas, *et al.* is based on an understanding of the interactions between the control system and the physical system. They model the behavior of a physical system as a linear dynamical system and use the model to determine the effects of control commands on the physical parameters of the system in question. Their approach assumes that an attack on a control system produces abnormal behavior in the physical system by having negative effects on the system parameters; thus, they use sequential detection theory to detect the negative effects. Our approach models the interactions between a control system and a physical system in terms of the evolutions of values of logical and continuous variables stored in the RAM variable memory of the control system. A statistical estimation technique is used to obtain a series of parameters that are used with logistic regression formulas to form a probability mass function for each variable stored in control system memory. For a control command to be deemed normal, the network packet that conveys it should cause an evolution of values of a logical or continuous variable that is deemed to be normal by the probabilistic model.

Naess, *et al.* propose an intrusion detection approach that uses high-level application-based policies implemented at the middleware level. The misuse policies are based on attack signatures, procedural-based policies that use execution patterns of monitored components, and interval-based policies that look for anomalies in parameter values and method invocation frequencies. Procedural-based policies are not comparable with our statistical approach, nor are misuse policies and interval-based policies that deal with method invocation frequencies. Our research suggests that interval-based policies take into account the state of the physical system when setting parameter thresholds. Naess, *et al.* discuss maximum and minimum value policies that look for parameter values that lie outside the range of allowable values. For instance, if the allowed set point for the linear position of a control rod used to adjust the reactivity of a nuclear reactor core [21] should be an even value between 6 and 24, a maximum and minimum value policy would classify a set point of 24 as normal. However, if the value of reactivity is high, moving the control rod from a low value to a linear position of 24 is abnormal and possibly very dangerous.

The approach of Naess, *et al.* incorporates the delta value and maximum average policies, which are used to detect unexpected variations in parameter values over a short amount of time and excesses of maximum distance from a moving average for each measurement, respectively. A consideration of the state of a physical system would enable delta value and maximum average policies to produce corrective responses that are initiated by control systems upon an equipment fault or breakage. To our knowledge, such corrective responses often involve set points that cause large and abrupt changes to parameter values. Naess, *et al.* also use interval-based policies that employ cumulative distribution functions to detect rare values given a history of normally-distributed values. Thus, these policies compare the next value of a parameter with some number of previous values of the same parameter. In our experience, the next normal value of a parameter also depends on the current values of other parameters that characterize a physical system. In a nuclear power plant, for example, the next value of the position of a turbine bypass valve depends on the current value of the pressure in the reactor vessel. Our approach addresses this issue by considering the complete state of a physical system when estimating a probability distribution for the next value of a logical or continuous variable.

Naedele and Biderbost [14] describe an approach for reducing the security-related events that occur in a process control environment to quantitative metrics, which are understandable by system operators with limited computer security expertise. The quantitative metrics are presented to system operators during plant operation, enabling them to assess if an attack is taking place. Naedele and Biderbost's approach and the proposed approach both consider the dynamics of a digitally-controlled physical system when estimating the normalcy of network packets. However, the two approaches differ in how they estimate the normalcy of network packets. Naedele and Biderbost's approach uses humans for pattern matching while the proposed approach engages statistical estimation theory. We believe that the proposed approach is better because it supports real-time detection while the human analysis of events takes at least a few seconds. Consider, for example, a malicious network packet that opens a circuit breaker to desynchronize a power generator in the electrical power grid. While Naedele and Biderbost's approach would likely detect the malicious network packet only after circuit breaker has been opened, the proposed approach would detect the packet before it is processed by the control system that controls the circuit breaker.

3.   Statistical Approach for Anomaly Detection

This section presents our statistical approach for anomaly detection. In particular, it describes the mathematical modeling and statistical parameter estimation techniques, and the estimation-inspection algorithm.

3.1   Mathematical Modeling

The RAM variables of control systems can be expressed as a matrix W whose elements model logical or continuous variables that store process measurement data or actuator control data along with set points:

$$W = \begin{bmatrix} x_1 \ x_2 \ \cdots\cdots\cdots\cdots\cdots\cdots \\ \cdots\cdots\cdots\cdots\cdots\cdots\cdots \\ \cdots\cdots\cdots\cdots\cdots\cdots x_l \\ x_{l+1} \ x_{l+2} \ \cdots\cdots\cdots\cdots \\ \cdots\cdots\cdots\cdots\cdots\cdots\cdots \\ \cdots\cdots\cdots\cdots\cdots\cdots x_m \\ x_{m+1} \ x_{m+2} \ \cdots\cdots\cdots\cdots \\ \cdots\cdots\cdots\cdots\cdots\cdots\cdots \\ \cdots\cdots\cdots\cdots\cdots\cdots x_n \\ x_{n+1} \ x_{n+2} \ \cdots\cdots\cdots\cdots \\ \cdots\cdots\cdots\cdots\cdots\cdots\cdots \\ \cdots\cdots\cdots\cdots\cdots\cdots x_g \end{bmatrix}$$

The elements x_1, x_2, $\ldots$, x_l model input register variables; the elements x_{l+1}, x_{l+2}, $\ldots$, x_m model holding register variables; the elements x_{m+1}, x_{m+2}, $\ldots$, x_n model discrete input variables; and the elements x_{n+1}, x_{n+2}, $\ldots$, x_g model coil variables. A control system can hold as many as 65,536 variables of each type. If q is the number of control systems in a process control network, then $l = 65,536q$, $m = 2l$, $n = 3l$ and $g = 4l$. In a real-world control system, it may be the case that not all the input register variables, holding register variables, discrete input variables and coil variables are needed; consequently, not all of them are defined.

Logical variables and continuous variables in RAM variable memory, and, thus, the elements of matrix W are mapped to process parameters (i.e., variables characterizing the operation of physical equipment and/or physical processes) according to specific schemes (i.e., cyber-physical mappings) that depend on the communication protocol being used. In some byte-oriented protocols (e.g., Modbus), cyber-physical mappings are defined *ad hoc* by control engineers and are applied during device configuration. Other protocols (e.g., IEC 61850 [6]) have the cyber-physical mappings defined in their specifications. Process parameters are related to each other by mathematical formulas based on the processes taking place in the physical side of the system.

A cyber-physical mapping associates the physical or chemical relations between process parameters with functional relations among logical variables and continuous variables in RAM variable memory, and, thus, with the functional relations among the elements of matrix W. The functional relations, in turn, determine the logical data and continuous data assigned to sensor or actuator variables during the controlled operation of a physical system. Thus, given a process in the physical side of a controlled system along with a cyber-physical mapping, a value assigned to an element of matrix W can be explained by consulting a set of other elements of W under the assumption that the analysis is being performed on a safe operation of the controlled physical system.

The fundamental thesis of this research is that for every possible combination of values of W elements, including the current value of $W[i][j]$, $W[i][j]$ may take any one of its possible values with a probability that varies from 0 to 1. We refer to the probability in question as the "normalcy probability." A normal transition flow step occurs when $W[i][j]$ takes a value whose associated normalcy probability is non-zero. Thus, a network packet that is about to write to $W[i][j]$ is classified as normal if it causes a normal transition of the current value of $W[i][j]$, i.e., it writes a value to $W[i][j]$ whose associated normalcy probability is non-zero. In the statistical context, we refer to the elements of matrix W as $W[i][j]$ and $x_1, x_2, \ldots, x_g$ when we treat them as dependent variables and exposure variables, respectively. The estimation-inspection algorithm, which is described later in this section, estimates the probability distribution of the values of $W[i][j]$ given $x_1, x_2, \ldots, x_g$ and checks that a network packet that writes to $W[i][j]$ conveys a value for $W[i][j]$ whose associated normalcy probability is non-zero.

The possible values of each $W[i][j]$ lie in $\{min\,(W[i][j]), min\,(W[i][j]) + 1, \ldots, min\,(W[i][j]) + h\}$, where $min\,(W[i][j]) + h = max\,(W[i][j])$. We use the term "possible value" because each logical variable, by definition, may assume the value 0 or 1, while each continuous variable takes values from a defined interval that depends on the process parameter to which it is mapped. In a nuclear power plant, for example, the continuous variable mapped to the reactor vessel pressure may take values that vary from 0 psi at plant start-up to a maximum value of 1,000 psi when the plant is operating at 100% thermal power. Similarly, if the maximum synchronous speed of a two-pole AC induction motor is 1,500 rpm, then the applied voltage frequency, which is used control the actual rotational speed of the motor, may assume values from 0 Hz to 25 Hz. Note that $W[i][j]$ can take negative values because it is possible for process measurements and actuator control data to have negative values.

We use stochastic vectors to store the probability distributions of $W[i][j]$ values. These stochastic vectors are defined by:

$$
V_{W[i][j]} = \left\{ \begin{bmatrix} p_0 \\ p_1 \\ \cdot \\ \cdot \\ \cdot \\ p_h \end{bmatrix} \mid p_0 + p_1 + ... + p_h = 1 \right\} \tag{1}
$$

Let $p_k = V_{W[i][j]}[k]$ be the normalcy probability that $W[i][j]$ takes the value $min\,(W[i][j]) + k$ where $k \in \{0, 1, \ldots, h\}$. Thus, $p_0 = V_{W[i][j]}[0]$ is the normalcy probability that $W[i][j]$ takes the value $min\,(W[i][j])$; $p_1 = V_{W[i][j]}[1]$ is the normalcy probability that $W[i][j]$ takes the value $min\,(W[i][j]) + 1$; and so on.

We use a probability mass function $\Gamma_{W[i][j]}$ to model the normal data transition flows that may potentially be followed by element $W[i][j]$. The probability mass function $\Gamma_{W[i][j]}$ is defined by:

$$
\Gamma_{W[i][j]} : x_1 \times ... \times x_{l+1} \times ... \times x_{m+1} \times ... \times x_{n+1} \times ... \times x_g \to V_{W[i][j]} \tag{2}
$$

The estimation part of the estimation-inspection algorithm uses logistic regression integrated with maximum likelihood estimation in an inductive machine learning process to estimate a series of statistical parameters. These statistical parameters in conjunction with logistic regression formulas form a practical definition of the probability mass function $\Gamma_{W[i][j]}$ for each $W[i][j]$. The inspection part of the estimation-inspection algorithm uses the probability mass function $\Gamma_{W[i][j]}$ to estimate the normalcy probability of a specific value $min\,(W[i][j]) + k$ that a network packet is about to write to $W[i][j]$.

3.2   Statistical Parameter Estimation

As described later, an element $W[i][j]$ may take any one of its possible values with a probability that depends on $x_1, x_2, \ldots, x_g$ and the statistical parameters $\alpha(s)$ and $\beta(s)$. The parameters $\alpha(s)$ are intercept terms while $\beta(s)$ are coefficient terms. We estimate the statistical parameters using applied logistic regression analysis integrated with maximum likelihood estimation [5, 9]. The first step is to run a model of the controlled physical system normally and without any attacks. The values of the logical and continuous variables in control system RAM are recorded in a database as they evolve over time.

Next, we have different individuals run the model multiple times. Despite undergoing similar training and certification regimens, different nuclear reactor operators usually adjust process parameters in different ways to reach the desired operational states. Furthermore, process-related events may be handled differently, but are considered normal operations as long as the desired tasks are performed correctly. What is important is that the model be used to generate a sample of network packets that characterizes the population of network packets during normal operation of the controlled physical system.

For each program variable modeled by $W[i][j]$, we create a database view with rows of the form $\{\varphi(W[i][j]), x_1, x_2, ..., x_g\}$, where $\varphi(W[i][j])$ denotes the next value of $W[i][j]$. $\varphi(W[i][j])$ is extracted from a network packet transmitted over a process control network that is about to write $W[i][j]$, while the record of values of $x_1, x_2, \ldots, x_g$ is a snapshot of the current values of the elements of matrix W just before the network packet changes the value of $W[i][j]$ to $\varphi(W[i][j])$.

We now consider the case where $W[i][j]$ models a continuous variable. If (in statistical terms) each possible value of $W[i][j]$ is considered to be an outcome category, then ordinal logistic regression is applicable because the categories (in general) are ordered in controlled physical systems. In a nuclear power plant, for example, the possible values of continuous variables mapped to process parameters (e.g., reactor vessel pressure, reactor water level, neutron population in the reactor core and steam flow rate) are ordered. In ordinal logistic regression, comparisons between the contiguous values of a dependent variable play a key role in estimating their probabilities of occurrence. Since the possible values of $W[i][j]$ lie in $[min\,(W[i][j]),\, min\,(W[i][j]) + h]$, there are h possible comparisons between contiguous values of $W[i][j]$. Consequently, according to ordinal logistic regression, there are h intercept terms α in the ordinal logistic model $\alpha_1, \alpha_2, ..., \alpha_h$.

An intercept term α_k is defined for each value $min\,(W[i][j]) + k$ of $W[i][j]$ such that $k \neq 0$. Later in this section we will see that α_k is used to estimate the probability that $W[i][j]$ takes the value $min\,(W[i][j]) + k$. We will also show that there is no α_0 defined for $min\,(W[i][j])$. Since the logistic model under consideration is ordinal rather than polytomous, there is only one coefficient term β_a associated with each exposure variable x_a where $a \in \{1, 2, \ldots, g\}$. Furthermore, there is a unique set of coefficient terms $\beta_1, \beta_2, \ldots, \beta_g$ defined for all values $min\,(W[i][j]) + k$ of $W[i][j]$. Like the intercept term α_k, the coefficient terms $\beta_1, \beta_2, \ldots, \beta_g$ are also used to estimate the probability that $W[i][j]$ takes the value $min\,(W[i][j]) + k$.

Given $x_1, x_2, \ldots, x_g$, the probability that $W[i][j]$ takes a value greater than or equal to $min\,(W[i][j]) + k$ is:

$$P\left(\varphi(W[i][j]) \geq min\,(W[i][j]) + k \mid W\right) = \frac{1}{1 + e^{-\left(\alpha_k + \sum_{a=1}^{g} \beta_a x_a\right)}} \tag{3}$$

As a matter of fact, we are interested in $min\,(W[i][j]) + k \geq 1$ because $P\,(\varphi(W[i][j]) \geq 0 \mid W) = 1$. Similarly, the probability that $W[i][j]$ takes a value greater than or equal to $min\,(W[i][j]) + k + 1$ given $x_1, x_2, ..., x_g$ is:

$$P\,(\varphi(W[i][j]) \geq min\,(W[i][j]) + k + 1 \mid W) = \frac{1}{1 + e^{-\left(\alpha_{k+1} + \sum_{a=1}^{g} \beta_a x_a\right)}} \quad (4)$$

Equations (3) and (4) are used to derive the probability that $W[i][j]$ takes the value $min\,(W[i][j]) + k$ given $x_1, x_2, ..., x_g$. The probability is given by:

$$P(\varphi(W[i][j]) = min(W[i][j]) + k \mid W) = P(\varphi(W[i][j]) \geq min(W[i][j]) +$$
$$k \mid W) - P(\varphi(W[i][j]) \geq min(W[i][j]) + k + 1 \mid W) \quad (5)$$

Upon substituting Equations (3) and (4) into Equation (5), we obtain:

$$P\,(\varphi(W[i][j]) = min\,(W[i][j]) + k \mid W) =$$
$$\frac{1}{1 + e^{-\left(\alpha_k + \sum_{a=1}^{g} \beta_a x_a\right)}} - \frac{1}{1 + e^{-\left(\alpha_{k+1} + \sum_{a=1}^{g} \beta_a x_a\right)}} \quad (6)$$

For the case where $k = 0$ and the value of $W[i][j]$ whose probability of occurrence is being estimated is $min\,(W[i][j])$, the minuend in Equation (6) is 1 because $P\,(\varphi(W[i][j]) \geq min(W[i][j]) \mid W) = 1$. This explains why no α_0 is defined for $min\,(W[i][j])$ (i.e., when $k = 0$).

Next, we discuss the development of the likelihood function $L_{W[i][j]}$ for an element $W[i][j]$. The function $L_{W[i][j]}$ represents the joint probability for the likelihood of observing the data of the d rows in the database view. Assuming that the rows of the database view are numbered from 1 to d, let y_{bk} be an indicator variable defined on the bth row as follows:

$$y_{bk} = \begin{cases} 1 & \text{if in the } b^{\text{th}} \text{ row, } \varphi(W[i][j]) = min\,(W[i][j]) + k \\ 0 & \text{if in the } b^{\text{th}} \text{ row, } \varphi(W[i][j]) \neq min\,(W[i][j]) + k \end{cases} \quad (7)$$

The joint probability for the likelihood of observing the data in the database view is:

$$\prod_{b=1}^{d} \prod_{k=0}^{h} P\,(\varphi(W[i][j]) = min\,(W[i][j]) + k \mid W)^{y_{bk}} \quad (8)$$

Equation (8) estimates the individual contribution made by each row to the probability that $\varphi(W[i][j])$ is $min\,(W[i][j]) + k$, and then combines the individual likelihood contributions made by each row. Clearly, each row contributes the probability of one value $min\,(W[i][j]) + k$ taken by $W[i][j]$ because only one of the indicator variables is equal to 1. Upon substituting Equation (6) into Equation (8), we obtain:

$$\prod_{b=1}^{d} \prod_{k=0}^{h} \left(\frac{1}{1 + e^{-\left(\alpha_k + \sum_{a=1}^{g} \beta_a x_a\right)}} - \frac{1}{1 + e^{-\left(\alpha_{k+1} + \sum_{a=1}^{g} \beta_a x_a\right)}}\right)^{y_{bk}} \quad (9)$$

The values of the exposure variables $x_1, x_2, \ldots, x_g$ in Equation (9) are available from the database view because each individual row is processed by the equation. Therefore, after performing the multiplications of the probabilities contributed by each individual row, the likelihood function $L_{W[i][j]}$ appears as a function of the statistical parameters, and is given by:

$$L_{W[i][j]} (\alpha_1, \alpha_2, \ldots, \alpha_h, \beta_1, \beta_2, \ldots, \beta_g) \qquad (10)$$

We estimate the values of the statistical parameters $\alpha_1, \alpha_2, \ldots, \alpha_h, \beta_1, \beta_2, \ldots, \beta_g$ that maximize $L_{W[i][j]}$ using the maximum likelihood technique [11]. We organize the parameters of the likelihood function $L_{W[i][j]}$ as a vector $\theta = (\theta_1, \theta_2, \ldots, \theta_{h+g})$. Maximizing $L_{W[i][j]} (\theta)$ is equivalent to maximizing $ln [L_{W[i][j]} (\theta)]$. If $r \in \{1, 2, ..., h + g\}$ and θ_r is the rth element of vector θ, the values of the statistical parameters that maximize $L_{W[i][j]} (\theta)$ are the solutions of a system of equations of the form:

$$\frac{\partial ln [L_{W[i][j]} (\theta)]}{\partial \theta_r} = 0 \qquad (11)$$

where the fraction is a partial derivative of the natural logarithm of the likelihood function $L_{W[i][j]}$ with respect to θ_r. The solutions of the system of equations yield estimates of the parameters $\alpha_1, \alpha_2, \ldots, \alpha_h, \beta_1, \beta_2, \ldots, \beta_g$. Armed with the estimated values of the parameters, we return to Equation (6) and estimate the probability that $W[i][j]$ takes the value $min (W[i][j]) + k$ given the current values of the elements of matrix W. This is an integral component of the estimation-inspection algorithm, which is presented below.

Estimating $p_k = (P (\varphi(W[i][j]) = min (W[i][j]) + k \mid W))$ and storing p_k in $V_{W[i][j]}[k]$, for each $k \in \{0, 1, \ldots, h\}$, fills all the positions of stochastic vector $V_{W[i][j]}$. Iterating this procedure over every possible tuple of values of exposure variables $x_1, x_2, \ldots, x_g$ associates each tuple with a stochastic vector $V_{W[i][j]}$, which leads to the computation of the probability mass function $\Gamma_{W[i][j]}$.

We now consider the case where $W[i][j]$ models a logical variable that takes a value of 0 or 1. Since a logical variable matches the definition of a dichotomous measure in a statistical context, dichotomous logistic regression can be applied. In a dichotomous logistic model, there is only one intercept term α defined for the two possible values of $W[i][j]$, and only one coefficient term β_a associated with each exposure variable x_a where $a \in \{1, 2, \ldots, g\}$. Furthermore, a unique set of coefficient terms $\beta_1, \beta_2, \ldots, \beta_g$ is defined for the two possible values of $W[i][j]$. Upon applying the logistic function of the dichotomous logistic model, we obtain the probability that an element $W[i][j]$ takes the value 1:

$$P (\varphi(W[i][j]) = 1|W) = \frac{1}{1 + e^{-\left(\alpha + \sum_{a=1}^{g} \beta_a x_a\right)}} \qquad (12)$$

The probability that $W[i][j]$ takes the value 0 is given by:

$$P (\varphi(W[i][j]) = 0|W) = 1 - P (\varphi(W[i][j]) = 1|W) = 1 - \frac{1}{1 + e^{-\left(\alpha + \sum_{a=1}^{g} \beta_a x_a\right)}} \qquad (13)$$

We arrange the rows of the database view so that for the first c rows: $\varphi(W[i][j]) = 1$, and for the remaining $d - c$ rows: $\varphi(W[i][j]) = 0$. Let $P(X_b)$ denote $P(\varphi(W[i][j]) = 1 \mid W)$ for the bth row. Also in a dichotomous logistic model, the joint probability for the likelihood of observing the data in the database view is given by the likelihood function $L_{W[i][j]}$ defined by:

$$\prod_{b=1}^{c} P(X_b) \prod_{b=c+1}^{d} 1 - P(X_b) \tag{14}$$

Equation (14) estimates the individual likelihood contribution made by each row numbered from 1 to c to the probability that $W[i][j]$ takes the value 1, along with the individual likelihood contribution made by each row numbered from $c+1$ to d to the probability that $W[i][j]$ takes the value 0; it then combines the individual likelihood contributions made by each row. The values of the exposure variables $x_1, x_2, \ldots, x_g$ in Equation (14) are available from the individual rows of the database view. Upon multiplying the probabilities contributed by each row, we obtain the likelihood function $L_{W[i][j]}$ defined by:

$$L_{W[i][j]}(\alpha, \beta_1, \beta_2, ..., \beta_g) \tag{15}$$

Next, we estimate the values of the statistical parameters $\alpha, \beta_1, \beta_2, \ldots, \beta_g$ that maximize $L_{W[i][j]}$ using maximum likelihood estimation. We apply the unconditional likelihood technique instead of the conditional technique because the number of statistical parameters in the model is usually small relative to the number of rows in the database view. Furthermore, the conditional likelihood technique does not allow the estimation of the intercept term α, which, as can be seen from Equations (12) and (13), is indispensable to estimating the probability that $W[i][j]$ takes values of 1 and 0, respectively. If we denote the parameters of the likelihood function $L_{W[i][j]}$ as $\theta = (\theta_1, \theta_2, \ldots, \theta_{g+1})$, then the values of the statistical parameters that maximize $L_{W[i][j]}(\theta)$ are the solutions of a system of equations of the form given by Equation (11).

In this case, θ_r is the rth individual parameter for $r \in \{1, 2, \ldots, g + 1\}$. The solutions of the system of equations give the estimates of the statistical parameters $\alpha, \beta_1, \beta_2, ..., \beta_g$. With the statistical parameter estimates in hand, we use Equations (12) and (13) to estimate the probability that $W[i][j]$ takes the values 1 and 0, respectively, given the current values of the elements of matrix W. This is also an integral component of the estimation-inspection algorithm.

Estimating $p_1 = P(\varphi(W[i][j]) = 1 \mid W)$ and $p_0 = P(\varphi(W[i][j]) = 0 \mid W)$, and storing p_1 and p_0 in $V_{W[i][j]}[1]$ and $V_{W[i][j]}[0]$, respectively, fills both the positions of the stochastic vector $V_{W[i][j]}$. Iterating over every possible tuple of values of the exposure variables $x_1, x_2, \ldots, x_g$ associates each of them with a stochastic vector $V_{W[i][j]}$, which leads to the computation of the probability mass function $\Gamma_{W[i][j]}$.

Algorithm 1 : Assess the normalcy of a network packet payload.

Part I

1: **for all** $W[i][j]$ that models a program variable that is defined **do**
2:     **if** $W[i][j]$ models a continuous variable **then**
3:         estimate the associated statistical parameters $\alpha_1, \alpha_2, \ldots, \alpha_h, \beta_1, \beta_2,$ $\ldots, \beta_g$ using ordinal logistic regression and maximum likelihood estimation
4:     **end if**
5:     **if** $W[i][j]$ models a logical variable **then**
6:         estimate the associated statistical parameters $\alpha, \beta_1, \beta_2, \ldots, \beta_g$ using dichotomous logistic regression and maximum likelihood estimation
7:     **end if**
8: **end for**

Part II

1: $U \Leftarrow payload$
2: $Norm \Leftarrow true$
3: **for all** $W[i][j]$ such that $\varphi(W[i][j]) \in U$ **do**
4:     $k \Leftarrow \varphi(W[i][j]) - min(W[i][j])$
5:     **if** $W[i][j]$ models a continuous variable **then**
6:         $p_k \Leftarrow \frac{1}{1+e^{-(\alpha_k+\Sigma_{a=1}^g \beta_a x_a)}} - \frac{1}{1+e^{-(\alpha_{k+1}+\Sigma_{a=1}^g \beta_a x_a)}}$
7:     **end if**
8:     **if** $W[i][j]$ models a logical variable and $k = 1$ **then**
9:         $p_k \Leftarrow \frac{1}{1+e^{-(\alpha+\Sigma_{a=1}^g \beta_a x_a)}}$
10:     **else if** $W[i][j]$ models a logical variable and $k = 0$ **then**
11:         $p_k \Leftarrow 1 - \frac{1}{1+e^{-(\alpha+\Sigma_{a=1}^g \beta_a x_a)}}$
12:     **end if**
13:     **if** $p_k = 0$ **then**
14:         $Norm \Leftarrow false$
15:         break *for* loop
16:     **end if**
17: **end for**
18: **return** $Norm$

3.3   Estimation-Inspection Algorithm

The first part of the estimation-inspection algorithm (see Part I of Algorithm 1) is concerned with estimating the statistical parameters (intercept terms α(s) and coefficient terms β(s)) and is, therefore, conducted during the learning phase. As indicated in Line 1 (Part I), the algorithm estimates a specific set of statistical parameters for each element of the matrix W that models a program variable defined in a control system. As discussed above, the algorithm applies ordinal logistic regression integrated with maximum likelihood estimation on a learning data set to estimate the intercept and coefficient terms of the ordinal logistic model developed for an element of matrix W that models a continuous variable (Lines 2–4). The algorithm applies dichotomous logistic regression integrated with maximum likelihood estimation on a learning data set to estimate the intercept term and the coefficient terms of the dichotomous logistic model developed for an element of matrix W that models a logical variable (Lines 5–7).

Part II of the algorithm is concerned with scrutinizing network packets in a process control network. To assess the normalcy of a network packet, the algorithm conducts its statistical analysis in relation to each variable that is written by the network packet (Line 3). The algorithm checks if the program variable written by the network packet is a continuous variable (Line 4) or a logical variable (Lines 8, 10). This information along with the value of index k computed in Line 4 are used to identify: (i) the type of logistic model and, thus, the corresponding logistic regression formula applicable to the network packet; and (ii) the intercept terms $\alpha(s)$ and coefficient terms $\beta(s)$ of the applicable logistic model defined for the variable by the packet.

If the program variable written by the network packet is a continuous variable, the algorithm plugs the intercept terms $\alpha(s)$ and coefficient terms $\beta(s)$ along with the current values of the exposure variables $x_1, x_2, \ldots, x_g$ into the formula of the ordinal logistic model and produces an estimate of the normalcy probability of the specific value that the network packet writes to the continuous variable in question (Line 6). If the program variable written is a logical variable, the algorithm plugs the intercept term α and coefficient terms $\beta(s)$ along with the current values of the exposure variables $x_1, x_2, \ldots, x_g$ into the formula of the dichotomous logistic model to estimate the normalcy probability of value 1 (Line 9) or value 0 (Line 11) depending on whether 1 or 0 is written to the logical variable, respectively.

If the normalcy probability of the value written to the program variable under consideration is greater than zero, the algorithm conducts its statistical analysis in relation to the next variable that the network packet under inspection will write, if any. If this is not the case, i.e., the estimate of the normalcy probability is equal to zero, the algorithm interrupts the scrutinization process and classifies the network packet as abnormal (Lines 13–16).

4.   Experimental Evaluation

A small testbed was used to generate a data set for the inductive machine learning process used by the estimation-inspection algorithm and to conduct an experimental evaluation of the algorithm. The control system employed in the testbed comprised Linux PC-based PLCs [20], specifically, MatPLCs [22] installed on general-purpose Linux machines with x86 CPUs. Custom MatPLC modules were employed in the master mode to control and monitor a limited number of simulated components of an ABWR. These modules implemented control logic for processing MatPLC points (inputs, outputs, internal coils and registers). The MatPLC points were mapped to physical I/O parameters and, therefore, represented the link between the MatPLC modules in master mode and the parameters of simulated ABWR components. Network communications were implemented using the Modbus protocol over TCP/IP.

Sensors and actuators were emulated using custom MatPLC modules running in the slave mode. A MatPLC human-machine interface (HMI) GNU image manipulation program toolkit (GTK) module was used to read and write MatPLC points corresponding to supervisory network operations of a power plant. We conducted continuous simulations [2] of the mechanisms used to insert or withdraw a control rod (namely, the joint operation of an AC induction motor that produces a torque and a ball screw that transforms rotational motion into linear motion), a motor-driven water pump used to inject water within the reactor core, and limited portions of the nuclear fission process that involve reactivity [21] and core flow (i.e., water in the reactor core).

A prototype implementation of the estimation-inspection algorithm was deployed and activated in the MatPLCs and the simulated ABWR components were run normally using the control system and network. The main purpose of the test was to assess if the algorithm would mistakenly classify normal network packets as abnormal and, thus, generate false positives. To assess the effectiveness of the algorithm in detecting attacks, a series of memory errors were inserted in the Modbus implementation running on the MatPLCs and attack code was developed to exploit the errors.

The attacks launched on the MatPLCs included stack overflow exploits with shellcode injection, stack overflow exploits with arc injection, heap overflow exploits with shellcode injection, frame pointer overwrites with shellcode injection, format bug exploits with shellcode injection that corrupted function pointers in the global offset table, indirect pointer overwrites with shellcode injection that corrupted function pointers in the global offset table, and exploits of out-of-boundary array indices with shellcode injection. Inertial attacks [10] were also mounted on the simulated AC induction motor along with exclusion attacks that violated a functional dependency between the (limited) simulated control rod insertion and withdrawal system and the (limited) simulated reactor feedwater system.

We obtained a false alarm rate of zero false positives/hour, which we believe is a clear indication of the need to test the estimation-inspection algorithm on a data set comprising network packets sniffed from the process control network of a real power plant. Conversely, this initial result may indicate that the algorithm has potential to be highly effective.

We also obtained a detection probability of 98%, i.e., 98% of the malicious network packets were detected by the algorithm. When possible, we crafted network packets so as to inject shellcode one byte at a time. A few of these bytes managed to pass undetected because they were indeed normal process data in defined states of the simulated ABWR components. All the network packets that injected memory addresses were detected by the algorithm. In summary, all the attacks launched in the test were detected by the estimation-inspection algorithm.

5. Conclusions

The estimation-inspection algorithm is intended to protect cyber-physical systems such as power plants from application-level computer network attacks. The algorithm uses statistical techniques to determine if the payload of a network packet that is about to be processed by a control system is normal or abnormal based on the evolution of the variable that the network packet will modify. Experimental results with a small testbed demonstrate that the algorithm yields a detection probability of 98% with a zero false positive rate.

It is necessary to conduct additional tests of the estimation-inspection algorithm. In particular, the algorithm should be tested using packets collected from the process control network of a real power plant.

Acknowledgements

This work was supported in part by NSF Grant CNS 0614771. The research of Julian Rrushi was partially supported by scholarships from the University of Milan and (ISC)^2.

References

[1] A. Cardenas, S. Amin and S. Sastry, Research challenges for the security of control systems, *Proceedings of the Third USENIX Workshop on Hot Topics in Security*, 2008.

[2] F. Cellier and E. Kofman, *Continuous System Simulation*, Springer, New York, 2006.

[3] S. Cheung, B. Dutertre, M. Fong, U. Lindqvist, K. Skinner and A. Valdes, Using model-based intrusion detection for SCADA networks, *Proceedings of the SCADA Security Scientific Symposium*, 2007.

[4] General Electric Company, Advanced Boiling Water Reactor (ABWR), Fairfield, Connecticut (www.gepower.com/prod_serv/products/nuclear_en ergy/en/new_reactors/abwr.htm).

[5] D. Hosmer and S. Lemeshow, *Applied Logistic Regression*, Wiley, Hoboken, New Jersey, 2000.

[6] International Electrotechnical Commission, IEC 61850-7-410: Communication Networks and Systems for Power Utility Automation, Part 7-410: Hydroelectric Power Plants – Communication for Monitoring and Control, Geneva, Switzerland, 2007.

[7] H. Javitz and A. Valdes, The NIDES Statistical Component Description and Justification, SRI Project 3131 Annual Report, SRI, Menlo Park, California, 1994.

[8] S. Kay, *Fundamentals of Statistical Signal Processing, Volume 2: Detection Theory*, Prentice Hall, Upper Saddle River, New Jersey, 1998.

[9] D. Kleinbaum, L. Kupper, L. Muller and A. Nizam, *Applied Regression Analysis and Multivariable Methods*, Duxbury Press, Pacific Grove, California, 2007.

[10] J. Larsen, SCADA security, presented at *Blackhat DC*, 2008.

[11] E. Lehmann and G. Casella, *Theory of Point Estimation*, Springer, New York, 2003.

[12] J. Marcum, A statistical theory of target detection by pulsed radar, *IRE Transactions on Information Theory*, vol. 6(2), pp. 59–267, 1960.

[13] Modbus IDA, MODBUS Application Protocol Specification v1.1a, North Grafton, Massachusetts (www.modbus.org/specs.php), 2004.

[14] M. Naedele and O. Biderbost, Human-assisted intrusion detection for process control systems, *Proceedings of the Second International Conference on Applied Cryptography and Network Security*, pp. 216–225, 2004.

[15] E. Naess, D. Frincke, A. McKinnon and D. Bakken, Configurable middleware-level intrusion detection for embedded systems, *Proceedings of the Second International Workshop on Security in Distributed Computing Systems*, vol. 2, pp. 144–151, 2005.

[16] D. Nicol and P. Heidelberger, Parallel execution for serial simulators, *ACM Transactions on Modeling and Computer Simulation*, vol. 6(3), pp. 210–242, 1996.

[17] J. Rrushi and R. Campbell, An intrusion detection system for operation in nuclear power plants, presented at the *Fourth ITI Workshop on Dependability and Security*, 2007.

[18] J. Rrushi and R. Campbell, Using deception to facilitate intrusion detection in nuclear power plants, *Proceedings of the Third International Conference on Information Warfare and Security*, 2008.

[19] J. Rrushi and K. Kang, Mirage theory: A deception approach to intrusion detection in process control networks, *Proceedings of the NATO Symposium on Information Assurance for Emerging and Future Military Systems*, 2008.

[20] K. Stouffer, J. Falco and K. Scarfone, Guide to Industrial Control Systems (ICS) Security, Special Publication 800-82, Final Public Draft, National Institute of Standards and Technology, Gaithersburg, Maryland, 2008.

[21] U.S. Department of Energy, DoE Fundamentals: Handbook of Nuclear Physics and Reactor Theory, DOE-HDBK-1019/1-93, Washington, DC, 1993.

[22] C. Wuollet, A. Romanenko, H. Jack, J. Baum, J. Orozco and M. de Sousa, MatPLC (mat.sourceforge.net), 2006.

III

INFRASTRUCTURE SECURITY

Chapter 12

NONDEDUCIBILITY-BASED ANALYSIS OF CYBER-PHYSICAL SYSTEMS

Thoshitha Gamage and Bruce McMillin

Abstract   Controlling information flow in a cyber-physical system (CPS) is challenging because cyber domain decisions and actions manifest themselves as visible changes in the physical domain. This paper presents a nondeducibility-based observability analysis for CPSs. In many CPSs, the capacity of a low-level (LL) observer to deduce high-level (HL) actions ranges from limited to none. However, a collaborative set of observers strategically located in a network may be able to deduce all the HL actions. This paper models a distributed power electronics control device network using a simple DC circuit in order to understand the effect of multiple observers in a CPS. The analysis reveals that the number of observers required to deduce all the HL actions in a system increases linearly with the number of configurable units. A simple definition of nondeducibility based on the uniqueness of low-level projections is also presented. This definition is used to show that a system with two security domain levels could be considered "nondeducibility secure" if no unique LL projections exist.

Keywords: Cyber-physical systems, information flow security, nondeducibility

1.   Introduction

Cyber-physical systems (CPSs) are systems with pure cyber components that are highly integrated with pure physical components. However, in certain cases, the high integration causes information leakage to unauthorized parties mainly due to physical manifestations. This is especially true when it comes to preserving the confidentiality of high-level (HL) user interactions.

Gas distribution and electrical power distribution networks are examples of CPSs. Much of the work related to CPSs has focused on maintaining integrity in SCADA systems [3, 10]. However, in the case of a distributed system, confidentiality is also important because information about the system state can be used by an adversary to determine where to attack the system. Preventing

C. Palmer and S. Shenoi (Eds.): Critical Infrastructure Protection III, IFIP AICT 311, pp. 169–183, 2009.

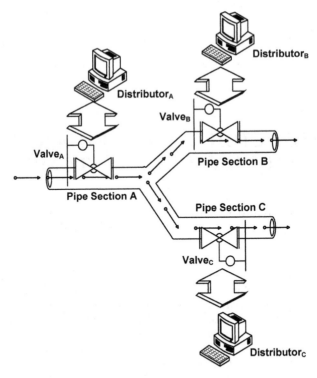

Figure 1. Gas pipeline with three distributors.

the unauthorized disclosure of sensitive information via physical interactions has opened up a new dimension of security – How much can an observer learn about a system by examining its physical operation?

To clarify the issue, consider the gas distribution pipeline system in Figure 1. When Distributor$_C$ applies a change at Valve$_C$, flow changes occur throughout the network. Knowing the topology of the system and how it operates, a rival distributor (Distributor$_B$), who is also fed by the same main distributor (Distributor$_A$), may be able to derive gas flow values in Distributor$_C$'s network. Thus, the confidentiality of Distributor$_C$'s actions is compromised and unintended information leakage occurs between the two competing distributors.

CPSs have inherent obfuscation features that can leave a low-level (LL) observer in doubt about the actions that could have contributed to a physical change. These features can be used to prevent information leakage. This paper focuses on measuring the confidentiality of CPSs using information flow coupled with physical commodity flow analysis.

2.   Information Flow Properties

Confidentiality, integrity and availability are three major security goals. Several formal security models (e.g., Bell-LaPadula, Biba and HRU models) have been proposed. However, most of these models focus on access control, which on its own, is insufficient to preserve information flow security.

The Bell-LaPadula model, for example, does not restrict HL actions from being observed by LL users; this indirectly violates the "no write down" (*–security) property [4]. Covert channels exist even in the best-designed systems [5]. Furthermore, interactions between the cyber and physical aspects of a CPS can lead to information flow security violations [13].

Information flow properties, also termed "possibilistic security properties" [7], are useful for describing the confidentiality of systems. These properties define ways for restricting unintended information disclosure between different user groups, primarily an HL user group with a secret to preserve, and an LL user group that should not acquire the secret.

Noninterference [6], noninference [9] and nondeducibility [11] are the three principal information flow properties.

Noninterference is the most restrictive of the three properties. It requires HL inputs not to interfere with LL outputs.

Noninference is a less restrictive property. It states that, for every legal "execution" of a system, the execution produced by purging all HL actions should also be a legal trace. Note that an execution is an interleaved sequence of system inputs and outputs of the system.

Nondeducibility, the least restrictive of the three properties, describes the ability to deduce HL inputs based on LL outputs.

The amount of information deducible about HL actions depends on several factors. This paper examines the effect of the number of LL observers on the level of deducibility. A simple DC circuit model is used to conduct a comprehensive analysis on the deducibility property for systems that permit physical observations.

3.   Nondeducibility

Sutherland's definition of nondeducibility [11] states that, given two information functions $f_1()$ and $f_2()$, a set of state transition sequences Σ, a particular state sequence and the existence of a certain state sequence with a known output on $f_2()$, then information flows from $f_1()$ to $f_2()$ if and only if:

$$(\exists \sigma \in \Sigma)(\exists_{\mathfrak{z}} : f_2^{-1}(\mathfrak{z}) \neq \lambda), \forall \bar{\sigma} \in \Sigma : f_1(\sigma) = f_1(\bar{\sigma}) \, (f_2(\bar{\sigma}) \neq \mathfrak{z}) \qquad (1)$$

A state sequence is also called an "execution" [1].

To better understand Equation (1), consider two functions, *projection* and *trace*, which are defined as follows. Given a certain user group G, an execution of the system σ and an initial state q_0, the *projection* function $proj(G, \sigma, q_0)$ provides a sequence of outputs of σ that G is permitted to see. The *trace* function $trace(\sigma, q_0)$ takes σ and q_0 as inputs and yields all the input commands (or events) in σ. These functions are borrowed from the state machine (or event machine) abstraction of systems, which is frequently used by the information flow security research community [1, 7, 8, 14]. The implicit notion of "permit" allows the subcategorization of user groups based on security clearances. In classical theory, these are a set of HL subjects/users G_{HL}/U_{HL} and a set of LL subjects/users G_{LL}/U_{LL}.

With reference to Equation (1), consider $f_1() \equiv proj()$ and $f_2() \equiv trace()$. Further, assume that an LL user $u_i \in G_{LL}$ sees the same projection output $\mathcal{X}$ for two different executions σ_i and σ_j ($proj(u_i, \sigma_i, q_0) = proj(u_i, \sigma_j, q_0)$) but sees different trace results. Knowing how the system behaves, u_i can rule out certain HL input commands because they are incapable of producing $\mathcal{X}$. However, u_i is unable to deduce the specific HL input action that caused $\mathcal{X}$. Thus, the "uniqueness of output events" impacts the deducibility, which, in turn, leads to the following lemma.

LEMMA 1 *Given a set of executions Σ and two information functions $f_1()$ and $f_2()$, information does not flow from $f_1()$ to $f_2()$ if and only if function $f_1()$ does not produce any unique outputs.*

Proof: The negation of Equation (1) describes the requirement for information not to flow between functions. In doing so, the universal quantifiers in the equation become existential quantifiers and vice versa.

$$\neg\{(\exists \sigma \in \Sigma)(\exists_{\mathfrak{z}} : f_2^{-1}(\mathfrak{z}) \neq \lambda), \forall \bar{\sigma} \in \Sigma : f_1(\sigma) = f_1(\bar{\sigma}), (f_2(\bar{\sigma}) \neq \mathfrak{z})\}$$
$$= (\exists \sigma \in \Sigma)(\exists_{\mathfrak{z}} : f_2^{-1}(\mathfrak{z}) \neq \lambda), \forall \bar{\sigma} \in \Sigma : f_1(\sigma) = f_1(\bar{\sigma}) \Rightarrow (f_2(\bar{\sigma}) \neq \mathfrak{z})$$
$$= (\forall \sigma \in \Sigma)(\forall_{\mathfrak{z}} : f_2^{-1}(\mathfrak{z}) \neq \lambda), \neg\{\forall \bar{\sigma} \in \Sigma : f_1(\sigma) = f_1(\bar{\sigma}) \Rightarrow (f_2(\bar{\sigma}) \neq \mathfrak{z})\}$$
$$= (\forall \sigma \in \Sigma)(\forall_{\mathfrak{z}} : f_2^{-1}(\mathfrak{z}) \neq \lambda), \exists \bar{\sigma} \in \Sigma : \neg\{f_1(\sigma) = f_1(\bar{\sigma}) \Rightarrow (f_2(\bar{\sigma}) \neq \mathfrak{z})\}$$
$$= (\forall \sigma \in \Sigma)(\forall_{\mathfrak{z}} : f_2^{-1}(\mathfrak{z}) \neq \lambda), \exists \bar{\sigma} \in \Sigma : f_1(\sigma) = f_1(\bar{\sigma}) \wedge (f_2(\bar{\sigma}) = \mathfrak{z}).$$

Lemma 1 describes the requirement for information flow not to occur between two information functions of a system. In other words, for every HL action $\mathfrak{z}$ of a system that produces a certain LL observation $\mathcal{X}$, if it is possible to find another execution with the same $\mathcal{X}$ but that was caused by a different HL action, the system preserves the nondeducibility of input actions. This result is used in the discussion of observability and the number of observers requirement later in this paper.

4.   Motivation

Given a CPS, suppose that it is possible to identify and distinguish between different user groups based on their security clearances and to determine the information or actions that need to be kept secret. Using Lemma 1, what is the minimum number of LL observers required to fully deduce all the HL actions of the CPS?

This paper answers the question using a distributed power electronics control device (FACTS) network as an example CPS. FACTS stands for flexible AC transmission systems. FACTS devices are installed at strategic locations along power distribution networks, primarily to increase fault tolerance and avoid cascading failures [2]. The devices are configurable and programmable, and are capable of injecting or absorbing active and reactive power from a set of transmission lines under their control.

When a faulty line is detected, FACTS devices cooperate with other devices on the network to derive distributed power flow redistribution decisions. Once the decisions are made, changes are applied to the corresponding physical transmission lines to re-stabilize the overall network. Thus, some aspects of the cyber domain decisions eventually manifest themselves in the physical domain as flow changes in power lines. Prior work [12] has shown that, in terms of information flow security, an external observer could deduce the local action on a particular power line or lines, and infer the overall state of the system based on external flow change measurements. However, this paper does not address the question of how many cooperating observers are required to fully discover changes in the system state.

5.   Deducible Observations

Modeling an actual AC power distribution network for the purpose of analysis is a difficult task. To simplify the analysis, we model the power distribution network as a simple DC circuit. In this model, the variable resistors R_i denote configurable/programmable devices and the edges between resistors denote transmission lines. External observers position themselves at connection points and other strategic locations to observe flow changes along the edges. Each R_i is considered to be an HL user ($\forall i : R_i \in U_{HL}$) while each observer is considered to be an LL user ($\forall j : \text{Observer}_j \in U_{LL}$). The HL input commands $\acute{I}$ for the system are the changes to resistance $\forall i : R_i \uparrow, R_i \downarrow \in \acute{I}$, while the LL observable outputs $\acute{O}$ are the voltage and current readings $V \uparrow, V \downarrow, I \uparrow, I \downarrow \in \acute{O}$.

The system dynamics of the DC circuit model adequately reflect the actual system and, in terms of real power, can be extended to the power grid [2]. Due to their high cost, FACTS devices are deployed sparsely in a real network. Thus, the minimum number of observers required to fully deduce the system state can characterize the information security of the system. The analysis considers two topologies, series-connected and parallel-connected networks. Each topology has basic and extended network configurations.

This model considers the steady-state behavior of the system and assumes that only one $\acute{i}_i \in \acute{I}$ occurs at a given time. This input command can lead to several LL observable changes at different observation points. Thus, an execution σ in this case, consists of a single HL input action followed by the resulting LL observable events. Furthermore, it is also assumed that the LL observers have sufficient knowledge of the system and topology to derive the expected outcome for each HL input. The voltage source is assumed to be maintained constant throughout the analysis.

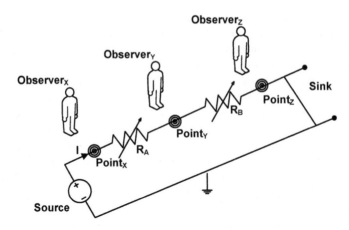

Figure 2.   Two-resistor series-connected circuit.

5.1   Series-Connected Circuits

Figure 2 shows a two-resistor series-connected DC circuit with three observation points. Note that the resistors correspond to variable power electronic devices.

Table 1.   Low-level observation matrix for a series-connected circuit.

	LL Observations			
HL	$V_y \uparrow$	$V_y \downarrow$	$I_y \uparrow$	$I_y \downarrow$
$R_A \uparrow$		$\checkmark$		$\checkmark$
$R_B \uparrow$		$\checkmark$		$\checkmark$
$R_A \downarrow$	$\checkmark$		$\checkmark$	
$R_B \downarrow$	$\checkmark$		$\checkmark$	

Table 1 presents the LL observation matrix for a two-resistor series circuit with one deducible observer. Note that $\acute{I} = \{R_A \uparrow, R_A \downarrow, R_B \uparrow, R_B \downarrow\}$ while $\acute{O} = \{I \uparrow, I \downarrow, V_y \uparrow, V_y \downarrow\}$. As a result, there are four legal executions $\sigma_k : 1 \leq k \leq 4$ corresponding to each HL input command. These are denoted as rows in Table 1. The first entry of each row denotes the corresponding trace, $trace(\sigma_k, q_0)$, for each execution σ_k. The remaining row entries correspond to projections.

LEMMA 2 *In a base series-connected circuit with two configurable units, the placement of any number of observers preserves nondeducibility.*

Proof: Consider two executions $\sigma_1 = \{R_A \uparrow, V_y \downarrow, I_y \downarrow\}$ and $\sigma_2 = \{R_B \uparrow, V_y \downarrow, I_y \downarrow\}$. Without loss of generality, assume that Observer$_y$ in Figure 2 sees the projection $\{V_y \downarrow, I_y \downarrow\}$, which, according to Lemma 1, corresponds to

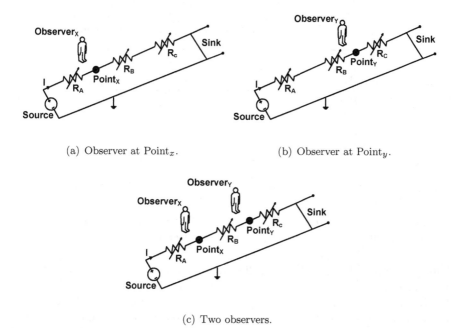

(a) Observer at Point$_x$.

(b) Observer at Point$_y$.

(c) Two observers.

Figure 3. Three-resistor series circuit with two deducible observers.

$f_1(\sigma) \equiv proj(U_{LL}, \sigma_1, q_0)$. The corresponding trace for σ_1 yields $R_A \uparrow$ where $f_2(\sigma) \equiv trace(\sigma_1, q_0)$. However, there exists another execution σ_2 with the same projection, $f_1(\bar{\sigma}) = \{V_y \downarrow, I_y \downarrow\}$, but with a different trace $f_2(\bar{\sigma}) = R_B \uparrow$.

For Observer$_y$ in Figure 2, the only distinct projections are $\{V_y \downarrow, I_y \downarrow\}$ and $\{V_y \uparrow, I_y \uparrow\}$. However, neither of them are unique projections because there is another execution for each case with the same projection but caused by a different trace (see Table 1). Thus, in Observer$_y$'s view, there are no unique LL projections, which preserves nondeducibility.

A "deducible observer" is an observer who can take multiple readings (e.g., voltage and current) that can be used to deduce HL information. Note that Observer$_x \in U_{LL}$ at the source and Observer$_z \in U_{LL}$ at the sink do not observe any voltage changes due to the nature of the layout. In contrast, Observer$_y \in U_{LL}$ can see voltage changes, albeit with multiple possibilities. Thus, Observer$_y$ is the only "deducible observer" in this network.

Figure 3 shows an extended series circuit, which is derived from Figure 2 by incorporating an additional resistor $R_C \in U_{HL}$. In the analysis that follows, only deducible observers are considered (Observer$_x$ and Observer$_y$). Figure 3(a) shows a three-resistor series-connected DC circuit with a single deducible observer at Point$_x$ and Figure 3(b) shows the same circuit with a single deducible observer at Point$_y$. Table 2 summarizes the LL observations for the extended circuit.

Table 2.   Observation matrix for an extended series circuit.

HL	Vₓ↑	Vₓ↓	Vy↑	Vy↓	I↑	I↓
R_A ↑		√		√		√
R_B ↑	√			√		√
R_C ↑	√		√			√
R_A ↓	√		√		√	
R_B ↓		√	√		√	
R_C ↓		√		√	√	

LEMMA 3 *A series circuit with $n \geq 3$ configurable units is fully deducible with a minimum of n distinct readings and $n - 1$ observers.*

Proof: To prove Lemma 3, it is sufficient to show that there is a violation of Lemma 1. From Table 2, consider the execution $\sigma = \{R_A \uparrow, V_x \downarrow, V_y \downarrow, I \downarrow\}$. By Lemma 1, for the Observer$_x$ and Observer$_y$ combination, the collective projection of σ is $f_1(\sigma) = \{V_x \downarrow, V_y \downarrow, I \downarrow\}$. According to Table 2, this is a unique projection that allows the observers to deduce $f_2(\sigma) = R_A \uparrow$. In fact, all the collective projections for this observer combination are unique. This, in turn, leads to full deducibility of all HL actions with two observers and three distinct readings.

For Observer$_x$ at Point$_x$, the projection $\{V_x \uparrow, I \downarrow\}$ is compatible with the traces $R_B \uparrow$ and $R_C \uparrow$. Similarly, the projection $\{V_x \downarrow, I \uparrow\}$ is compatible with the traces $R_B \downarrow$ and $R_C \downarrow$. By Lemma 1, the actions of R_B and R_C are nondeducible from Observer$_x$'s point of view. However, for the same observer, the projections $\{V_x \downarrow, I \downarrow\}$ and $\{V_x \uparrow, I \uparrow\}$ are unique corresponding to traces $R_A \uparrow$ and $R_A \downarrow$. Thus, whenever R_A makes an HL change, Observer$_x$ can deduce it exactly. In summary, Observer$_x$ is able to deduce R_A but not R_B or R_C. Similarly, it is not hard to see that Observer$_y$ at Point$_y$ in isolation (Figure 3(b)) can deduce the actions of R_C but not those of R_A or R_B (see Table 2). For this reason, the network is "partially deducible."

It is not difficult to see that every additional resistor appended to the circuit in Figure 3(c) produces at least one additional distinct reading that would require one additional observer. Thus, the number of observers and distinct readings required to fully deduce the network increase linearly with the number of configurable units. Since changes to I are equally visible to any observer, the number of observers required is always one less than the number of configurable units.

Note that multiple configurable units are located after Point$_x$ and only one configurable unit before Point$_x$. Given an observation point, configurable unit locations before and after the observation point are called "pre-locations" and "post-locations," respectively. Similarly, for Point$_y$, there are multiple pre-locations but only one post-location.

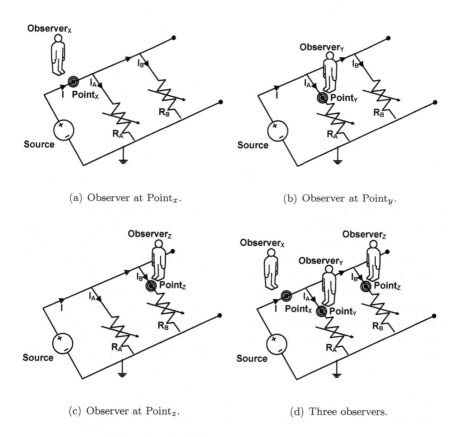

(a) Observer at Point$_x$.

(b) Observer at Point$_y$.

(c) Observer at Point$_z$.

(d) Three observers.

Figure 4. Parallel circuit with three observers.

5.2 Parallel-Connected Circuits

Figure 4 shows all the possible single observer scenarios for a two-resistor parallel-connected DC circuit with three deducible observers. It is not possible to observe any V changes at any of the "deducible points." However, Observer$_x$ at the source can be considered to be a deducible observer because the total current I branches into two currents I_A and I_B along the parallel links of the circuit. The corresponding LL observation matrix is presented in Table 3.

LEMMA 4 *For a base parallel-connected circuit with two parallel resistors, any combination of two observers is sufficient to fully deduce the circuit.*

Proof: This network also violates the condition of Lemma 1. Consider the scenario of multiple cooperating observers shown in Figure 4(d). Without loss of generality, consider the execution $\sigma = \{R_A \uparrow, I_A \downarrow, I \downarrow\}$. By Lemma 1, $f_1(\sigma) = \{I_A \downarrow, I \downarrow\}$ and $f_2() = R_A \uparrow$ for the observer combination Observer$_x$ and Observer$_y$. From Table 3, it is clear that this projection is unique. This

Table 3.   Observation matrix for a parallel circuit with three observers.

HL	$I_A \uparrow$	$I_A \downarrow$	$I_B \uparrow$	$I_B \downarrow$	$I \uparrow$	$I \downarrow$
		LL Observations				
$R_A \uparrow$		$\checkmark$				$\checkmark$
$R_B \uparrow$				$\checkmark$		$\checkmark$
$R_A \downarrow$	$\checkmark$				$\checkmark$	
$R_B \downarrow$			$\checkmark$		$\checkmark$	

allows the two collaborative observers to deduce the exact HL action ($R_A \uparrow$). Further examination of Table 3 reveals that this is true for all other executions of the network. In fact, any combination of two observers can deduce all the HL actions; thus, with just two observers, the entire network is deducible.

Note that a single deducible observer at Point$_z$ (Figure 4(c)) cannot derive any information about R_A's actions. This is because there are no corresponding observations for traces $R_A \uparrow$ and $R_A \downarrow$ in the $I_B \uparrow$ and $I_B \downarrow$ columns in Table 3. However, for Observer$_z$, R_B's actions are deducible. Similarly, a single observer at Point$_y$ cannot deduce anything about R_B's actions (see Figure 4(b)) but can deduce R_A's actions. As for Observer$_x$ in Figure 4(a), $I \downarrow$ is consistent with either $R_A \uparrow$ or $R_B \uparrow$ whereas $I \uparrow$ is consistent with $R_A \downarrow$ and $R_B \downarrow$. Thus, a single observer is able to "partially deduce" the network.

Figure 5 shows a three-resistor parallel-connected DC circuit with five deducible observers. Table 4 shows the corresponding LL observation matrix.

LEMMA 5 *For a pure parallel-connected circuit with n parallel resistors, a minimum of n strategically-placed observers are required to fully deduce the circuit.*

Proof: To prove that only three observers are sufficient to fully deduce the network in Figure 5(f), we use Lemma 4 and consider one additional parallel path compared with Figure 4(d). However, not all combinations of three observers provide full deducibility. For example, an observer combination such as Observer$_x$, Observer$_y$ and Observer$_v$ cannot even notice the actions of R_B or R_C. For this observer combination, $\{I_V \downarrow, I \downarrow\}$ is a legal projection that is compatible with two traces $R_B \uparrow$ and $R_C \uparrow$. Thus, the placement of observers is also important.

There are two post-locations and one pre-location for Observer$_v$'s view of the system. Interestingly, Observer$_v$ cannot observe pre-location changes and any post-location change preserves nondeducibility. Similarly, Observer$_x$ has three post-locations and, as the last two columns of Table 4 show, a single observable change is compatible with any of these post-locations. Furthermore, an observer along a parallel path can only observe changes in that particular path.

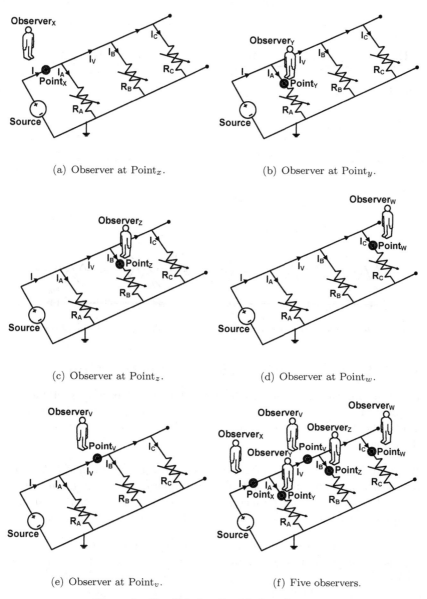

(a) Observer at Point$_x$.

(b) Observer at Point$_y$.

(c) Observer at Point$_z$.

(d) Observer at Point$_w$.

(e) Observer at Point$_v$.

(f) Five observers.

Figure 5. Parallel circuit with five observers.

6. Summary of Results

This section summarizes the results for DC circuits with series-connected and parallel-connected units.

Table 4. Observation matrix for a parallel circuit with five observers.

HL	$I_A\uparrow$	$I_A\downarrow$	$I_B\uparrow$	$I_B\downarrow$	$I_C\uparrow$	$I_C\downarrow$	$I_V\uparrow$	$I_V\downarrow$	$I\uparrow$	$I\downarrow$
LL Observations										
$R_A\uparrow$		✓								✓
$R_B\uparrow$				✓				✓		✓
$R_C\uparrow$						✓		✓		✓
$R_A\downarrow$	✓								✓	
$R_B\downarrow$			✓				✓		✓	
$R_C\downarrow$					✓		✓		✓	

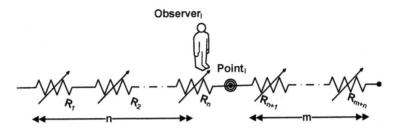

Figure 6. Series system with $n + m$ configurable units and one observer.

6.1 Circuits with Series-Connected Units

Figure 6 shows a pure series-connected system with Observer$_i$ at Point$_i$ with n pre-location paths and m post-location paths. Lemmas 2 and 3 can be used to prove the following theorem related to observability for series-connected configurable units.

THEOREM 1 *(Observability of Series-Connected Configurable Units): In a purely series-connected system with $n + m$ configurable units where $n + m \geq 3$, a single change seen by an Observer$_i$ is consistent with a change α in one of the n pre-locations or a change β in one of the m post-locations with $\alpha = \bar{\beta}$.*

Proof: This theorem is proved using mathematical induction.
Base Case 1: From Lemma 2 (Figure 3(a)) with $n = 1$, $m = 2$, $\alpha =\uparrow$ and $\beta =\downarrow$, we see that $R_1 \uparrow$, $R_2 \downarrow$, $R_3 \downarrow$ is consistent with $V \downarrow$ and $R_1 \downarrow$, $R_2 \uparrow$, $R_3 \uparrow$ is consistent with $V \uparrow$. Thus, the claim is true for the base case.
Base Case 2: From Lemma 2 (Figure 3(b)) with $n = 2$, $m = 1$, $\alpha =\uparrow$ and $\beta =\downarrow$, we see that $R_1 \uparrow$, $R_2 \uparrow$, $R_3 \downarrow$ is consistent with $V \downarrow$ and $R_1 \downarrow$, $R_2 \downarrow$, $R_3 \uparrow$ is consistent with $V \uparrow$. Thus, the claim is true for the base case.
Inductive Hypothesis: Assume that the claim holds for a system with $n + m$ resistors.
Inductive Step: If the observation point is moved by one location to the right, the system consists of $n + 1$ pre-locations and $m - 1$ post-locations. Since no

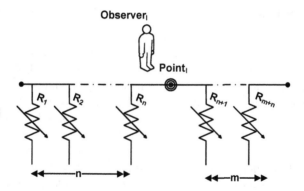

Figure 7. Parallel system with $n + m$ configurable units and one observer.

other parameter of the system is changed and the claim holds for the $n+m$ configuration, the claim holds for a system with $(n+1)+(m-1)$ configurable units.

6.2 Circuits with Parallel-Connected Units

Parallel-connected topologies are highly relevant to AC power distribution networks. These topologies can be modeled using pure parallel-connected configurable units in our DC model. Figure 7 shows a pure parallel-connected system with Observer$_i$ at Point$_i$ with n pre-location paths and m post-location paths.

- For a parallel-connected system with a single change at a time, an observation made by Observer$_i$ is consistent with m post-location path unit changes.

- For the same system, changes in any of the n pre-location path units are not visible to Observer$_i$.

- Two or more actions at any post-locations may compensate each other and cancel out the likelihood of an observation being made at Point$_i$. Thus, a set of changes at post-locations can also be hidden from Observer$_i$.

Lemmas 4 and 5 can be used to prove the following theorem for parallel-connected networks. The proof, which is not presented here, employs mathematical induction.

THEOREM 2 *(Observability of Parallel Connected Configurable Units): For a pure parallel-connected system consisting of n pre-location paths and m post-location paths with respect to an Observer$_i$, a minimum of m + n observers are required to fully deduce all HL actions. A combination of n pre-location deducible observers and m − 1 post-location deducible observers must be selected in addition to Observer$_i$.*

7.   Conclusions

This paper has attempted to provide a new perspective on information flow properties in systems with cyber-physical interactions. In particular, it has presented a detailed analysis of the minimum number of observers required to fully deduce HL actions in a CPS. Furthermore, a simplified definition of nondeducibility based on the uniqueness of LL projections has been presented. The results of the analysis lead to two corollaries related to the minimum number of "deducible observers" required to fully deduce a system.

COROLLARY 1 *To fully deduce all HL actions, a series-connected system with k configurable units requires a minimum of k distinct readings and k–1 deducible observers.*

COROLLARY 2 *To fully deduce a parallel system with $k = n+m$ configurable units, an Observer$_i$ requires a minimum of n pre-location observers and m–1 post-location observers. Thus, including Observer$_i$, a minimum of $k = n+(m-1)+1$ observers are required.*

The observer-based view of the system can be considered as an LL domain view of the HL actions in a CPS. The focus of this paper has been on full deducibility of a CPS. However, certain HL actions are accurately deducible with fewer observers than identified above. For example, whenever Observer$_x$ in Table 2 sees $\{V_x \downarrow, I \downarrow\}$, he can deduce that $R_A \uparrow$ was the cause. This is termed as "partial deducibility."

Our future work will analyze the effect of multiple, simultaneous HL changes on nondeducibility. Also, it will investigate hybrid series/parallel networks with a variety of configurations.

Acknowledgments

This work was partially supported by NSF MRI Award CNS 0420869, CSR Award CCF-0614633 and the Missouri S&T Intelligent Systems Center.

References

[1] B. Alpern and F. Schneider, Defining liveness, *Information Processing Letters*, vol. 21(4), pp. 181–185, 1985.

[2] A. Armbruster, M. Gosnell, B. McMillin and M. Crow, Power transmission control using distributed max-flow, *Proceedings of the Twenty-Ninth International Conference on Computer Software and Applications*, vol. 1, pp. 256–263, 2005.

[3] K. Barnes and B. Johnson, Introduction to SCADA Protection and Vulnerabilities, Technical Report INEEL/EXT-04-01710, Idaho National Engineering and Environmental Laboratory, Idaho Falls, Idaho, 2004.

[4] D. Bell and L. LaPadula, Secure Computer Systems: Mathematical Foundations, MITRE Technical Report 2547, Volume I, The MITRE Corporation, Bedford, Massachusetts, 1973.

[5] R. Focardi and R. Gorrieri, Classification of security properties (Part I: Information flow), in *Foundations of Security Analysis and Design, Tutorial Lectures*, R. Focardi and R. Gorrieri (Eds.), Springer, Berlin-Heidelberg, Germany, pp. 331–396, 2001.

[6] J. Goguen and J. Meseguer, Security policies and security models, *Proceedings of the IEEE Symposium on Security and Privacy*, pp. 11–22, 1982.

[7] J. McLean, A general theory of composition for a class of "possibilistic" properties, *IEEE Transactions on Software Engineering*, vol. 22(1), pp. 53–67, 1996.

[8] N. Nagatou and T. Watanabe, Run-time detection of covert channels, *Proceedings of the First International Conference on Availability, Reliability and Security*, pp. 577–584, 2006.

[9] C. O'Halloran, A calculus of information flow, *Proceedings of the First European Symposium on Research in Computer Security*, pp. 147–159, 1990.

[10] P. Pires and L. Oliveira, Security aspects of SCADA and corporate network interconnections: An overview, *Proceedings of the International Conference on the Dependability of Computer Systems*, pp. 127–134, 2006.

[11] D. Sutherland, A model of information, *Proceedings of the Ninth National Computer Security Conference*, pp. 175–183, 1986.

[12] H. Tang and B. McMillin, Security of information flow in the electric power grid, in *Critical Infrastructure Protection*, E. Goetz and S. Shenoi (Eds.), Springer, Boston, Massachusetts, pp. 43–56, 2007.

[13] H. Tang and B. McMillin, Security property violation in CPS through timing, *Proceedings of the Twenty-Eighth International Conference on Distributed Computing Systems*, pp. 519–524, 2008.

[14] A. Zakinthinos and E. Lee, A general theory of security properties, *Proceedings of the IEEE Symposium on Security and Privacy*, pp. 94–102, 1997.

Chapter 13

STACK-BASED BUFFER OVERFLOWS IN HARVARD CLASS EMBEDDED SYSTEMS

Kristopher Watts and Paul Oman

Abstract   Many embedded devices used to control critical infrastructure assets are based on the Harvard architecture. This architecture separates data and program memory into independent address spaces, unlike the von Neumann architecture, which uses a single address space for data and program code. Buffer overflow attacks in desktop and server platforms based on the von Neumann model have been studied extensively. However, buffer overflows in Harvard architectures have only just begun to receive attention. This paper demonstrates that stack-based buffer overflow vulnerabilities exist in embedded devices based on the Harvard architecture and that the vulnerabilities are easily exploited. The paper shows how the reversal in the direction of stack growth simplifies attacks by providing easier access to critical execution controls. Also, the paper examines defense techniques used in server and desktop systems and discusses their applicability to Harvard class machines.

Keywords: Embedded systems, Harvard architecture, buffer overflows

1. Introduction

The buffer overflow is a well-researched attack vector. However, most research has focused on high performance processors based on the von Neumann memory model. The von Neumann model uses a single address space for data and program code [4]. On the other hand, the Harvard architecture – which is widely used in embedded devices – separates data and program memory into independent address spaces [15]. The independent data address space allows the data segment to grow and be manipulated without regard to the location of the program memory. Because the address space in a von Neumann machine is shared by data and program code, the program must take steps to prevent data from interfering with program code. This paper examines the Harvard and von Neumann architectures and demonstrates how stack-based vulnerabilities in Harvard class machines render them vulnerable to buffer overflow exploits.

C. Palmer and S. Shenoi (Eds.): Critical Infrastructure Protection III, IFIP AICT 311, pp. 185–197, 2009.
© IFIP International Federation for Information Processing 2009

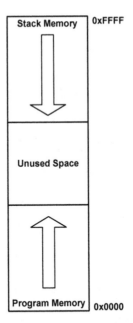

Figure 1.   von Neumann memory model.

2.   Stack-Based Buffer Overflows

Buffer overflow vulnerabilities have been documented since the early 1970's [2], but the most celebrated exploit involved the Morris worm of 1988 [11], which opened a Pandora's box of buffer overflows and other exploits. Stack-based buffer overflows were popularized by Levy (aka Aleph One) in his 1996 paper, "Smashing the Stack for Fun and Profit" [1]. A buffer overflow is an artifact of dynamic memory and occurs when a program attempts to write "too much" data to a specified location. The effect of writing excess data is that the extra data spills over the boundary of allocated space, possibly overwriting other important data. The effect of an overflow on a running program depends on where the allocated space exists within memory and how the space is used by the system and/or program. Levy's paper, which focused exclusively on von Neumann class architectures, examined overflows that occur in dynamic memory structures used by C-like languages.

A stack is a data structure with the property that the last item placed on the stack is the first item to be removed. A stack has two principal operations, Push and Pop. Push places a new item on top of the stack; Pop removes an item from the top of the stack.

The arrangement of a stack in memory varies according to the processor architecture and compiler implementation. A von Neumann machine almost always has a stack that starts in high address memory and grows into low address memory (Figure 1). On the other hand, a Harvard class machine

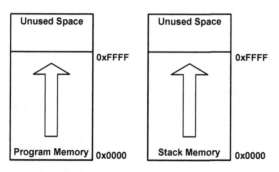

Figure 2.   Harvard memory model.

usually has a stack that starts in low address memory and grows into high address memory [4, 15] (Figure 2).

Many modern programming languages use a stack to support dynamic calling mechanisms such as function calls. The stack stores the state of the machine prior to a dynamic jump. Specifically, whenever a function is invoked, the state of the machine is saved by pushing the processor registers on the stack along with bookkeeping items associated with the machine state (e.g., the current stack top pointer and return address for code execution). The result is a clean processor that is ready to execute the called function.

Each logical memory segment on a stack that is associated with an instance of a function is called a "frame." After a function has finished executing, the variables belonging to the previous function are popped off the stack and placed back in the processor; this effectively moves the function frame from the stack to the processor registers and status words. The return pointer is removed from the stack when a function exits; this pointer gives the address where execution resumes after the function has terminated. Thus, the execution sequence relies on the integrity of the stack. Corrupting the stack can cause a processor to execute unintended code, process invalid data or crash. Interested readers are referred to [8] for a discussion of stack-based buffer overflow exploits in von Neumann architectures.

The memory organization for an executing program is also dependent on the operating system and compiler. For instance, in an IA32 Linux system (von Neumann architecture), the executable code of a process usually starts at memory location 0x08000000 and the stack begins at 0xBFFFFFFF and grows downward in memory [10]. Note, however, that the actual starting locations vary for different IA32 Linux versions.

Many environments, such as multitasking operating systems, use virtual memory systems to simplify the execution environment. The resulting "virtual address space" creates the illusion that each process can access the entire address space without interfering with other processes. These systems may complicate the physical memory organization, but simplify the operation of the stack from the point of view of an executing process. Virtual memory is not discussed in this paper because it is typically not supported by Harvard architectures.

3.   Harvard Architecture

The Harvard architecture is prevalent in small devices and embedded systems, but is relatively rare in higher capacity systems due to the cost of incorporating large amounts of integrated CPU memory. Harvard class microprocessors are used for low-power, high-reliability embedded applications such as microcontrollers, sensors and actuators. Examples include vehicle engine controllers, flight systems, mobile communication systems and remote sensing equipment. Embedded control devices are ubiquitous in critical infrastructure components and are becoming increasing common in consumer products. Security research, however, has historically focused on desktop and server environments, and has only recently turned its attention to embedded systems.

This paper focuses on the Intel 8051 Harvard class microprocessor [14]. Introduced by Intel in 1980 as a logical extension to its 8048 microprocessor, the Intel 8051 exemplifies all the characteristics of a Harvard class processor – a comparatively small instruction word, small program space and a minuscule data space. The original chip contains 4 KB of ROM and 128 bytes of RAM, both integrated into the chip.

We use the C8051F530 embedded system development kit from Silicon Laboratories, which is based on the Intel 8051 architecture. The development kit contains a complete board with an interface to the processor, several output ports and a Keil C compiler for the Intel 8051. The board also contains a JTAG port that provides direct access to ROM and RAM during processor execution (primarily for debugging purposes). The JTAG-based debugging system enables programmers to inspect the machine state during execution and to view the entire RAM contents. The board also contains an integrated universal asynchronous receiver transmitter (UART) that communicates with the processor and delivers data to the running program.

4.   Stack Frames

As described earlier, the stack frame associated with a function call contains critical data that describes the status of the function and the flow of execution. The data placed in a frame is dependent on the programming language, operating system and compiler that are involved. The return pointer is a critical piece of data that is placed on the stack prior to each function call. The stack frame is an ideal location for the return pointer because each frame is associated with a single instance of a function. Compilers may store variables, processor registers and function parameters differently within a frame, but all compilers save the return pointer on the stack in some form or another.

The organization of stack frames is relatively consistent in compilers for von Neumann machines; however, compilers designed for Harvard architectures (e.g., Keil 8051 C compiler) organize stack frames in a non-conventional manner

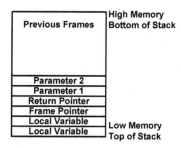

Figure 3. von Neumann stack organization.

[9]. Specifically, the Keil C compiler attempts to pre-allocate the stack space required for function calls. The stack frames built by Keil C are minimal and do not reside on top of the stack (unlike frames built by a GNU C compiler, for example [13]). Instead, Keil C frames exist lower in the stack and below the global variables. A frame pointer associated with a function call does not reside within a frame, but is instead pushed to the top of the stack.

The basic frame structure follows the order of operations outlined by a processor function call. Most modern processors automatically push the return pointer on the stack when a CALL instruction is encountered. The compiler must then produce a function header that saves the other processor registers. This task is left to the compiler instead of being integrated within the CALL instruction so that intelligent optimization routines can reduce the number of pushes and pops if registers are not needed during function execution.

Figure 3 presents an example of a frame produced by the GNU C compiler executing on an IA32 processor. Note that the first items pushed on the stack before a function call are the function parameters (placed on the stack by the calling function). The next items are the return pointer and the frame pointer of the previous function (note, however, that not all compilers and processors store the frame pointer). The last items placed on the stack are the local variables of the function.

It is important to note that, because the stack for the IA32 architecture starts in high memory and grows down, contiguous writes to local variables (e.g., a character array) begin writing in low memory and progress to high memory towards the locations of the return pointer and frame pointer. For example, the strcpy() function (which copies one array to another) creates a buffer overflow vulnerability in the IA32 architecture by overwriting the return pointer and causing the processor to return to a location different from what was intended. Exploit writers use such a misdirected return to gain control of an executing machine, essentially by modifying the execution path of a program.

Not all compilers and processors store the frame pointer. Harvard architectures produce a frame that is organized differently from that produced by a von Neumann machine. Early Harvard architectures rarely stored the frame pointer because the data space was small enough to preclude the need for additional reference points. Moreover, since the stack is in a separate address space, it

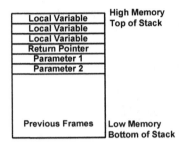

Figure 4. Harvard stack organization.

can begin at low memory and grow into high memory – the direction of stack growth is opposite to that for a von Neumann machine.

Figure 4 shows a typical frame in a Harvard architecture. The structure is similar to that of a von Neumann machine frame (with local variables on top of the stack). However, because a Harvard architecture stack grows from low memory to high memory, contiguous writes are made in the same direction as stack growth and, thus, do not approach the return pointer in the frame. As a result, it is impossible to overwrite a return pointer through a typical buffer overflow, except when the return pointers are placed above the local variables.

5.   Buffer Overflow Exploits

Exploiting a buffer overflow vulnerability requires an intimate knowledge of stack behavior, execution procedures and the programming environment. The stack frame organization is especially significant because variables that are critical to the continued operation of a function may have to be overwritten to get to the targeted address. The change in the direction of stack growth in a Harvard architecture creates a more complex exploit environment because the buffer overflow moves away from the return pointer instead of towards it.

This section describes the process of overwriting a return pointer via a buffer overflow and examines how the process differs for the Harvard and von Neumann architectures. Our experiments used the C8051F530 development kit for the Intel 8051 microprocessor along with the Keil C compiler. The Keil C compiler employs several defensive techniques for inhibiting buffer overflow, which will be discussed in more detail later in this paper.

A simple terminal application connected to the UART (called the "Echo" program) was used to explore buffer overflows. The Echo program incorporates a UART and hardware timer drivers along with interface functions for gathering and sending data to the UART. The UART driver is an interrupt-driven system that transfers data to and from the UART port asynchronously. A simple echo routine is used to pull data from the UART buffers as a string terminated by a newline character. The function that pulls strings from the UART is similar to the `getline()` function in the GNU C library. After a complete string has been input, the string is copied into another buffer using the `strcpy()` function

```
Function func{
    char buff1[32];
    char buff2[16];
    while(1){
        ...
        GetStringFromUART(buff1);
        strcpy(buff2, buff1);
        PutStringToUART(buff2);
        ...
    }
}
```

Figure 5. Echo program pseudocode.

and the new buffer is sent back to the terminal. If a user were to connect to the embedded device through a terminal program (e.g., HyperTerminal), the program would simply display what the user types.

The GNU C library `strcpy()` function was implemented as a known vector for buffer overrun exploits because it insecurely copies one array to another – it does not perform any bounds checking. Interested readers are referred to [8] for a complete list of C library vulnerabilities and to [7] for a comparison of vulnerability detection tools.

Our Echo program uses a `func()` function to create two buffers of different sizes and then invokes `strcpy()` to insecurely copy data from a larger buffer to a smaller buffer – a classic coding error. The Echo program also contains an orphaned function, `owned()`, which continuously echoes the string "owned!" to the UART. The `owned()` function is considered to be orphaned because it is not called by any other function and is unreachable via normal execution paths. Our test program uses a stack-based buffer overflow to redirect the execution of the Echo program from `func()` to `owned()`. Once the redirection occurs, execution never exits `owned()`, and an endless stream of "owned!" text is produced, which indicates that the exploit is successful.

Figure 5 shows the Echo program. Variables `buff1` and `buff2` are defined as global space for arrays of size 32 and size 16, respectively. Thus, a buffer of size 32 is copied to a buffer of size 16 without bounds checking. The result is that up to 15 bytes of data can be written beyond the bounds of `buff2` on the stack plus a null terminator. The overwritten data can contain important control identifiers that dictate the flow of execution and data passed to other functions. As shown in Figure 3, a successful buffer overflow in the frame of a von Neumann machine enables an attacker to access all the variables defined after the buffer along with the return pointers and frames located deeper in the stack. The exact opposite is true for Harvard architectures. The reversed direction of code growth means that an attacker has access only to the data defined after the overflowed buffer. Note, however, that subtle nuances in stack implementation may create exploitable vulnerabilities.

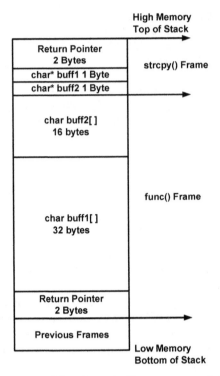

Figure 6. Mapping a buffer overrun exploit.

In general, it is relatively difficult to successfully gain control of a process without causing an illegal instruction or reference to unallocated memory. Figure 6 shows a stack representation (similar to the GNU C compiler) for the Atmega AVR, which is also a Harvard architecture. The global variables are placed at the base of the stack before any functions are allocated.

Note that strcpy() is called by func() and is passed two parameters with the addresses of the source (buff1) and destination (buff2) buffers. The strcpy() function repeatedly references the parameters within its frame during the copying process; thus, any corruption of the values causes the function to write data to incorrect locations. In order to gain control of the process, an attacker must write a value into the two bytes containing the return pointer for strcpy(). This causes strcpy() to return to a location of the attacker's choosing (in our case, the orphaned function that repeatedly outputs "owned!"). The challenge is to get to the location of the return pointer without corrupting the parameters passed to strcpy() by including the proper values for the two parameters in the source buffer. The overflow writes valid data to the two parameters used by strcpy(); the overwritten parameters must contain the correct values that allow strcpy() to proceed normally and successfully write to the memory locations containing the return pointer.

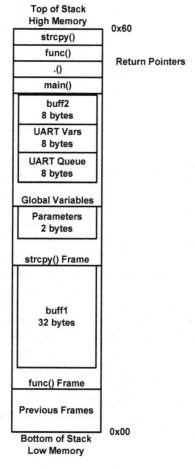

Figure 7. Stack structure of Echo program.

Figure 6 suggests that a Harvard architecture that places the return address on top of the stack should be easy to exploit. However, this is difficult in practice because of the efforts taken by compiler writers to organize memory effectively. The Keil C compiler for the Intel 8051 is an excellent example of a non-standard stack arrangement devised to simplify the use of limited RAM [9]. The Keil C compiler does not include return pointers in stack frames, but instead rearranges global variables in a way that essentially pre-allocates space for function variables. It moves the global variables towards the top of the stack, above the space where local function variables reside and, instead of placing return pointers inside stack frames, aggregates them at the very top of the stack above the global variables. Thus, stack frames constructed by the Keil C compiler are not reentrant.

Figure 7 shows the actual stack mapping for the Echo program. Because of the arrangement of global variables by the Keil C compiler, an overflow of buff2 allows direct access to the return pointers. An attacker can directly access the uppermost return pointer without regard for the other return pointers that may be destroyed – this is because the uppermost return pointer is the first to be loaded. In fact, the attacker can gain immediate control merely by loading the uppermost return pointer with a valid location.

6.   Exploit Payloads

As described above, it is possible to conduct a successful exploit on a Harvard architecture embedded system. However, the "payload" of the exploit is an issue that deserves consideration. Specifically, what would an attacker hope to execute that is not already in the ROM of the embedded system? Developing a "worthwhile" exploit is more difficult than in a traditional von Neumann architecture where the processor makes no distinction between data and code.

An exploit on a von Neumann system can deliver custom code within the overflow string and jump to that code, enabling the attacker to insert functionality that was never present in the original program. At first glance, this does not seem possible in a Harvard architecture because the code is "frozen" in ROM or flash memory, and the processor only manipulates data in the data address space. The memory separation effectively eliminates the ability of an attacker to inject custom code into the execution stream. The attacker must instead use the functionality already present in the system. However, there are some well-researched analogs to building an effective payload for Harvard architectures. For example, it is possible to create a buffer overflow that performs a `return-to-libc` attack, which then injects entirely new code into the data segment of an Atmega based wireless sensor [5].

Non-executable stacks have been implemented in BSD, Linux, Solaris and Windows Vista as a method for combating exploits. Such an implementation requires the processor to permit memory segments to be designated as non-executable (newer X86 processors and processors belonging to the SPARC family support this feature). A non-executable stack is constructed by setting the no-execute (NX) bit for the appropriate memory segments. When a memory segment has the NX bit set, the processor refuses to execute data as instructions in the memory segment. The result is a Harvard-like memory organization where a section of memory is designated as non-executable data space. While the address spaces are not entirely separate, the characteristics of the two segments in memory loosely equate to the program and data address spaces encountered in the Harvard architecture.

Attackers have developed methods for defeating non-executable memory segments by utilizing available functionality. Specifically, instead of pushing custom instructions into the machine, execution is directed to pre-existing functionality. The strategy of using existing code to circumvent no-execute protection is leveraged in a `return-to-libc` attack [12]. This type of attack manipulates the stack so that it is intact and functional when the return pointer redirects execution to a function within the program. Exploit writers have used the `return-to-libc` attack to cause programs to invoke remote shells, download toolkits and execute commands on a host system even when the system has non-executable memory enabled. The `return-to-libc` attack is analogous to identifying functionality within the data space of a Harvard class machine and causing the program to return to the desired functionality with the stack in a valid state. An example is redirecting execution to an update routine used to change data in embedded system memory. The routine is already present in the machine; however, clever manipulation of the stack enables the attacker to upload a new ROM image of his/her choosing.

7.   Defense Techniques

Several techniques have been devised to guard against buffer overflows, most of them involve strict bounds checking or surrounding buffers with verifiable values. The values placed on the stack are called "canaries" (from the old practice of using birds to detect deadly gas in coal mines). To detect an overflow, a variable with a known value is placed before and after the variables in a stack frame. If an overflow occurs, the variable placed after the buffer is overwritten and its value is, therefore, altered. Before the executing function exits, it checks the value of this canary variable. The program is terminated if the value has changed, thwarting an attempt at forcing a redirected function return.

Several canary implementations have been devised. Systems used in von Neumann architectures, such as the randomized canaries employed by Stack-Guard [3] and ProPolice [13], protect stack frames and mitigate attacks that redirect execution. StackGuard modifies the GNU C compiler so that an integer value is inserted just before the return pointer in each stack frame and another copy of the integer is placed before the local variables. Comparing the two values before function return helps determine if an overflow has occurred, at which point the program is terminated. ProPolice, used in BSD and the GNU C version 4.1 compiler, incorporates a traditional random canary system and reorganizes the placement of variables within frames. By reorganizing variables and placing buffers at the beginning of frames, the compiler makes it more difficult to overwrite return pointers without destroying critical data.

Canary systems are not limited to protecting entire frames and detecting overflows. The Keil C compiler prevents overflows from occurring by performing a bounds check on every write to a buffer; this involves an integrity check of the null byte located at the end of the buffer. To accomplish this, the compiler translates array assignments into complete function calls that perform the bounds check and determine if the write is allowed. This method works well for null terminated strings. However, if a program allows nulls to be written to a buffer, an attacker can simply write a null byte to the location of the check value. The check routine would interpret the null value as an intact canary and permit the write. While this method is effective for simple character array operations and null terminated strings, it is not appropriate for all systems. The Keil C canary method also dramatically increases the overhead of write operations. A normal translation of an array write produces five to seven machine instructions. Since the Keil C compiler translates the array operation into a complete function call, it produces ten to fifteen instructions, including several (slow) memory operations.

Mitigating overflows using canaries comes with a significant performance penalty. The security of a randomized canary is based on the statistical improbability of correctly guessing its value; this requires the invocation of a random number generation routine, which takes time. Canary values also consume stack space and require extra instructions to be executed before and after function calls. Other canary systems that protect individual buffers instead of entire frames involve considerable overhead. Small systems that rely on buffered input/output can be dramatically slowed by the decreased speed of operations on buffers. Interestingly, the Keil C compiler is targeted specifically at small embedded systems, which are usually input/output driven and rely on fast asynchronous interaction with external devices.

8.   Conclusions

Stack-based buffer overflow vulnerabilities existing in the Harvard architecture can be exploited in much the same manner as in von Neumann systems. However, the process of exploiting a vulnerability is tricky, and delivering or identifying an exploit payload can be relatively complicated.

The memory management model used in the Harvard architecture changes the direction of writes in relation to stack growth; this simplifies the task of obtaining control of the instruction path. Memory space limitations may require compiler writers to be frugal with stack allocation, often leading to the clustering of key variables. In the case of the Keil C compiler, the non-standard placement of global variables permits direct access to the complete list of return pointers, which actually simplifies the exploit. The separation of data and program space in the Harvard architecture limits the ability of an attacker to inject operational code, but it does not limit the ability to redirect execution. Once an attacker has control of execution, he/she can find code to execute as in the case of a `return-to-libc` attack. Embedded systems commonly have the ability to dynamically update their code. The dynamic update systems are used for remote patching, feature updates and general fixes. Such a system can be exploited, for example, by using a buffer overflow to enter an update routine and then introduce unauthorized code into the embedded device.

Exploit writers have traditionally focused on powerful desktop and server systems, but attackers are increasingly targeting smaller devices, including embedded systems based on the Harvard architecture. Generalized protection mechanisms such as canaries are effective, but come with significant overhead that can impact the real-time performance of embedded systems, especially those used to control critical infrastructure assets.

Acknowledgements

This research was partially supported by NSF Scholarship for Service (SFS) Grant DUE 0621348.

References

[1] Aleph One, Smashing the stack for fun and profit, *Phrack*, vol. 49(14), 1996.

[2] J. Anderson, Computer Security Technology Planning Study, ESD-TR-73-51, Vol. 1, Deputy for Command and Management Systems, HQ Electronic Systems Division, United States Air Force, Hanscom Field, Bedford, Massachusetts, 1972.

[3] C. Cowan, C. Pu, D. Maier, J. Walpole, P. Burke, S. Beattie, A. Grier, P. Wagle and Q. Zhang, StackGuard: Automatic adaptive detection and prevention of buffer overflow attacks, *Proceedings of the Seventh USENIX Security Symposium*, pp. 63–78, 1998.

[4] S. Eisenbach, *Functional Programming: Languages, Tools and Architectures*, Ellis Horwood, Chichester, United Kingdom, 1987.

[5] A. Francillon and C. Castelluccia, Code injection attacks on Harvard-architecture devices, *Proceedings of the Fifteenth ACM Conference on Computer and Communications Security*, pp. 15–26, 2008.

[6] Q. Gu and R. Noorani, Towards self-propagate mal-packets in sensor networks, *Proceedings of the First ACM Conference on Wireless Network Security*, pp. 172–182, 2008.

[7] N. Hanebutte and P. Oman, An evaluation of static source code analyzers for automated vulnerability detection, *Proceedings of the Ninth IASTED International Conference on Software Engineering and Applications*, pp. 112–117, 2005.

[8] N. Hanebutte and P. Oman, Software vulnerability mitigation as a proper subset of software maintenance, *Journal of Software Maintenance and Evolution*, vol. 17(6), pp. 379–400, 2006.

[9] Hitex, C51 Primer: An Introduction to the Use of the Keil C51 Compiler on the 8051 Family, Coventry, United Kingdom (www.hitex.com/fileadmin/img/download/c51_primer_290404.pdf), 2004.

[10] J. Koziol, D. Litchfield, D. Aitel, C. Anley, S. Eren, N. Mehta and R. Hassell, *The Shellcoder's Handbook*, Wiley, Indianapolis, Indiana, 2004.

[11] D. Seeley, A tour of the worm, *Proceedings of the Winter USENIX Conference*, pp. 287–304, 1989.

[12] Solar Designer, `return to-libc attack`, *Bugtraq*, 1997.

[13] R. Stallman, Using the GNU Compiler Collection, GNU Press, Boston, Massachusetts (gcc.gnu.org/onlinedocs/gcc-4.3.3/gcc.pdf), 2003.

[14] J. Waclawek, The unofficial history of 8051 (www.efton.sk/t0t1/history8051.pdf), 1996.

[15] W. Wolf, *Computers as Components: Principles of Embedded Computing System Design*, Morgan Kaufmann, San Diego, California, 2001.

Chapter 14

SECURE CROSS-DOMAIN TRAIN SCHEDULING

Mark Hartong, Rajni Goel and Duminda Wijesekera

Abstract   Track configurations at cross-domain interchange points, train performance characteristics and cross-domain authentication often produce significant train delays that can impact large segments of a railroad network. This paper presents a model that captures the behavior of trains and the track infrastructure. The model enables railroad signal engineers to quickly estimate the required trust management system performance that will support safe, secure and efficient railroad operations.

Keywords: Railroads, trains, cross-domain scheduling, security

1.   Introduction

Railroads are a major component of the U.S. transportation infrastructure. According to the Association of American Railroads [2], more than 1.7 trillion ton-miles of freight was transported by rail in 2007.

Unlike other transportation modes, trains operate with a single degree of freedom. They are constrained to travel on a single track and are unable to pass other trains operating on the same track except where there are sidings.

Since the early 1820s, various methods for scheduling, dispatching and controlling cross-domain train operations have been devised. These range from simple systems to complex stochastic models that optimize asset locations, times of movement and paths through the rail network. However, the operations research community has largely ignored the issue of cross-domain trust management system performance when trains reach an interchange point. With the implementation of secure positive train control (PTC) [17] in the U.S. railroad system, cross-domain scheduling, train movement and authority management must all work in concert.

This paper proposes a deterministic model that provides railroad signal engineers with the ability to quickly estimate the required trust management

C. Palmer and S. Shenoi (Eds.): Critical Infrastructure Protection III, IFIP AICT 311, pp. 199–211, 2009.
© IFIP International Federation for Information Processing 2009

system performance, while precluding train-to-train collisions and optimizing traffic flow at an interchange. The solution facilitates cost containment, a critical consideration for U.S. railroad companies.

2.　　Related Work

Several algorithmic approaches for position, scheduling and routing optimization have been developed since the mid 1970s [5, 9, 37]. These approaches and others have been incorporated in computer dispatch systems from major suppliers such as Alstom, Advanced Railway Concepts, Digital Concepts, GE Transportation, Siemens and Anslado STS. However, details of these systems are proprietary and the exact mechanisms they use for position, scheduling and routing optimization are not known to the research community. Despite the lack of information, it is safe to assume that the proprietary systems engage exact, heuristic and simulation strategies similar to those described by Sutewong [39].

Global visibility of the rail network and rail traffic enables dispatchers to discern bottlenecks in advance, permitting traffic to be rerouted securely, safely and efficiently. This contributes to an increase in overall system velocity (average rate at which trains move through the network) and, consequently, an increase in railroad network throughput. The improved utilization directly translates to cost savings for railroad companies and consumers.

While the positioning problem associated with freight and passenger trains is similar, there are significant differences in the scheduling and routing problems. Passenger service is constrained to fixed schedules and constant routes. Freight service, on the other hand, does not have these restrictions. Since railroad routing is a highly constrained network optimization problem that has confounded traditional optimization methods, we limit the scope of our analysis. No attempts will be made to develop new or improved dispatching methodologies or to examine complex network topologies. Instead, we consider only a single line of track approaching an interchange point with no other topological additions (including merging or branching routes) other than a single siding track off the main line. This enables us to consider the track connecting the railroads through the interchange point as a "single track railroad." Several approaches (e.g., [12, 16, 22–24, 30, 31, 33, 34, 36]) can then be used to minimize the impact of delays.

The security of rail networks and the integration of trust management systems have been the subject of several research efforts (see, e.g., [8, 10, 15, 18–21, 44]). However, these efforts have not made significant progress in integrating secure train control and scheduling or providing railroad signal engineers with the ability to evaluate performance and ensure safe train operations.

3.　　Interchange and Cross-Domain Operations

Determining a global solution to the dispatch problem requires the consideration of cross-domain security mechanisms. This is complicated by the structure of the United States rail industry. Since railroad companies are distinct commercial entities, they have separate dispatch, scheduling and trust management systems in their respective domains. These differences are most pronounced at interchanges – fixed, geographically-dispersed points where the tracks belonging to one railroad company interconnect with the tracks of another company, and where crews, locomotives and consists are exchanged. Secure exchanges between domains require the ability of the dispatcher in each domain to authenticate the communicating entities and to ensure message integrity.

Before a train can be authorized to pass from one railroad domain to another, the following two activities must occur:

- The train and the crew leaving the first domain for the second domain must be authenticated before a movement authority can be granted by a dispatcher to allow the cross-domain movement.

- Track space must be available to allow the issuance of the movement authority.

For a train moving from one domain to another, delays in the authentication process will delay the granting of the current movement authority as well as subsequent movement authorities. This, in turn, will delay the scheduled movement of subsequent trains. Minimizing or eliminating authentication delays reduces delays in the granting and issuance of movement authorities, which, in turn, reduces traffic delays.

Our choice of unidirectional analysis is deliberate. In high traffic density areas, where large volumes of rail traffic are exchanged between domains, multiple main tracks are often used at the interchange point, with one main track carrying traffic from Domain A to Domain B and a second main track carrying traffic from Domain B to Domain A. Each main track can, therefore, be analyzed as a separate unidirectional track. Single main tracks used for interchange points are generally found on low density lines, where the directional movement of cross-domain traffic is spatially and temporally separated to minimize the numbers of meets and passes; this reduces the number and size of expensive sidings. High degrees of spatial and temporal separation also permit the cross-domain analysis to be treated as unidirectional.

3.1   Interchange Movement

Figure 1 shows two railroad companies (Railroad A and Railroad B) that have a common interchange point. The trains can belong to any company. Train 1 (T_X), Train 2 (T_{X+1}) and Train 3 (T_{X+2}) through Train N (T_{X+N}) are moving sequentially along tracks operated by Railroad A to the interchange point. The movement of train T_X requires the possession of a valid movement authority (M_X) from the dispatcher (DS). In the situation involving a single main track with a single siding, four possible situations may be encountered by T_{X+1} that follows T_X:

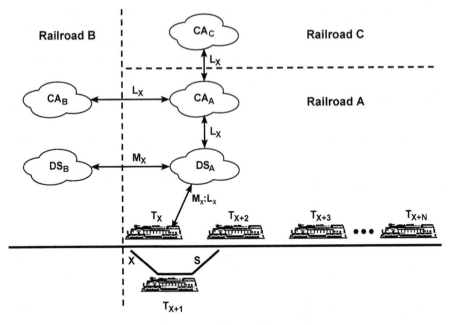

Figure 1. Railroad interchange point.

- **The main track and siding are clear:** In this situation, T_{X+1} may take the main track or siding and proceed to the interchange point without any delay.

- **The main track is clear and the siding is blocked:** In this situation, T_{X+1} may take the main track and proceed to the interchange point without any delay.

- **The main track is blocked and the siding is clear:** In this situation, T_{X+1} may take the siding and proceed to the interchange point without any delay.

- **The main track and siding are blocked:** In this situation, T_{X+1} may have to wait until the main track or siding are clear in order to proceed to the interchange point.

If T_X is already at the limits of its movement authority M_X at the interchange point, then T_X stops and remains stopped until a new authority to proceed is received. To preclude a train-to-train collision between the head of T_{X+1} and the tail of T_X, T_{X+1} must receive a notification to stop before it proceeds beyond the safe stopping distance BD_{X+1}. The movement of subsequent trains such as T_{X+2}, T_{X+3} ...T_{X+N} must then be rescheduled to preclude collisions and the overrun of their authority limits as necessary.

A delay of T_X at the interchange point is mitigated by the availability of Siding S. If the train dispatcher DS_A for Railroad A is aware in advance of an authentication delay associated with T_X, the dispatcher could direct T_X to Siding S, allowing T_{X+1} to proceed along the main line to the interchange point. However, even if the dispatcher was able to safely divert T_X to Siding S, any delay of T_{X+1} at the interchange point would still delay $T_{X+2} \ldots T_{X+N}$.

The cross-domain delay is the sum of the propagation delay between the dispatchers, the processing time required by the communicating entities and the authentication delay that results from the additional overhead associated with the transmission of data required for cross-domain certification and integrity. The propagation and processing delays are fixed and unavoidable, being functions of the media through which the data is transmitted. The authentication delay, however, is a function of the security protocols used to provide cross-domain certification.

The two most commonly-used protocols in the railroad industry are ATCS-200 and TCP/IP that operate in the 40 MHz, 160 MHz or 220 MHz radio-frequency bands. ATCS-200 is a railroad-specific communications protocol designed by the Association of American Railroads as part of the Advanced Train Control System (the precursor to PTC). TCP/IP is the standard TCP/IP v4 (RFC 793) or v6 (RFC 2460).

ATCS and TCP/IP follow the classical three-way handshake to establish and terminate connections over possibly unreliable links. The three-way handshake begins by A initiating a connection by sending a message to B. Next, B responds with an acknowledgment. At this point, A sends another message to B confirming that A received B's acknowledgment. The connection between A and B is established when B receives the second message from A that confirms the acknowledgement from B. Each protocol has its own set of vulnerabilities and countermeasures [4, 11].

3.2 Cross-Domain Certification

Entry into Domain B is controlled by Dispatcher B. Dispatcher B must approve a movement authority M_X for train T_X. The request for M_X and the response of Dispatcher B are routed through Dispatcher A (of Domain A). Prior to accepting the request for M_X, the authenticity of T_X and the integrity of the request must be verified to the satisfaction of Dispatcher B. This is accomplished by pre-establishing a trust relationship between the certificate authorities of Domain A (CA_A) and Domain B (CA_B) and Dispatcher A and Dispatcher B. Before it begins operations, train T_X is assigned a certificate L_X via a separate secure channel.

The movement authority authentication process for T_X (shown in Figure 2) begins when T_X submits an M_X request to Dispatcher A. This process is described in Algorithm 1.

The algorithm assumes that Dispatchers A and B have established a secure trust relationship. Based on the response from Dispatcher B, Dispatcher A determines the appropriate moves of T_X as well as moves of subsequent trains

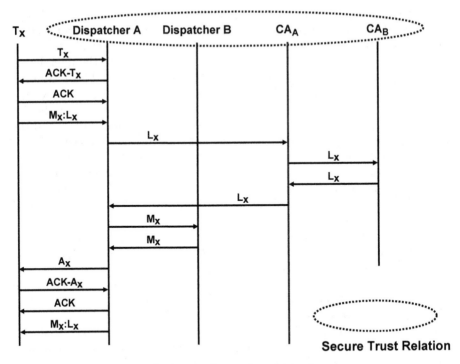

Figure 2. Authentication and authorization process.

$T_{X+1} \dots T_{X+N}$. The total delay time associated with authentication and authority issuance is the time elapsed from when M_X is submitted to Dispatcher A to when the approved or disapproved M_X is received by T_X.

The cross-domain authentication and authority process uses open wireless networks to relay data. This exposes the process to a variety of network attacks, which may be classified as passive or active. Passive attacks involve the surreptitious gathering of information, which may facilitate more serious (active) attacks. Active attacks, which specifically target data transmission, can have an immediate impact on cross-domain operations.

Active attacks often involve denial-of-service. Additionally, they may involve an exploitation attempt associated with the sender (identity theft, where an unauthorized user adopts the identity of a valid sender); a weakness associated with the receiver (malicious association, where an unsuspecting sender is tricked into believing that a communications session has been established with a valid receiver); or a weakness associated with the communication path (man-in-the-middle attack, where the attacker emulates the authorized receiver for the sender – the malicious assertion, and emulates the authorized transmitter for the authorized sender – identity theft). These attacks are primarily geared at disrupting integrity in the form of user authentication (assurance that the party is who it says it is); data origin authentication (assurance that the data

---

Algorithm 1 : Movement Authority Authentication Algorithm.

Grant Authority ()
begin

      Dispatcher A and Train T_X authenticate each other;

      T_X signs M_X using L_X;

      T_X submits $M_X{:}L_X$ to Dispatcher A;

      Dispatcher A submits L_X to Certificate Authority CA_Y;

      repeat

            Certificate Authority CA_Y validates L_X or

            Certificate Authority CA_Y queries next Certificate Authority;

      until L_X is validated or no more Certificate Authorities remain to query;

      if L_X is valid then

            Dispatcher A submits M_X to Dispatcher B;

            Dispatcher B approves or disapproves M_X;

            Dispatcher B returns M_X to Dispatcher A;

            Dispatcher A and Train T_X authenticate each other;

            Dispatcher A signs M_X with its certificate L_A;

            Dispatcher A submits $M_X{:}L_A$ to T_X;

            if M_X authorizes the move then

                  T_X executes M_X

            else T_X does not move;

      else Dispatcher A disapproves M_X;

end

---

came from where it says it did); and data integrity (assurance that the data has not been modified). Countermeasures implemented for these attacks add additional time delays.

The simple model presented in this paper does not describe the mechanisms used to prevent or mitigate the numerous wireless attacks to which the cross-domain authority and issuance process is susceptible. In general, protection against attacks on message integrity is achieved using cryptographic hash functions. Any input modification would produce a different hash value, which would be detected by the receiver when the computed hash value is not equal to the received hash value.

Protection against identity attacks involves the application of authentication mechanisms that provide accountability for user actions and are considered in terms of user authentication and data origin authentication. User authentication involves the corroboration of the identity of the originator in real time, while data origin authentication involves the corroboration of the source of the data (but provides no timeliness guarantees). User authentication methods range from time-invariant methods such as weak passwords to time-variant cryptographic methods. Data origin authentication provides assurances regarding both integrity and authentication, which rely on the use of symmetric or asymmetric digital signatures.

3.3   Authentication Delays

The potential for a collision between trains T_{X+1} and T_X is affected by the velocity of T_{X+1}, time of release of T_X, communication and processing delays associated with information exchanges between CA_A and CA_B, processing delays for dispatchers DS_A and DS_B, and PTC system processing times PTC_A and PTC_B. The velocity V_{X+1} of train T_{X+1} directly affects its safe stopping distance BD_{X+1}. As V_{X+1} increases, BD_{X+1} increases, requiring greater separation of trains T_X and T_{X+1} to preclude a collision. Stopping distances for various types of (freight and passenger) trains have been studied extensively (see, e.g., [3, 25, 35]).

Commercial tools are available for calculating safe braking distances and can be integrated with dispatch system behavior. The tools include the RailSim Train Performance Calculator (TPC) from Systra Consulting and the Train Operation and Energy Simulator (TOES) from the Association of American Railroads. The models used by the tools are quite complex and account for variables such as rail friction, engine latency, in-train forces, track geometry, brake pipe propagation and blended braking. However, these tools are expensive, which limits their availability. Accordingly, we adopt a simplified braking model to illustrate the basic concepts.

The simplified model assumes a straight and level track, but otherwise reflects the same variables that are used in [43] to predict braking distances for the European Train Control System (ETCS) system. The work in [43] is an improvement over the predictive braking curves based on the International Union of Railways (UIC) 546 Standard [6]. A similar U.S. standard [26] is currently under development. Efforts are underway to develop braking algorithms that model track geometry and consist behavior more realistically (see, e.g., [14, 28, 29, 38, 40, 45, 46]).

In order to prevent delays, either the siding or the main track must be clear prior to the arrival of a following train. The authentication delays for a train occupying a siding or mainline block and the clearance time for the train to clear the block must be less than or equal to the time it takes for a following train to cover its braking distance, i.e.,

$$Authentication\ Delay + Time\ to\ Clear\ T_X \leq Time\ to\ Stop\ T_{X+1} \qquad (1)$$

The term *Time to Clear* T_X (t_{Clear}) is computed as:

$$t_{Clear} = \sqrt{\frac{2(L_f - L_s)}{a_{Clear}}} \qquad (2)$$

where L_f is the final location of the tail of train T_X (i.e, the interchange point); L_s is the starting location of the tail of T_X; $L_f - L_s$ is the length of T_X; and a_{Clear} is the acceleration of T_X.

The acceleration a_{Clear} is given by:

$$a_{Clear} = \frac{F - R}{M} \qquad (3)$$

where F is the tractive force of the locomotives of T_X in lbs/ton; R is the resistance of T_X in ft lbs; and M is the mass of a train car in T_X in tons.

The value of R, which expresses the resistive force, is estimated using the Davis Equation. This equation was originally developed in the mid 1920s for estimating locomotive resistance. The resistance R (lbs/ton) is currently estimated using the new version of the equation, which was created in the 1970s [26]:

$$R = 0.6 + \frac{20}{w} + 0.01V + \frac{KV^2}{wn} \tag{4}$$

where w is the weight of the train per number of axles; V is the velocity in mph; K is a drag coefficient, which has a value of 0.07 when the train is accelerating; and n is the number of axles.

The safe stopping distance is the point ahead of the target that an oncoming train T_{X+1} must begin to brake in order to preclude a collision with the rear of train T_X. This point, denoted by L_b, where the braking of T_{X+1} begins is computed as:

$$L_b = L_h + Vt + \frac{1}{2}Ka_{Stop}t^2 \tag{5}$$

where L_h is the location at which the head of train T_{X+1} is stopped (i.e., the interchange point); V is the initial velocity of T_{X+1}; t is the duration of the deceleration of T_{X+1}; K is the deceleration factor, which is equal to 1.4667; and a_{Stop} is the deceleration of T_{X+1}.

The deceleration a_{Stop} is given by:

$$a_{Stop} = \frac{F + R}{M} \tag{6}$$

where F is the braking force of the consist cars of T_{X+1} in lbs/ton; R is the resistance of T_{X+1} in ft lbs; and M is the mass of a train car in T_{X+1} in tons.

Train T_{X+1} can continue its movement to the interchange point if the length of time taken for T_X to receive its authority and move beyond the interchange point is less than the time it takes to stop T_{X+1}. These computations support the evaluation of a worst-case traffic density scenario and minimize the chance of a signal passed at danger. Rail operations can continue safely as long as the associated trust management systems support the required intra-domain security and traffic-scheduling constraints, and sufficient track space is available.

4. Conclusions

The approach presented in this paper addresses the performance issue once authorization has been requested and received by a train waiting at the interchange point to cross domains. However, it does not address the global sequencing of trains between two domains. In general, the movement of trains within a railroad domain is not optimized for behavior at an interchange point, but rather to support the most efficient use of the domain's rail assets (cars, locomotives and track). This operations research problem has been the focus of considerable study [1, 7, 13, 27, 32, 41, 42] and is outside the scope of this work. It is necessary to construct a more general model for estimating tactical cross-domain authentication and authorization performance. The expansion and integration of tactical and strategic scheduling and routing is a logical extension of the current work. However, since a closed form solution will be unlikely, statistical techniques will have to be applied to solve the problem. Additional work is also required to integrate quality of service constraints, different train types with different operating characteristics, and more complicated track geometries.

Several implementation-related issues have not been fully addressed in this work. In an operational environment, where rail traffic is both heavy and dense, the volume of operational and environmental data that must be transmitted may exceed the communications bandwidth. The required bandwidth capabilities can only be determined in the context of the railroad operating environment and the particular implementation mechanisms. If appropriately chosen and considered in the light of organizational and environmental factors, the combination of managerial, operational and technical controls can synergistically ensure a safe, secure and interoperable rail system. Efforts in this area and in the related security requirements would provide valuable data for detailed system design and cost evaluation.

References

[1] L. Anderegg, S. Eidenbenz, M. Gantenbein, C. Stamm, D. Taylor, B. Weber and P. Widmeyer, Train routing algorithms: Concepts, design choices and practical considerations, *Proceedings of the Fifth Workshop on Algorithm Engineering and Experiments*, pp. 106–118, 2003.

[2] Association of American Railroads, Class I Railroad Statistics, Washington, DC (www.aar.org/~/media/AAR/Industry%20Info/Statistics200906 10.ashx), 2009.

[3] D. Barney, D. Haley and G. Nikandros, Calculating train braking distance, *Proceedings of the Sixth Australian Workshop on Safety Critical Systems and Software*, vol. 3, pp. 23–29, 2001.

[4] S. Bellovin, Security problems in the TCP/IP protocol suite, *ACM SIGCOMM Computer Communication Review*, vol. 19(2), pp. 32–48, 1989.

[5] A. Billionnet, Using integer programming to solve the train-platforming problem, *Transportation Science*, vol. 37(2), pp. 213–222, 2003.

[6] British Standards Institution, EN 15179: Railway Applications; Braking; Requirements for the Brake System of Passenger Coaches, Document BS 05/19984709 DC, London, United Kingdom, 2005.

[7] M. Carey and I. Crawford, Scheduling trains on a network of busy complex stations, *Transportation Research, Part B: Methodological*, vol. 41(2), pp. 159–178, 2007.

[8] A. Carlson, D. Frincke and M. Laude, Railway security issues: A survey of developing railway technology, *Proceedings of the International Conference on Computer, Communications and Control Technologies*, vol. 1, pp. 1–6, 2003.

[9] T. Crainic, J. Ferland and J. Rousseau, A tactical planning model for rail freight transportation, *Transportation Science*, vol. 18(2), pp. 165–184, 1984.

[10] C. Craven, A brief look at railroad communication vulnerabilities, *Proceedings of the Seventh IEEE Conference on Intelligent Transportation Systems*, pp. 245–249, 2004.

[11] P. Craven and A. Craven, Security of ATCS wireless railway communications, *Proceedings of the IEEE/ASME Joint Rail Conference*, pp. 227–238, 2005.

[12] A. D'Ariano, M. Pranzo and I. Hansen, Conflict resolution and train speed coordination for solving real-time timetable perturbations, *IEEE Transactions on Intelligent Transportation Systems*, vol. 8(2), pp. 208–222, 2007.

[13] M. Dessouky, Q. Lu, J. Zhao and R. Leachman, An exact solution procedure to determine the optimal dispatching times for complex rail networks, *IEE Transactions*, vol. 38(2), pp. 141–152, 2006.

[14] B. Friman, An algorithm for braking curve calculations in ERTMS train protection systems, *Proceedings of the Tenth International Conference on Computer System Design and Operation in the Railway and Other Transit Systems*, pp. 421–429, 2006.

[15] General Accounting Office, Critical Infrastructure Protection: Challenges and Efforts to Secure Control Systems, Report to Congressional Requesters, GAO-04-354, Washington, DC, 2004.

[16] S. Graff and P. Shenkin, A computer simulation of a multiple track rail network, presented at the *Sixth International Conference on Mathematical Modeling*, 1987.

[17] M. Hartong, R. Goel and D. Wijesekera, Communications-based positive train control systems architecture in the USA, *Proceedings of the Sixty-Third IEEE Vehicular Technology Conference*, vol. 6, pp. 2987–2991, 2006.

[18] M. Hartong, R. Goel and D. Wijesekera, Communications security concerns in communications-based train control, *Proceedings of the Tenth International Conference on Computer System Design and Operation in the Railway and Other Transit Systems*, pp. 693–703, 2006.

[19] M. Hartong, R. Goel and D. Wijesekera, Securing positive train control systems, in *Critical Infrastructure Protection*, E. Goetz and S. Shenoi (Eds.), Springer, Boston, Massachusetts, pp. 57–72, 2007.

[20] M. Hartong, R. Goel and D. Wijeskera, Security and the U.S. rail infrastructure, *International Journal of Critical Infrastructure Protection*, vol. 1, pp. 15–28, 2008.

[21] M. Hartong, R. Goel and D. Wijesekera, Trust-based secure positive train control (PTC), *Journal of Transportation Security*, vol. 1(4), pp. 211–268, 2008.

[22] A. Higgins and E. Kozan, Modeling train delays in urban networks, *Transportation Science*, vol. 32(4), pp. 346–357, 1998.

[23] T. Ho, J. Norton and C. Goodman, Optimal traffic control at railway junctions, *IEE Proceedings on Electric Power Applications*, vol. 144(2), pp. 140–148, 1997.

[24] T. Ho and T. Yeung, Railway junction traffic control by heuristic methods, *IEE Proceedings on Electric Power Applications*, vol. 148(1), pp. 77–84, 2001.

[25] IEEE, IEEE Standard 1474.1-2004: IEEE Standard for Communications-Based Train Control (CBTC) Performance and Functional Requirements, Piscataway, New Jersey, 2004.

[26] IEEE, Draft Guide for the Calculation of Braking Distances for Rail Transit Vehicles, IEEE Draft Document P1698/D1.3, Piscataway, New Jersey, 2008.

[27] M. Khan, D. Zhang, M. Jun and J. Zhu, An intelligent search technique for the train scheduling problem based on genetic algorithms, *Proceedings of the International Conference on Emerging Technologies*, pp. 593–598, 2006.

[28] E. Khmelnitsky, On an optimal control problem of train operation, *IEEE Transactions on Automatic Control*, vol. 45(7), pp. 1257–1266, 2000.

[29] H. Krueger, E. Vaillancourt, A. Drummie, S. Vucko and J. Bekavac, Simulation within the railroad environment, *Proceedings of the Thirty-Second Winter Simulation Conference*, pp. 1191–1200, 2000.

[30] J. Lee, K. Sheng and J. Guo, A fast and reliable algorithm for railway train routing, *Proceedings of the IEEE Region 10 Conference on Computers, Communications, Control and Power Engineering*, vol. 2, pp. 652–655, 1993.

[31] M. Lewellen and K. Tumay, Network simulation of a major railroad, *Proceedings of the Thirtieth Winter Simulation Conference*, pp. 1135–1138, 1998.

[32] F. Li, Z. Gao, K. Li and L. Yang, Efficient scheduling of railway traffic based on global information of trains, *Transportation Research, Part B: Methodological*, vol. 42(10), pp. 1008–1030, 2008.

[33] Q. Lu, M. Dessouky and R. Leachman, Modeling train movements through complex rail networks, *ACM Transactions on Modeling and Computer Simulation*, vol. 14(1), pp. 48–75, 2004.

[34] M. Lubbecke and U. Zimmermann, Engine routing and scheduling at industrial in-plant railroads, *Transportation Science*, vol. 37(2), pp. 183–197, 2003.

[35] M. Malvezzi, P. Presciani, B. Allotta and P. Toni, Probabilistic analysis of braking performance in railways, *Proceedings of the Institution of Mechanical Engineers, Part F: Journal of Rail and Rapid Transit*, vol. 217(3), pp. 149–165, 2003.

[36] D. Parkes and L. Ungar, An auction-based method for decentralized train scheduling, *Proceedings of the Fifth International Conference on Autonomous Agents*, pp. 43–50, 2001.

[37] E. Petersen, Over-the-road transit time for a single track railway, *Transportation Science*, vol. 8(1), pp. 65–74, 1974.

[38] W. Rudderham, Longitudinal control system of the intermediate capacity transit system, *Proceedings of the Thirty-Third IEEE Vehicular Technology Conference*, pp. 183–190, 1983.

[39] W. Sutewong, Algorithms for Solving the Train Dispatching Problem for General Networks, Ph.D. Dissertation, Department of Industrial and Systems Engineering, University of Southern California, Los Angeles, California, 2006.

[40] H. Takeuchi, C. Goodman and S. Sone, Moving block signaling dynamics: Performance measures and re-starting queued electric trains, *IEE Proceedings on Electric Power Applications*, vol. 150(8), pp. 483–492, 2003.

[41] A. Tazoniero, R. Goncalves and F. Gomide, Decision making strategies for real-time train dispatch and control, in *Analysis and Design of Intelligent Systems Using Soft Computing Techniques*, P. Melin, O. Castillo, E. Gomez-Ramirez, J. Kacprzyk and W. Pedrycz (Eds.), Springer, Berlin-Heidelberg, pp. 195–204, 2007.

[42] J. Tornquist, Computer-based decision support for railway traffic scheduling and dispatching: A review of models, *Proceedings of the Fifth Workshop on Algorithmic Methods and Models for Optimization of Railways*, 2005.

[43] B. Vincze and G. Tarmai, Development and analysis of train brake curve calculation methods with complex simulation, *Proceedings of the Fifteenth International Exhibition of Electrical Equipment for Power Engineering, Electrical Engineering, Electronics, Energy and Resource-Saving Technologies and Household Electric Appliances*, 2006.

[44] J. Whittle, D. Wijeskera and M. Hartong, Executable misuse cases for modeling security concerns, *Proceedings of the Thirtieth International Conference on Software Engineering*, pp. 121–130, 2008.

[45] F. Yan and T. Tang, Formal modeling and verification of real-time concurrent systems, *Proceedings of the IEEE International Conference on Vehicular Electronics and Safety*, pp. 1–6, 2007.

[46] L. Zhang, P. Li, L. Jia and F. Yang, Study on the simulation for train operation adjustment under moving block, *Proceedings of the Eighth IEEE Conference on Intelligent Transportation Systems*, pp. 351–356, 2005.

IV

INFRASTRUCTURE MODELING
AND SIMULATION

Chapter 15

A HOLISTIC-REDUCTIONISTIC APPROACH FOR MODELING INTERDEPENDENCIES

Stefano De Porcellinis, Gabriele Oliva, Stefano Panzieri and Roberto Setola

Abstract   Modeling and analyzing critical infrastructures and their interdependencies are essential to discovering hidden vulnerabilities and threats. Several current approaches engage a holistic perspective and rely on abstract models; others incorporate a reductionistic perspective and focus on inter-domain and intra-domain interactions among elementary components. This paper proposes a mixed approach in which holism and reductionism coexist. A critical infrastructure is expressed at different, albeit interrelated, levels of abstraction, and intermediate entities that provide specific aggregate resources or services are introduced.

Keywords: Interdependencies, complex systems, holistic-reductionistic modeling

1.   Introduction

Infrastructures such as energy grids, transportation networks and telecommunications systems are vital to every facet of society [2]. A malfunction or disruption in any of these complex systems of systems can have serious impacts on the health, safety, security and economic well-being of citizens and on government functions [4].

In order to be effective, a critical infrastructure protection strategy requires detailed knowledge about the global behavior and intrinsic weaknesses of infrastructures and their components, especially in the presence of adverse events. Most infrastructure protection strategies leverage analysis and simulation. However, the complexity of the infrastructures [15] renders common systems analysis and simulation methodologies ineffective, especially due to the many interdependencies existing within and between infrastructures [1]. These interdependencies are often implicit, hidden and not well understood even by infrastructure owners and operators.

C. Palmer and S. Shenoi (Eds.): Critical Infrastructure Protection III, IFIP AICT 311, pp. 215–227, 2009.

Rinaldi, *et al.* [17] categorize interdependencies into four, not necessarily mutually exclusive, classes:

■ **Physical Interdependency:** Two infrastructures are physically interdependent when the operations of one infrastructure depend on the physical output(s) of the other.

■ **Cyber Interdependency:** An infrastructure has a cyber dependency if its state depends on information transmitted by means of the information infrastructure.

■ **Geographical Interdependency:** A geographical interdependency exists when elements of multiple infrastructures are in close spatial proximity. Adverse events affecting one element may generate cascading failures in one or more proximal infrastructures.

■ **Logical Interdependency:** Two infrastructures are logically interdependent when the state of one infrastructure depends on the state of the other because of control, regulatory or other mechanisms that are not physical, geographical or cyber in nature.

De Porcellinis, *et al.* [6] introduce an additional type of interdependency:

■ **Social Interdependency:** An infrastructure has a sociological interdependency when its operativeness is affected by the spreading of disorder related to human activities, i.e., the emergence and diffusion of collective behaviors that have a negative impact on the ability of the infrastructure to operate.

Nieuwenhuijs, *et al.* [14] treat only physical and functional dependencies as real dependencies; the others are viewed as common vulnerabilities that are shared by two or more infrastructures or components (and are, therefore, not considered to be dependencies). However, we believe that there is the need to represent failures and their spread in order to highlight criticalities and to identify adequate countermeasures and policies to prevent or mitigate their effects. This need derives from the fact that shared threats and propagating failures occur as a result of different mechanisms. Shared threats (e.g., an earthquake) derive from vulnerabilities that are shared due to particular conditions or properties of the elements (e.g., spatial proximity). In contrast, failures and the propagation of failures derive from direct or indirect interactions among the elements (e.g., fire is propagated from one element to other proximal elements that have "geographical" interactions with each other).

Several approaches have been introduced to address the problems posed by the complexity of infrastructures and their interdependencies. Holistic approaches treat infrastructures as unique entities; reductionistic approaches model systems as sets of interconnected elementary elements; other approaches use multiple formalisms and the agent-based paradigm to model infrastructures and components. The various modeling paradigms have their advantages, but

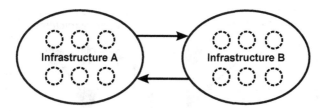

Figure 1. Holistic modeling.

all of them are limited in their ability to cope with the complex, multidimensional nature of critical infrastructures [6, 17].

De Porcellinis, *et al.* [5] have proposed a mixed holistic-reductionistic (MHR) approach to address this key limitation. The MHR approach merges the holistic and reductionistic paradigms into a single framework, thereby providing the benefits of both types of modeling approaches. This paper describes an enhancement of the MHR approach, which incorporates mediation mechanisms to enrich the original modeling paradigm. These mediation mechanisms constitute the basis of the mixed approach in which holism and reductionism coexist.

2. Modeling Interdependencies

The safety, security and dependability of critical infrastructures are strongly dependent on mutual interaction phenomena. Direct dependency mechanisms are easily identified and modeled in small portions of a critical infrastructure. However, in a large, complex infrastructure, direct and indirect dependencies among the various elements form multiple loops, which give rise to mutual dependency or "interdependency" mechanisms. Such interdependencies are difficult to understand, and manifest themselves only after the entire infrastructure has been modeled. At the same time, they pose serious threats to the stability of a critical infrastructure.

Several approaches have been proposed to model critical infrastructure interdependencies and their potential effects. They may be classified based on their use of three (possibly overlapping) perspectives: (i) holistic perspective; (ii) reductionistic perspective; and (iii) agent-based hybrid perspective.

2.1 Holistic Perspective

In the holistic perspective, each infrastructure is viewed as a single, monolithic entity (Figure 1) with well-defined boundaries and a (possibly reduced) set of functional properties. Infrastructures are assumed to interact with each other according to an identifiable (and limited) set of relationships.

The holistic perspective simplifies the identification of dependencies and interdependencies, which is a natural outcome of the modeling procedure. An example is the Input-Output Inoperability Model [9] based on the economic

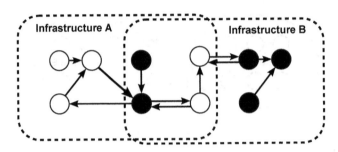

Figure 2.   Reductionistic modeling.

theory of Leontief [11], which expresses the cascading effects that a failure in one critical infrastructure induces in other critical infrastructures.

A holistic approach typically models interactions between elements at a high level of abstraction, usually based on statistical data, market rules, sociological trends and strategic policies. The high-level representation masks low-level interdependencies that are based on the exchange of physical quantities. In addition, the abstraction and simplification mechanisms often do not capture the structure and geographical scale of infrastructures and the dynamics of the various infrastructure components.

2.2   Reductionistic Perspective

A reductionistic approach identifies "elementary" components within an infrastructure and then describes the evolution of the entire system based on the "aggregated" behavior of these components. The elementary components, which are characterized by their own dynamics, receive/provide resources from/to other components. A failure in one component propagates to other components.

In the reductionistic perspective, the boundaries of each infrastructure tend to fade (Figure 2), but the interactions between components can be detected.

Reductionistic approaches are very powerful and well-suited to representing the complexities of cross-infrastructure interactions. However, the modeling effort can be overwhelming and massive computational resources are required, especially for large, complex infrastructures. Reductionistic approaches also require deep knowledge about the modeled systems and their interdependencies. This is problematic because, in addition to the large amount of data required, there often is a lack of detailed information about elements and their interdependencies. Thus, reductionistic approaches often simplify and/or reduce the scope of the analyses, which limits the applicability of the resulting infrastructure models.

2.3   Agent-Based Modeling

Agent-based modeling and simulation (ABMS) approaches model infrastructures and their elements as software agents. Each software agent implements a specific infrastructure component that interacts with other agents and the environment. The agent-based approach does not impose any limits on the granularity used to describe the decomposing/aggregating elements of an infrastructure, thereby providing an extremely flexible framework for modeling and analyzing complex systems.

Several agent-based simulation tools have been developed for analyzing critical infrastructures [16]. Notable examples include EPOCHS [10] and various ABMS tools created as a result of the CRESCO Project [18].

One of the key results of the CRESCO Project is a federated framework that can be leveraged by ABMS tools. The federated framework incorporates a two-layer architecture that enables the representation (within a single simulation environment) of different infrastructures and different functional aspects of their elements. The bottom layer of the framework contains simulators that simulate intra-domain relationships at a high level of detail (e.g., power flows and transients in an electrical power grid). The top layer contains agent-based simulators that simulate inter-domain interactions [3, 6] at high levels of abstraction. The "horizontal" simulators in the top layer implement components belonging to the same infrastructures modeled in the bottom layer. "Super agents" within these horizontal simulators are used as connectors between the two layers [18], permitting the access of detailed information from simulators in the bottom layer and data transfer to the "component" agents in the horizontal simulators.

The federated ABMS approach demonstrates how multi-scale modeling techniques can overcome the limitations of pure holistic and reductionistic approaches. However, in order to accomplish this, it is necessary to encapsulate the representation of the entire infrastructure and the services involved within unique black-box agents. At the same time, the federated ABMS approach requires all intra-domain dependencies to be modeled by dedicated simulators and super agents, which expose the resources and the behaviors resulting from functional inter-domain interactions to the multi-domain simulators.

3. Mixed Holistic-Reductionistic Approach

De Porcellinis, *et al.* [5] developed a mixed holistic-reductionistic (MHR) formulation to address the limitations of other approaches. MHR is designed to capture the dynamics that characterize an infrastructure while maintaining model complexity at a manageable level.

The MHR approach uses reductionistic techniques to model interdependencies between components, and a holistic paradigm to express the logical and functional dependencies involving infrastructures as a whole. Thus, an infrastructure is simultaneously represented within a common modeling paradigm as monolithic entity and as interconnected components. For example, a control room, which represents the "brain" of an infrastructure, can be viewed as a high-level entity. The same control room, with its buttons, lights and communication lines, can be modeled as a collection of interconnected components according the reductionistic (and physical) perspective.

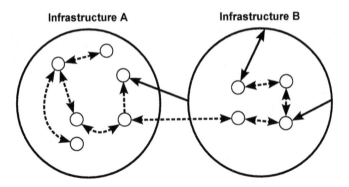

Figure 3. Mixed holistic-reductionistic modeling.

Figure 3 illustrates the mixed holistic-reductionistic perspective. The framework expresses the dependencies and interdependencies existing between reductionistic components belonging to the same or different infrastructures. At the same time, the framework also represents the high-level relations among the holistic views of different infrastructures.

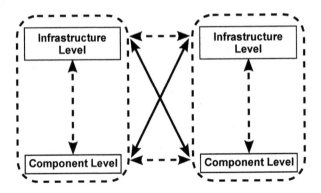

Figure 4. Interdependencies in the MHR approach.

The stack-like schema in Figure 4 shows how the holistic and reductionistic perspectives capture the "horizontal" relations among elements and the "vertical" dimension corresponding to a hierarchical decomposition (or aggregation), which is used to express the inner relationships existing within an infrastructure and its components. The MHR paradigm also uses "diagonal" links to explicitly model functional relationships between heterogeneous components and infrastructures, i.e., elements with different levels of granularity and belonging to different domains (solid lines in Figure 4). Indeed, diagonal relations can be expressed using horizontal and vertical dependencies, enabling the specification of all the links between the reductionistic components of one infrastructure and all the other involved elements. Note, however, that an explosion in complexity can occur due to the large number of interconnections that must be considered.

Also, many required links are generally hidden and may not be well understood from the point of view of a single component.

Representing dependencies and interdependencies using links between reductionistic components and the holistic view of an infrastructure leads to a simplified model. Moreover, only general information about the overall state of infrastructures is required, and there is no need to know the state of every component in the infrastructure.

As described above, each layer of an MHR model comprises several elements (or blocks) belonging to the holistic or reductionistic layers. All the elements with the layers conform to a common general model [6]:

- Elements exist in order to supply and/or consume tangible or intangible resources (e.g., goods, services and operativeness).

- Elements may suffer from faults or failures.

- Faults may propagate (or propagate their negative effects) based on various types of proximity.

- The ability of an element to provide the required resources depends on its operative condition, which is based on the availability of the resources it requires and on the severity of the failures that affect it.

The internal representation of a single block can be heterogeneous (e.g., rule-based system, dynamic system, finite state machine, etc.). The coupling of elements with different internal models is enabled by a common exposed interface.

4.   Mediating the Perspectives

Although the framework described in the previous section simplifies the resulting model, it is not rich enough to capture the complexity of the problem at hand. In fact, reductionistic elements often rely on specific functionalities instead of depending on the overall state of the infrastructure. For example, the operativeness of a node in a telecommunications network may depend on the efficiency of the UMTS service in its zone rather than on the global state of the infrastructure. The model described above is unable to handle relations involving such specific, yet high-level, system views.

The same problem has emerged in other fields. Recent research in genetics [8] has shown that the exact knowledge and sequencing of the genome is not enough to understand the complex behavior of the human body. Therefore, it has become necessary to study functional gene aggregates (proteins, RNA, etc.) [7, 12] in order to "mediate" interactions between the genes and the human body as a whole.

We employ a similar strategy to improve the modeling capabilities of MHR. In particular, we introduce an additional layer in the framework to better represent how the effect of the holistic representation is propagated into the reductionistic representation of the overall system. An element in the intermediate layer of the model represents a tangible or intangible (logical, organizational, etc.) entity that provides an "aggregate resource" or "service." These intermediate entities are called "service providers" because they are characterized by the functionality they provide.

Consider, for example, a simple computer network composed of interconnected servers and user terminals. Clearly, the ability to provide end-to-end VoIP communications depends not only on the physical path, but also on the VoIP status and quality of service. Creating an exact reductionistic model of the dependencies and interdependencies in this scenario is not a trivial endeavor. Moreover, if many different functionalities exist in the overall system, model creation may require several iterations. Traditional end-user services such as GSM, SMS and electrical power are only some of the possible aggregate resources provided by service providers. In fact, other support and management functionalities (e.g., supervisory control, emergency backup generation, fire protection, etc.) should be considered.

Based on the biological perspective, a service provider is not just the sum of its components, but an emerging entity whose bounds are not easily modeled. In fact, a reductionistic component of an infrastructure may have multiple service contributions (e.g., a router in a computer network that forwards network packets for many different services). Moreover, a service can be "transversal," i.e., not necessarily limited to a single infrastructure. For example, a service provider belonging to one infrastructure can provide outputs to external entities (e.g., power distribution), or, less frequently, a service provider can emerge from the cooperation of entities belonging to different infrastructures. Finally, some aggregate resources may be required only in critical situations (e.g., a "network reconfiguration" service that handles overloads in a power grid or an emergency power supply for a router in a telecommunications network). As described above, service providers are mediation entities created to represent how specific high-level functions of a critical infrastructure are provided to reductionistic elements. The aggregate resources provided by the different service providers can be interrelated. For example the operativeness of a telecontrol service can depend on the state of the power distribution system and the emergency power supply, or the efficiency of traffic redirection and monitoring services in the transportation infrastructure can be mutually dependent.

An important issue is how to reverse the (monodirectional) dependencies between service providers and reductionistic elements. In fact, specifying the exact contribution exerted by every reductionistic element on the different service providers may render the overall complexity unmanageable. Indeed, such inverse dependencies are complex and are mostly hidden from the point of view of a single service provider. Also, it is often the case that the control actions performed to grant an acceptable quality of such "services" are demanded by entities with a wider perspective (e.g., a control room). Therefore, it is more appropriate that a service provider relays data provided by a management entity (with an overall vision and able to filter the huge amount of reductionistic data) instead of considering the contribution of every single component.

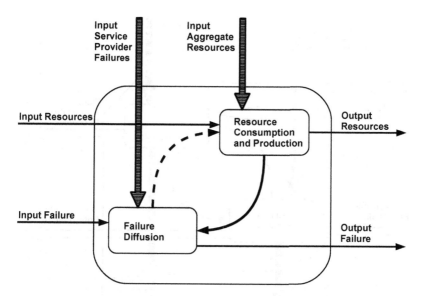

Figure 5. Reductionistic entity structure.

Such an approach takes into account the experience of human actors. It is more useful to engage this experiential knowledge within the holistic layer (e.g., via a rule-based system) rather than incorporating it within every service provider. Indeed, the operativeness of a service provider is largely influenced by the operative condition of the infrastructure and by the specific policies and management strategies adopted by the infrastructure owners and operators.

5. Mixed Holistic-Reductionistic Framework

The MHR framework has three possibly overlapping layers: (i) reductionistic layer; (ii) service layer; and (iii) holistic layer.

According to the reductionistic perspective, each infrastructure is decomposed into a web of interconnected elementary entities (or blocks). These entities receive and generate resources and propagate failures based on "proximities" of various types. Therefore, their behavior depends on the (mutual or not) interactions with other reductionistic elements. Moreover, their ability to operate properly depends on the availability and quality of aggregate resources (or services) offered by service providers (Figure 5).

Service providers are introduced as functional blocks to provide specific, yet high-level, functions to reductionistic elements belonging to the same or different infrastructures (Figure 6). Like reductionistic elements, service providers require and provide (aggregate) resources and may suffer from and propagate failures; this permits the modeling of complex, high-level failures (e.g., cyber attacks) that are difficult to model using a pure reductionistic perspective. The capability of each service provider is influenced by the operative condition of

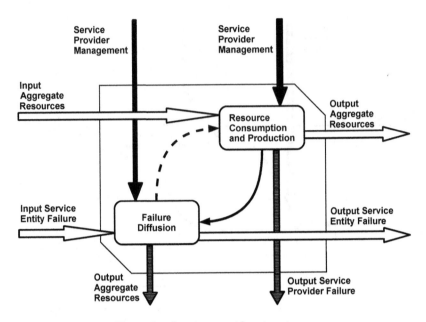

Figure 6. Service provider structure.

the infrastructures and by the policies and management strategies adopted in the specific context by infrastructure owners and operators.

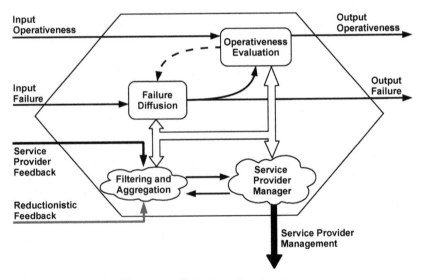

Figure 7. Holistic entity structure.

Holistic blocks (Figure 7) represent the holistic view of infrastructures. They interact with other holistic entities to exchange their operativeness. In this

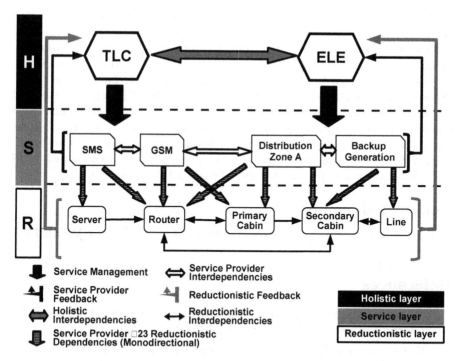

Figure 8. Example MHR architecture.

case, the failure block permits the modeling of sociologically-related events (e.g., strike, panic and malicious behavior) that are very difficult to model at a different level of abstraction. Holistic blocks influence the operative conditions of service providers based on the feedback received from reductionistic elements and on the overall state of the infrastructure. Moreover, every top node must provide adequate management service to the service providers by defining and executing appropriate control actions (e.g., flow redirection, parameter configuration, event-driven suspension/reactivation/recovery) in order to react to adverse events that may degrade or deny the aggregate resources provided by service providers and result in the cascading propagation of faults. Finally, a holistic node must be aware of the operativeness of its own service providers in order to obtain complete knowledge of the state of the infrastructure and update the overall operativeness accordingly.

Figure 8 shows an example MHR architecture. Note how the telecommunications (TLC) and electrical (ELE) infrastructures are naturally decomposed into holistic blocks, service providers and reductionistic entities.

6.   Conclusions

The proposed MHR approach facilitates the modeling of complex, heterogeneous infrastructures and their interdependencies by simultaneously expressing the holistic interactions between infrastructures and the mutual influence of their components expressed using a reductionistic perspective. Aggregated and intermediate entities are used to model complex relationships existing between elementary components and complex, high-level structures. Also, service providers are engaged to mediate interactions between the holistic and reductionistic representations of the infrastructures. The MHR approach is well suited to the analysis of complex scenarios and to the design of innovative infrastructure cooperation mechanisms that can enhance the ability of an infrastructure to operate properly in the presence of adverse events. Our future work will focus on using the MHR paradigm to model and analyze real-world scenarios in the context of the EU IST Project MICIE [13].

Acknowledgements

This research was partially supported by the EU IST Project MICIE FP7-ICT-225353/2008.

References

[1] M. Amin, Modeling and control of complex interactive networks, *IEEE Control Systems*, vol. 22(1), pp. 22–27, 2002.

[2] E. Brunner and M. Suter, *International CIIP Handbook 2008/2009: An Inventory of 25 National and 7 International Critical Infrastructure Protection Policies*, Center for Security Studies, ETH Zurich, Zurich, Switzerland, 2008.

[3] E. Casalicchio and E. Galli, Federated agent-based modeling and simulation: An approach for complex critical systems analysis, *Proceedings of the Twenty-Second Workshop on Principles of Advanced and Distributed Simulation*, p. 147, 2008.

[4] Commission of the European Communities, Green Paper: On a European Programme for Critical Infrastructure Protection, COM(2005)576 Final, Brussels, Belgium, 2005.

[5] S. De Porcellinis, S. Panzieri and R. Setola, Modeling critical infrastructure via a mixed holistic reductionistic approach, *International Journal of Critical Infrastructures*, vol. 5(1/2), pp. 86–99, 2009.

[6] S. De Porcellinis, R. Setola, S. Panzieri and G. Ulivi, Simulation of heterogeneous and interdependent critical infrastructures, *International Journal of Critical Infrastructures*, vol. 4(1/2), pp. 110–128, 2008.

[7] L. Dunlap, Advancing gene expression studies, *Genetic Engineering and Biotechnology News*, vol. 28(14), August 1, 2008.

[8] Y. Guo, G. Eichler, Y. Feng, D. Ingber and S. Huang, Towards a holistic, yet gene-centered analysis of gene expression profiles: A case study of human lung cancers, *Journal of Biomedicine and Biotechnology*, vol. 2006, pp. 1–11, 2006.

[9] Y. Haimes and P. Jiang, Leontief-based model of risk in complex interconnected infrastructures, *Journal of Infrastructure Systems*, vol. 7(1), pp. 1–12, 2001.

[10] K. Hopkinson, R. Giovanini and X. Wang, EPOCHS: Integrated commercial off-the-shelf software for agent-based electric power and communication simulation, *Proceedings of the Thirty-Fifth Winter Simulation Conference*, pp. 1158–1166, 2003.

[11] W. Leontief, *Input-Output Economics*, Oxford University Press, New York, 1966.

[12] D. Lockhart and E. Winzeler, Genomics, gene expression and DNA arrays, *Nature*, vol. 405(6788), pp. 827–836, 2008.

[13] MICIE, The MICIE Project, Rome, Italy (www.micie.eu).

[14] A. Nieuwenhuijs, E. Luiijf and M. Klaver, Modeling dependencies in critical infrastructures, in *Critical Infrastructure Protection II*, M. Papa and S. Shenoi (Eds.), Springer, Boston, Massachusetts, pp. 205–213, 2008.

[15] Office of Science and Technology Policy/Science and Technology Directorate, The National Plan for Research and Development in Support of Critical Infrastructure Protection, Executive Office of the President/Department of Homeland Security, Washington, DC, 2005.

[16] P. Pederson, D. Dudenhoeffer, S. Hartley and M. Permann, Critical Infrastructure Interdependency Modeling: A Survey of U.S. and International Research, Report No. INL/EXT-06-11464, Critical Infrastructure Protection Division, Idaho National Laboratory, Idaho Falls, Idaho, 2006.

[17] S. Rinaldi, J. Peerenboom and T. Kelly, Identifying, understanding and analyzing critical infrastructure interdependencies, *IEEE Control Systems*, vol. 21(6), pp. 11–25, 2001.

[18] R. Setola, S. Bologna, E. Casalicchio and V. Masucci, An integrated approach for simulating interdependencies, in *Critical Infrastructure Protection II*, M. Papa and S. Shenoi (Eds.), Springer, Boston, Massachusetts, pp. 229–239, 2008.

Chapter 16

ONTOLOGY-BASED CRITICAL INFRASTRUCTURE MODELING AND SIMULATION

Vincenzo Masucci, Francesco Adinolfi, Paolo Servillo, Giovanni Dipoppa and Alberto Tofani

Abstract   This paper describes a knowledge-based system (KBS) designed to support a federated environment for simulating critical infrastructure models. A federation of simulators is essentially a "system of systems," where each simulator represents an entity that operates independently with its own behavior and purpose. The interactions among the components of the federated system of systems exhibit critical infrastructure vulnerabilities as emergent behavior; these vulnerabilities cannot be analyzed and simulated by considering the behavior of each system component individually. The KBS, which is based on ontologies and rules, provides a semantic foundation for the federated simulation environment and enables the dynamic binding of different critical infrastructure models. The KBS-based simulation environment can be used to identify latent critical infrastructure interdependencies and to test assumptions about interdependencies.

Keywords: Modeling, simulation, ontology, federated environment

1. Introduction

The DIESIS Project, which is funded by the European Community, is currently investigating the feasibility of creating a European Infrastructure Simulation and Analysis Center (EISAC). EISAC would function as a distributed e-infrastructure for conducting interoperable federated simulations of critical infrastructures in support of risk analysis and management efforts. EISAC would connect various modeling and simulation communities through the deployment of high-level services. Despite the utmost importance of critical infrastructures to citizens, the economy and society at large, the understanding of critical infrastructures and their interdependencies is still relatively immature. Com-

C. Palmer and S. Shenoi (Eds.): Critical Infrastructure Protection III, IFIP AICT 311, pp. 229–242, 2009.

prehensive, systematic investigations of complex infrastructures demand joint efforts by researchers, infrastructure owners and operators, and government agencies to overcome obstacles such as the availability of models and data, interoperable simulation environments for multiple infrastructures, testbeds and benchmarks for protection solutions.

The main concepts and definitions related to critical infrastructure interdependencies are widely accepted (see, e.g., [19]). A report on European critical infrastructure disruptions [11], which classifies the cascading effects in critical infrastructures, emphasizes the importance of analyzing such events. However, the scale, complexity and coupling of critical infrastructures present numerous theoretical and practical challenges to the modeling, prediction, simulation and analysis of cause-and-effect relationships. Critical infrastructure systems are heterogeneous mixtures of dynamic, interactive, non-linear entities with unscheduled discontinuities and numerous other significant effects. Thus, the modeling and analysis of these systems requires the consideration of their large-scale, non-linear and time-dependent behavior.

The EISAC facility, which is intended to have the same functionality as the U.S. NISAC [20], will support collaborative activities in critical infrastructure protection and advance the state of the art in the field of federated simulation. One of the key requirements is a knowledge-based system (KBS) that would provide the semantic foundation for a federated simulation environment. A federation of simulators can be considered to be a "system of systems," where each simulator represents an entity that operates independently with its own behavior and purpose [12]. The interactions between simulators display emergent behavior that cannot be analyzed by simulating the individual entities in isolation.

This paper describes the design of a KBS for a federated critical infrastructure simulation environment being developed under the DIESIS Project. The KBS, which is based on ontologies and rules, provides a semantic foundation for the federated simulation environment and enables the dynamic binding of different critical infrastructure models. The KBS-based simulation framework can be used to identify latent critical infrastructure interdependencies and to test assumptions about interdependencies. In addition, it facilitates the development of strategies for operating critical infrastructures and articulating risk management policies.

2. Background

The IEEE High Level Architecture (HLA) Standard specifies a common architecture for distributed modeling and simulation, including a framework for the interconnection of interacting simulations. However, environments based on HLA and related approaches are not well-suited to simulating critical infrastructures. In particular, the coupling of simulators is based on a common data model, which must be implemented by all the involved simulators. Moreover, the data model is purely syntactic and does not provide semantic information about the modeled domains. The proposed federated simulation environment is specifically designed to address the semantic interoperability of critical infrastructure simulators.

Several modeling and simulation approaches have been developed to analyze critical infrastructure interdependencies. Pederson, *et al.* [16] categorize them as integrated and coupled approaches. Integrated approaches engage a single monolithic framework to express multiple infrastructures and their interdependencies. In contrast, coupled approaches model individual infrastructures separately and couple the individual models to analyze the infrastructures and their cascading effects.

NISAC uses several modeling approaches and simulation tools [1] ranging from detailed to abstract. NISAC also offers the Critical Infrastructure Protection Knowledge Management Portal (CIP KM Portal) that supports the rapid access of information (documents, presentations, media files and web links). The information is organized into multiple taxonomies covering programs, projects, infrastructures, models and tools. The DIESIS KBS is similar to the NISAC CIP KM Portal in terms of the model and infrastructure taxonomies. In addition, the DIESIS KBS will play a major role in federated simulations and facilitate the automatic acquisition of new knowledge about infrastructure interconnections and interdependencies.

Tolone, *et al.* [23] and others [5, 7] also focus on infrastructure interdependencies. The modeling and simulation approaches, which are based on comprehensive models of critical infrastructures, primarily support high-level analysis (also, see [3, 6, 13]). Marti, *et al.* [14] have developed an infrastructure interdependencies simulation (I2Sim) system based on integrated, supply and demand system models. I2Sim has been applied to several infrastructures (e.g., electrical power grid, water supply, telecommunications and transportation) to coordinate planning, response and recovery during large-scale disaster situations (e.g., earthquakes, hurricanes and terrorist attacks).

The Idaho National Laboratory (INL) has designed CIPR/sim simulators that allow emergency planners to visualize the real-time cascading effects of multiple infrastructure failures before an actual emergency occurs. CIPR/sim adheres to the IEEE HLA Standard and can import real-time data from numerous existing analysis modules, including the Real-Time Digital Simulator (for electrical power grid analysis), QualNet [21] (for telecommunications system analysis) and other tools for wind speed and flood surge analysis. CIPR/sim can be categorized as employing a coupled, high-fidelity modeling and simulation approach.

Several interesting approaches have been developed by European researchers as a result of national and EU initiatives. Klein, *et al.* [10] have proposed a comprehensive critical infrastructure modeling and simulation approach. Another notable contribution is the CRESCO architecture [9] developed under an Italian initiative. The CRESCO architecture provides facilities for defining and configuring simulation scenarios, analyzing critical infrastructure interdependencies, and integrating domain-specific models in order to simulate the detailed behavior of critical infrastructures. CRESCO engages two approaches

for modeling critical infrastructure interdependencies: CISIA, which is based on
an entity resource model [4]; and CIAB, which exploits an agent-based model
[2]. All these systems can be considered to use macroscopic approaches: a key
limitation is that the coupling of critical infrastructure domain simulators often
yields inadequate simulation results.

The approach of Tolone, *et al.* [23] is conceptually very similar to our work.
This service-oriented framework for integrated modeling and simulation also
uses meta knowledge to formalize agent behavior and inter-infrastructure relationships.

3.   Ontology-Based Modeling and Simulation

This section describes the formal processes involved in representing knowledge about critical infrastructures and their interconnections, and guiding KBS
development. The ontological framework used in the DIESIS KBS permits the
specification of domain knowledge (definition), the application of inference rules
(reasoning), and the generation of new knowledge from the knowledge base (de-
duction).

3.1   DIESIS Knowledge-Based System

The top-down design approach used for the DIESIS KBS is intended to pro-
mote flexibility. Domain ontologies express concepts in a highly specialized
manner and are often very detailed; consequently, it is difficult to merge ontologies into a general representation. However, as described below, the DIESIS
KBS can be integrated via existing standardized domain models in a bottom-
up fashion. Figure 1 presents the DIESIS KBS architecture, which is inspired
by [17, 18].

The DIESIS KBS design incorporates a meta knowledge infrastructure ontology (MKIONT), infrastructure ontologies (IONTs), a federation ontology
(FONT) and gateway components.

3.1.1   MKIONT.   The meta knowledge infrastructure ontology (referred to as MKIONT) defines a general template for expressing the basic concepts and relationships of critical infrastructures and their interconnections.
The MKIONT assumes that it is possible to model every critical infrastructure as a set of interconnected system components. Infrastructure ontologies
(IONTs) are defined by specializing the MKIONT definitions to specific critical infrastructure domains. The MKIONT template permits the representation
of cross-domain critical infrastructure interconnections and the related semantics. In particular, the abstract concepts and relationships defined within the
MKIONT are represented as classes (meta classes) and relations (properties)
that are specialized as IONTs and a federated ontology (FONT) by specifying sub-classes and sub-properties. Thus, the MKIONT template essentially
provides an object-oriented approach for defining the IONTs and FONT.

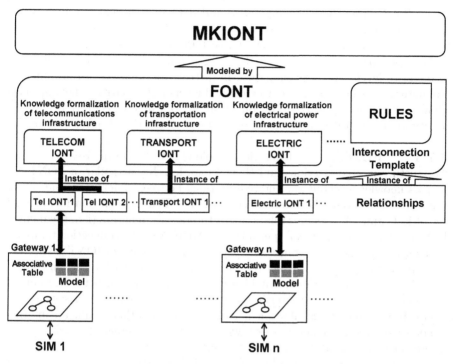

Figure 1. DIESIS KBS architecture.

In summary, the MKIONT provides: (i) a critical infrastructure template that captures basic concepts and relationships pertaining to a critical infrastructure; and (ii) an interconnection template that represents critical infrastructure interconnections and their relative semantics.

3.1.2 IONT.

An infrastructure ontology (IONT) represents knowledge about a particular critical infrastructure (e.g., telecommunications, transportation or electrical power). The IONT, which is derived from the MKIONT template, defines the set of concepts and properties used to formalize the critical infrastructure domain. The definition could rely on existing standards as in the case of the electrical power domain, for which the relative IONT has been defined with respect to IEC standards [15].

The MKIONT template is used to define IONTs for the considered critical infrastructures, ensuring the semantic interoperability of the different critical infrastructure models. An IONT is "simulator independent" because it conceptually models and formalizes the knowledge of a particular domain and because it is possible to define different IONTs for a domain to accommodate different levels of granularity. However, the various IONTS for a given domain are independent of each other and cannot be used in a federated simulation environment unless the appropriate interconnection rules are specified using a FONT (described below). The IONTs are instantiated by populating them with actual critical infrastructure components and data to represent specific critical infrastructure models (e.g., electrical power transmission/distribution grid of a particular zone, city or district). These IONTs are subsequently translated to the appropriate simulator models. In general, IONTs created at different granularity levels (for a given critical infrastructure domain) run on different simulators, each corresponding to a defined level of granularity. This approach allows for the modular composition of simulators in the federation and the ability to employ different levels of detail for a given critical infrastructure.

3.1.3   FONT.   A federation ontology (FONT) formalizes critical infrastructure interconnections and their semantics. In particular, a FONT expresses knowledge about the interconnections between different domains and the rules that govern the interconnections. The FONT definition includes all the objects and relationships relevant to a federated simulation (i.e., the defined IONTs). Therefore, a FONT specializes an MKIONT interconnection template that formalizes the interconnections between the elements of IONT instances.

Note that we distinguish between interconnections and interdependencies. An interconnection is an explicit identification of a relation between items of different domains (e.g., a router in a telecommunications network receives electricity from a power distribution network). On the other hand, an interdependency represents emergent behavior due to the interaction modalities of interconnected critical infrastructure networks.

Thus, the specification of all possible critical infrastructure interconnections is insufficient to generate interdependency phenomena in a federated simulation environment. To this end, the FONT enriches the definition of interconnections with semantic rules. In particular, a rule specifies how two critical infrastructure elements are interconnected (i.e., how one element depends on the other, enabling effects to propagate in different domains). For example, the FONT could define an interconnection named *isaLoad* between a router element (in the telecommunications domain) and a load element (in the electrical power domain). The semantics of this interconnection can be defined as follows: if a certain router in the telecommunications domain relates to a particular load in the electrical power domain via the *isaLoad* interconnection and the load is not fed, then the router is off." This rule is applicable to every router instance connected to a load instance (by a FONT relationship). Thus, the propagation of events between the two domains is enabled.

Figure 2 shows how rules, IONT instances and relationships (instances of the interconnections) permit the identification of critical infrastructure interdependencies. Domain experts develop a set of basic rules that express knowledge about cross-domain interconnections. These rules are used in an inference process with IONT instances and their relationships to simulate and analyze inter-domain interdependencies.

3.1.4   Gateways.   Gateway components provide bridges between the KBS and simulators of specific domains. Well-defined gateways make it

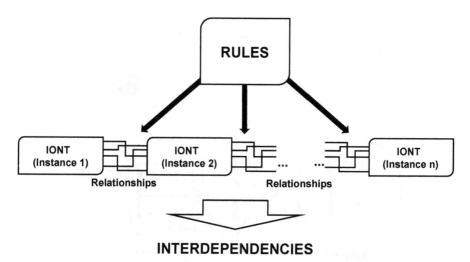

Figure 2. FONT rules.

possible to exploit the functionalities of the standalone simulators. Gateways also manage the input/output models of simulators in a federated environment.

A gateway has two components: a simulator model and an associative table. A simulator model is the simulator equivalent of an IONT instance. The domain IONT is an abstraction over a set of different simulator models, while an IONT instance has only one corresponding domain simulator model. For this reason a simulator model must be realized for each IONT instance in the KBS and for each simulator available for the domain.

An associative table exists for each IONT instance and its related simulator model. The table maps the objects defined in an IONT instance to specific simulator model objects.

3.2   KBS Development Process

The KBS development process has five steps: (i) MKIONT definition; (ii) domain IONT definition; (iii) IONT instantiation; (iv) FONT definition; and (v) FONT instantiation. The KBS development process starts with the MKIONT definition, which represents the highest abstraction level used in the KBS. As mentioned above, critical infrastructure IONTs are created using the MKIONT. To this end, the MKIONT critical infrastructure template can be used in two ways:

- **Derivative Template:** The first step in the IONT definition process is to import the MKIONT concepts and relationships. The IONT then specializes the MKIONT concepts and relationships (properties) to represent domain knowledge about the critical infrastructure.

- **Container Template:** The specific domain IONT is developed starting with existing standards and/or ontology definitions. Then, the defined

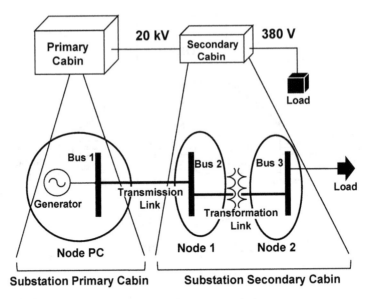

Figure 3.   IONT instantiation.

IONT is made MKIONT compliant. In particular, the MKIONT template is used as a container for the IONT knowledge definition. Note that the inclusion of the IONT in the MKIONT template ensures the applicability of the interconnection template to permit the definition of semantic interconnection bridges with other critical infrastructure components in a federated simulation environment.

The development of a domain IONT requires deep knowledge of the corresponding critical infrastructure. For this reason, the DIESIS KBS development team should include both knowledge engineers and domain experts. We developed a railway infrastructure IONT in collaboration with RFI (Italian Railway Infrastructure) experts; and telecommunications and electrical power IONTs in cooperation with the appropriate domain experts and managers. A domain IONT is subsequently instantiated to effectively model a real critical infrastructure network (e.g., electrical power grid of a city district). The topology and requirements of a real critical infrastructure are translated into IONT objects by populating the IONT ontological schema.

Figure 3 shows an IONT instantiation corresponding to an electrical power distribution infrastructure. The infrastructure topology and specifics are represented using the ontology formalism harnessed by the IONT schema.

The FONT must include all the domain IONTs in a federated simulation environment. It supports the semantic interoperability of IONTs in the federation by defining cross-domain interconnections enriched with semantic rules. In this way, an interconnection template is realized as a set of relationships between concepts of different IONTs. Next, rules are defined to govern the interactions between interconnected objects. Thus, developing the FONT involves three steps: (i) importing the domain IONTs; (ii) creating the interconnection template; and (iii) defining rules.

Finally, a FONT instance is created to serve as the core for a federated simulation session. Since DIESIS employs the Ontology Web Language (OWL) and Semantic Web Rule Language (SWRL), the acquired knowledge must be represented in terms of OWL classes, sub-classes, properties, sub-properties, restrictions on properties and SWRL rules. First, the concepts, relationships and constraints are expressed in natural language. Next, classes are created to represent the relevant concepts and sub-classes to express hyponym relationships. Then, properties are used to represent relationships between classes (object properties) and relationships between classes and datatypes (datatype properties). Eventually, restrictions on properties with respect to specific classes are defined. The ontology is then enriched with rules to enable a rule engine to infer new knowledge (assertions and facts).

4. Test Case

This section describes a test case related to the DIESIS Project that illustrates the flexibility and effectiveness of the proposed approach.

The proposed approach was used to define IONTs for the electrical power, telecommunications and railway transportation infrastructures. The IONTs were defined based on domain-specific standards. A FONT schema and rules were also defined to facilitate interoperability between the three domains from a semantic point of view. In particular, the FONT instance integrated the electrical power IONT with the telecommunications and railway IONTs to demonstrate how the proposed approach could be used to represent cross-domain interconnections.

This section presents a detailed description of the electrical power domain IONT, which was defined according to the IEC Common Information Model (CIM) Standard [8]. The CIM Standard, which is maintained as a UML model, enables applications software developed for electrical power transmission and distribution systems to exchange information about the configuration and status of electrical networks. The CIM Standard also defines a common vocabulary and ontology for the electrical power industry. The IEC 61970-301 Standard defines the core packages of the CIM with a focus on the needs of electricity transmission, where related applications include energy management, SCADA, planning and optimization systems. The IEC 61970-501 and 61970-452 Standards provide an XML specification of network model exchanges using RDF. The IEC 61968 Standard extends the CIM to meet the needs of electrical power distribution, where related applications include distribution management, outage management, planning, metering, work management, geographic information, asset management, customer information and enterprise resource planning systems.

Figure 4 presents the IONT created for the electrical power domain using the UML definitions of IEC COM objects [8].

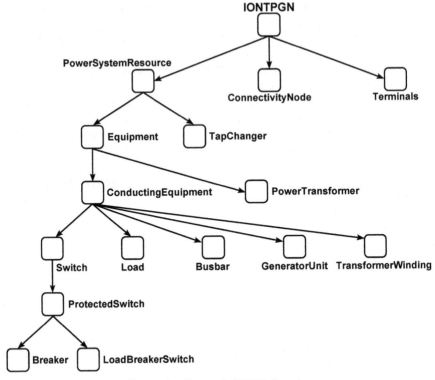

Figure 4. Example IONT domain.

Figure 5 shows the mappings of electrical power domain components and CIM objects. Interested readers are referred to [15] for the remaining OWL IONT classes and additional details. Note that the IONT defined for the electric power domain may be used to create models of real electrical power grids.

A FONT instance was used to integrate the electric domain IONT with IONT instances for the telecommunications and railway domains. Figure 6 shows an example where simple cross-domain interconnections are defined for these domains. Note that some components of the telecommunications and railway networks are fed through electrical network components. These components are represented as loads in the electrical network, and the interconnections are expressed using *isaLoad* OWL properties in the FONT instance. Other interconnections involve electrical network components that are telecontrolled using telecommunications network components. The scenario in Figure 6 was represented ontologically and formalized using OWL and SWRL. A rule engine such as Jess may be used to verify that the model addresses semantic interoperability (at least from the conceptual point of view). Our future work will focus on implementing gateways for each simulator to enable the federated simulation environment to manifest interdependency phenomena.

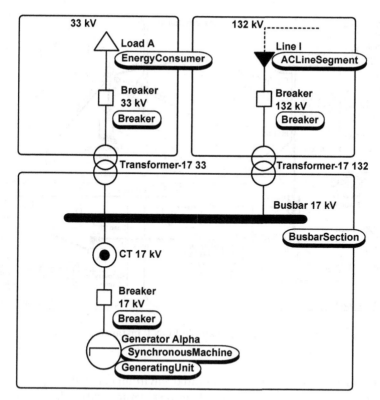

Figure 5. Mappings of electrical power domain and CIM objects [15].

5.   Conclusions

The DIESIS Project is developing techniques and tools for characterizing critical infrastructures and their interdependencies. The DIESIS KBS is designed to create abstractions of critical infrastructure domains and to represent and formalize their parameters and dependencies. The KBS is intended to be used in a federated simulation environment to study the behavior of infrastructures and their components under different conditions and constraints.

The KBS defines the meta knowledge infrastructure ontology (MKIONT), which serves as a template for modeling the considered critical infrastructure domains via infrastructure ontologies (IONTs). The MKIONT template provides the semantic layer for the definition of the federation ontology (FONT), which provides semantic consistency for interconnections among IONTs and contains rules that govern the interactions among interconnected objects. To initialize a federated simulation, it is necessary to define a simulator model for each IONT instance. A gateway provides the bridge between an IONT instance and a simulator model using an associative table. The KBS can exploit a reasoning engine to manage ontologies and rules (defined using OWL and SWRL) to enable the semantic interoperability of the infrastructure domains involved

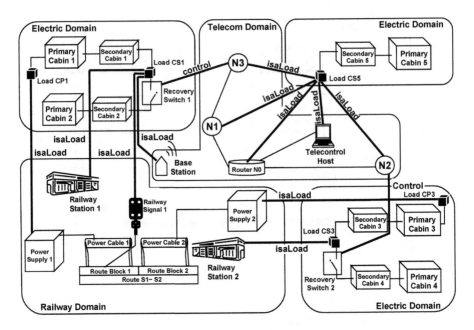

Figure 6.　Example FONT instance.

in a simulation. The resulting federated environment will support complex simulation scenarios involving multiple infrastructures with different semantics and granularities.

Acknowledgements

This research was partially supported by the European Community Seventh Framework Programme FP7/2007-2013 under Grant 212830. The authors also wish to acknowledge the contributions of the DIESIS Project members, especially Erich Rome (IAIS), Erol Gelenbe (Imperial College), Eric Luiijf (TNO) and Sandro Bologna (ENEA).

References

[1] T. Brown, Multiple modeling approaches and insights for critical infrastructure protection, in *Computational Models of Risks to Infrastructure*, D. Skanata and D. Byrd (Eds.), IOS Press, Amsterdam, The Netherlands, pp. 23–33, 2006.

[2] E. Casalicchio, E. Galli and S. Tucci, Federated agent-based modeling and simulation approach to study interdependencies in IT critical infrastructures, *Proceedings of the Eleventh IEEE International Symposium on Distributed Simulation and Real-Time Applications*, pp. 182–189, 2007.

[3] A. Chaturvedi, A society of simulation approach to dynamic integration of simulations, *Proceedings of the Thirty-Eighth Winter Simulation Conference*, pp. 2125–2131, 2006.

[4] S. De Porcellinis, R. Setola, S. Panzieri and G. Ulivi, Simulation of heterogeneous and interdependent critical infrastructures, *International Journal of Critical Infrastructures*, vol. 4(1/2), pp. 110–128, 2008.

[5] D. Dudenhoeffer, M. Permann and M. Manic, CIMS: A framework for infrastructure interdependency modeling and analysis, *Proceedings of the Thirty-Eighth Winter Simulation Conference*, pp. 478–485, 2006.

[6] F. Flentge and U. Beyer, The ISE metamodel for critical infrastructures, in *Critical Infrastructure Protection*, E. Goetz and S. Shenoi (Eds.), Springer, Boston, Massachusetts, pp. 323–336, 2007.

[7] O. Gursesli and A. Desrochers, Modeling infrastructure interdependencies using Petri nets, *Proceedings of the IEEE International Conference on Systems, Man and Cybernetics*, vol. 2, pp. 1506–1512, 2003.

[8] International Electrotechnical Commission, IEC 61970 Energy Management System Application Program Interface (EMS-API) – Part 301: Common Information Model (CIM) Base, Edition 1.0, Geneva, Switzerland, 2003.

[9] Italian National Agency for New Technologies, Energy and the Environment (ENEA), The CRESCO Project, Rome, Italy (www.cresco.enea.it).

[10] R. Klein, E. Rome, C. Beyel, R. Linnemann, W. Reinhardt and A. Usov, Information modeling and simulation in large interdependent critical infrastructures, presented at the *Third International Workshop on Critical Information Infrastructure Security*, 2008.

[11] E. Luiijf, A. Nieuwenhuijs, M. Klaver, M. van Eeten and E. Cruz, Empirical findings on critical infrastructure dependencies in Europe, presented at the *Third International Workshop on Critical Information Infrastructure Security*, 2008.

[12] M. Maier, Architecting principles for systems-of-systems (www.infoed.com /Open/PAPERS/systems.htm), 2008.

[13] J. Marti, J. Hollman, C. Ventura and J. Jatskevich, Design for survival real-time infrastructures coordination, presented at the *International Workshop on Complex Network and Infrastructure Protection*, 2006.

[14] J. Marti, J. Hollman, C. Ventura and J. Jatskevich, Design recovery of critical infrastructures: Real-time temporal coordination, *International Journal of Critical Infrastructures*, vol. 4(1/2), pp. 17–31, 2008.

[15] A. McMorran, An Introduction to IEC 61970-301 61968-11: The Common Information Model, Technical Report, Institute for Energy and Environment, Department of Electronic and Electrical Engineering, University of Strathclyde, Glasgow, United Kingdom, 2007.

[16] P. Pederson, D. Dudenhoeffer, S. Hartley and M. Permann, Critical Infrastructure Interdependency Modeling: A Survey of U.S. and International Research, Report No. INL/EXT-06-11464, Critical Infrastructure Protection Division, Idaho National Laboratory, Idaho Falls, Idaho, 2006.

[17] T. Rathnam, Using Ontologies to Support Interoperability in Federated Simulation, M.S. Thesis, School of Mechanical Engineering, Georgia Institute of Technology, Atlanta, Georgia, 2004.

[18] T. Rathnam and C. Paredis, Developing federation object models using ontologies, *Proceedings of the Thirty-Sixth Winter Simulation Conference*, pp. 1054–1062, 2004.

[19] S. Rinaldi, J. Peerenboom and T. Kelly, Identifying, understanding and analyzing critical infrastructure interdependencies, *IEEE Control Systems*, vol. 21(6), pp. 11–25, 2001.

[20] Sandia National Laboratories, National Infrastructure Simulation and Analysis Center (NISAC), Albuquerque, New Mexico (www.sandia.gov /mission/homeland/programs/critical/nisac.html).

[21] Scalable Network Technologies, QualNet, Los Angeles, California (www .scalable-networks.com/products/developer.php).

[22] R. Setola, S. Bologna, E. Casalicchio and V. Masucci, An integrated approach for simulating interdependencies, in *Critical Infrastructure Protection II*, M. Papa and S. Shenoi (Eds.), Springer, Boston, Massachusetts, pp. 229–239, 2008.

[23] W. Tolone, E. Johnson, S. Lee, W. Xiang, L. Marsh, C. Yeager and J. Blackwell, Enabling system of systems analysis of critical infrastructure behaviors, presented at the *Third International Workshop on Critical Information Infrastructure Security*, 2008.

Chapter 17

A FRAMEWORK FOR MODELING INTERDEPENDENCIES IN JAPAN'S CRITICAL INFRASTRUCTURES

Zaw Zaw Aung and Kenji Watanabe

Abstract   This paper discusses Japanese efforts related to critical infrastructure protection, including several case studies to clarify the risk components and countermeasures. An interdependency modeling framework that combines the inoperability input-output model (IIM) for economic interdependencies and Bayesian networks for operational dependencies is presented. Also, the paper provides new multidimensional measures for interpreting interdependency modeling results.

Keywords: Japan, interdependency modeling

1.   Introduction

The modeling and analysis of critical infrastructure interdependencies are challenging tasks. Traditionally, these tasks have been performed using qualitative and/or quantitative approaches. Qualitative approaches typically rely on expert knowledge and experience, often gleaned from interviews and expressed in loosely-structured terms. Nevertheless, these approaches have been used to good effect, especially when the expertise pertaining to critical infrastructure assets is engaged in a systematic manner. Quantitative approaches, on the other hand, often engage national input-output statistics for critical infrastructure dependency assessments. However, these statistics have certain limitations when they are used to analyze interdependencies existing between multiple critical infrastructures.

This paper discusses Japanese critical infrastructure protection efforts with an emphasis on interdependency analysis. Several case studies are presented to clarify the risk components related to Japan's critical infrastructures and the associated countermeasures. A framework for interdependency modeling that combines the inoperability input-output model (IIM) for economic interdependencies and Bayesian networks for operational dependencies is presented. Also,

C. Palmer and S. Shenoi (Eds.): Critical Infrastructure Protection III, IFIP AICT 311, pp. 243–257, 2009.
© IFIP International Federation for Information Processing 2009

Table 1. Critical infrastructure sectors in Japan and the United States [7].

Japanese CI Sectors	United States CI Sectors
1. Government Services	1. Government Facilities
2. Communications (and Broadcasting)	2. Communications
3. Finance (and Insurance)	3. Banking and Finance
4. Air Transportation	4. Transportation Systems
5. Railway System	5. Energy
6. Electric Power	6. Public Health and Health Care
7. Gas	7. Water
8. Medical Services	8. Dams
9. Water Supply	9. Agriculture and Food
10. Logistics (Road Transportation not incl. Private Transportation)	10. Chemical
	11. Commercial Facilities
	12. Emergency Services
	13. Information Technology
	14. Postal and Shipping
	15. Nuclear Reactors, Materials and Waste
	16. Defense Industrial Base
	17. National Monuments
	18. Critical Manufacturing

the paper specifies new multidimensional measures for interpreting interdependency modeling results.

2. Overview

Table 1 lists the Japanese and U.S. critical infrastructure sectors. Note that only ten sectors are identified as being critical in Japan as opposed to eighteen sectors in the United States. Earthquake-prone Japan has extensive experience dealing with natural disasters. Japan's well-established emergency management and disaster recovery practices have been naturally extended to critical infrastructure protection. Consequently, in the Japanese context, most critical infrastructure protection efforts engage existing anti-disaster measures articulated via "system of systems" approaches. Note, however, that critical infrastructure protection is distinguished from emergency management and disaster recovery efforts by emergent information technology (IT) threats.

The Japanese National Information Security Center (NISC) was established in April 2005 as the central coordinating entity for IT security efforts. NISC has four crucial functions [17]: (i) planning fundamental government-wide strategies for IT security policy; (ii) promoting comprehensive security measures for government agencies; (iii) providing incident handling functions for government agencies; and (iv) enforcing critical information infrastructure protection. NISC

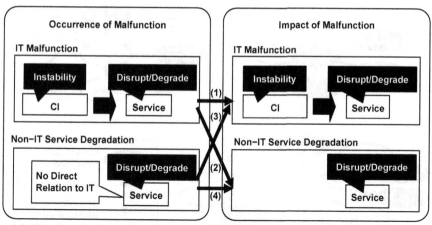

1, 2: IT malfunction in one CI affects other CI
3, 4: Non–IT service degradation affects other CI

Figure 1. NISC interdependency analysis scope [7].

also coordinates information exchange between the various Japanese stakeholders as well as foreign entities.

One of the principal NISC committees is the Critical Infrastructure Technical Committee, which has 26 members from industry, research organizations, academia and government. A 2007 study by the Technical Committee [7] confirmed the propagation of adverse effects of disruptions or malfunctions in one critical infrastructure sector to other sectors.

Figure 1 illustrates the scope of the interdependency analysis conducted by the NISC Technical Committee. The occurrence of an IT malfunction in one or more critical infrastructure sectors can cause service disruptions and/or degradation in other sectors. Services that have no direct relation to IT can also be degraded. Consequently, the Technical Committee emphasized the importance of comprehensively analyzing the interdependencies existing between the ten critical infrastructure sectors.

Of the ten critical infrastructure sectors in Japan, broadcasting, railway system, electric power, gas, medical services, water supply and logistics are termed as highly-independent (robust) systems. On the other hand, communications, finance, air transportation and government services are termed as low independence (weak) systems. Note that communications and broadcasting is defined as a single sector. However, they are treated separately because of their different dependency characteristics.

Figure 2 presents the results of the interdependency analysis conducted by the NISC Technical Committee [7]. The dark circles represent sectors with low independence; the dotted arrows represent time-varying dependencies. Note that communications, electric power and water supply are the major supporting sectors for many other critical infrastructure sectors. Electric power plays the largest role in supporting other critical infrastructures. Communications

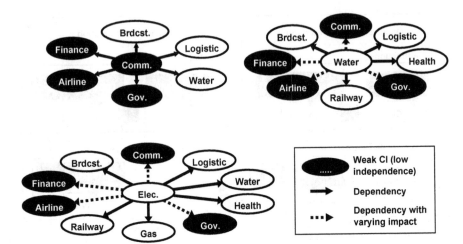

Figure 2.   Interdependency analysis results [7].

has a smaller role compared with electric power, the reason being that some sectors (e.g., the railway system) use their own communications networks for operations and do not rely on the public communications network. Consequently, a public communications network disruption has little, if any, impact on these infrastructures. Nevertheless, it is important to note that all the dependencies on the communications sector are direct dependencies (arrows) that represent high vulnerability.

3.   Risk Components

The prototypical expression for risk in the homeland security context is written as:

$$Risk = Threat \times Vulnerability \times Consequence$$

where the total risk is the combination or the Cartesian product of all relevant threat types, system weaknesses (vulnerabilities) and consequences that occur when the damage-inducing mechanisms associated with the threats interact with the vulnerabilities [6]. This section discusses a number of case studies along with the various risk components – threats, vulnerabilities and consequences – in the context of Japan's critical infrastructure sectors. Figure 3 outlines the various discussion points.

3.1   2004 Niigata Chuetsu Earthquake

The Niigata Chuetsu earthquake occurred at 5:56 p.m. on October 23, 2004 (Saturday) in an isolated mountainous region. A total of 48 fatalities and 643 serious injuries were reported [11]. Approximately 278,000 households lost electricity, water and gas supply. Cell phone service was disrupted as a result

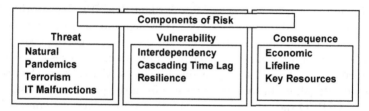

Figure 3. Risk components in Japan's critical infrastructures.

of the power outage (backup systems for cell towers only supply power for one day).

The most notable case was the first-ever derailment of a high-speed bullet train. The main shock occurred as the northbound train traveling in excess of 200 km/hr was exiting a tunnel just south of Nagaoka. The bullet train took more than 1.5 km to stop; fortunately, no injuries resulted from the derailment. The Joetsu Shinkansen line, which carries 360,000 passengers per day, was out of service until early 2005 [11]. The Tokyo Stock Market dropped considerably on the Monday following the earthquake, with Japan Rail East suffering large stock losses. This highlights the societal interdependence with the economic sector.

Table 2. Operational levels at 217 manufacturing plants.

Operational Level	0%	≤50%	≤70%	≤100%	100%
November 4, 2004	24 (11%)	19 (9%)	21 (10%)	48 (22%)	105 (48%)
November 15, 2004	2 (1%)	7 (3%)	15 (7%)	39 (18%)	154 (71%)
December 1, 2004	0 (0%)	4 (2%)	3 (1%)	17 (8%)	193 (89%)

The Niigata Sanyo Electronic Semiconductor plant with 1,500 workers was closed until December 22, 2004. The shutdown cost the parent company 50 billion yen in direct losses and 37 billion yen in indirect losses. The Nihon Seiki automobile parts plant was unable to resume its motorcycle speedometer assembly line, which caused Honda Motor Company to halt production at four plants elsewhere in Japan; Yamaha Motor Company was also affected [8]. Table 2 shows the changes in operational level (as a percentage of operations before the earthquake) for 217 manufacturing plants in the region at three different times after the earthquake.

3.2   2007 Chuetsu Offshore Earthquake

The Chuetsu offshore earthquake (magnitude 6.6) occurred at 10:13 a.m. local time on July 16, 2007 in the Niigata region. Eleven deaths and at least 1,000 injuries were reported; 342 buildings were completely destroyed, mostly older wooden structures [3].

The Kashiwazaki-Kariwa Nuclear Power Plant (KKNPP), the world's largest nuclear power generation facility, which is owned and operated by the Tokyo Electric Power Company (TEPCO), was affected by the earthquake. KKNPP produces power for approximately 30 percent of Japanese homes [2]. The earthquake started a small fire at the sprawling Kashiwazaki-Kariwa nuclear complex and caused 312 gallons of radioactive water from the plant to spill into the Sea of Japan. TEPCO did not announce the leak until nearly 12 hours after the earthquake struck. On July 18, TEPCO announced that the leak was actually 50% more radioactive than originally estimated [15]. The plant was closed for testing [16] and remained completely shut down for more than twenty months after the earthquake. The area, ordinarily with a strong tourism industry in the summer months, was hit hard by cancellations due to fears about the nuclear plant. This highlights the policy/procedural interdependence and the societal interdependence with the economic sector.

Two days after the earthquake, Toyota announced that it would stop production at all its factories for the rest of the week because of the damage to the Riken automobile parts plant in Kashiwazaki, Niigata. Nissan shut down two of its factories; Mitsubishi Motors and Fuji Heavy Industries also scaled back production [13].

3.3   1995 Tokyo Subway Gas Attack

At 8:15 a.m. on March 20, 1995, three Tokyo subway lines were simultaneously affected by the release of lethal Sarin gas by the Aum Shinrikyo cult. Twelve people died and 5,000 were injured, most of them with long-term health consequences. Post-attack police raids led to the discovery of several tons of chemicals, enough to kill more than four million people [18].

Japan has not faced any bioterrorism-related events since the Aum Shinrikyo attack. However, several willful attacks have been executed by individuals. One of the worst attacks occurred on June 8, 2008 [4]. Tomohiro Kato, 25, hit three people with a two-ton truck near Akihabara Station, Tokyo. He then jumped on top of one of the men he had hit with his vehicle and stabbed him several times. He proceeded to walk towards Akihabara Train Station slashing pedestrians at random, eventually killing seven people and injuring ten others. Because of Japan's densely-populated cities and crowded stations, bioterrorism or any other type of willful attack on the public can lead to a significant number of casualties.

3.4   2005 Tokyo Stock Exchange Failure

On November 1, 2005, a problem with newly-installed software designed to improve the Tokyo Stock Exchange's ability to deal with higher trading volumes shut down the exchange for almost an entire trading day. On December 8, 2005, a trader at Mizuho Securities issued an order to sell 610,000 shares of J-Com (a job recruiting company) at 1 yen a share. The intention was to sell one share at 610,000 yen (approx. $5,000). Mizuho Securities personnel discovered the error within 85 seconds of the order being placed and made four attempts to cancel it, but the attempts were rejected by the Tokyo Stock Exchange. Mizuho Securities finally managed to buy back most of the erroneous order.

Upon consulting with Fujitsu, the system vendor, the Tokyo Stock Exchange found that the system was unable to cancel sell orders while taking buy orders. Nor was the system programmed to accept cancellation orders on newly listed stocks. Investors purchased about 100,000 of the nonexistent shares, which resulted in a loss to Mizuho Securities of about $225 million to reimburse buyers and cancel the order [5, 14]. Cyber attacks and natural disasters are the primary concerns as far as critical infrastructures are concerned. However, human error, system flaws and improper procedures can also lead to disastrous effects.

3.5 Other Events

The following are some of the other key incidents recorded in Japan since 2002:

- Dam break (2002)

- Banking system integration malfunction (2002)

- Air traffic control system malfunction (2003, 2008)

- Nationwide ATM network malfunction (2004)

- IP telephony interruption (2004)

- Fire department emergency number outage (2004)

- Erroneous tests on hepatitis virus infected blood (2005)

- Securities trading system malfunction (2005, 2006, 2008)

- Airline check-in system malfunction (2007)

- Railway automatic ticket gate malfunction (2007)

- Newspaper printing system malfunction (2007)

- Railway routing control equipment malfunction (2008)

- Public telephone communications malfunction (2008)

3.6 Generating Potential Scenarios

Based on the incidents described above, we provide some scenarios that define the scope of our study. Note that it is important to distinguish between the terms "common failure" and "interdependency." In the case of a natural disaster (e.g., an earthquake), multiple critical infrastructures are affected due to a common failure. In contrast, an interdependency between critical infrastructures leads to a cascading failure due to the networked infrastructures. Scenarios of interest include:

- A strong earthquake affects a major national highway and restoration work requires several days.

- A power plant is destroyed by a severe typhoon resulting in insufficient power supply to an urban area.

- An attack at a Tokyo station disrupts railway service.

- A flood contaminates the water supply system and cleaning efforts require several days.

4.　Modeling Interdependencies

This section describes an interdependency modeling framework that combines the inoperability input-output model (IIM) for economic interdependencies and Bayesian networks for operational dependencies.

4.1　Inoperability Input-Output Model

Leontief received the 1973 Nobel Prize for Economics for developing his input-output model of the economy. Leontief's model facilitates the analysis of the interconnectedness between various sectors of an economy and the forecasting of the effects of a change in one economic sector on another. The inoperability input-output model (IIM) based on Leontief's seminal work was developed by Haimes and co-workers [1, 9]. The IIM formulation is given by:

$$q = A^*q + c^* = (I - A^*)^{-1}c^*.$$

The terms in the IIM equation are defined as follows:

- q is the inoperability vector expressed in terms of normalized economic loss. The elements of q represent the ratio of unrealized production (i.e., "business-as-usual" production minus degraded production) with respect to the "business-as-usual" production level of the industry sectors.

- A^* is the interdependency matrix that indicates the degree of coupling of the industry sectors. Each element indicates how much additional inoperability is contributed by the column industry to the row industry.

- c^* is a demand-side perturbation vector expressed in terms of the normalized degraded final demand (i.e., "business-as-usual" final demand minus actual final demand divided by the "business-as-usual" production level).

Interested readers are referred to [10] for details about the derivation of the model and the model components.

Table 3. Total requirements of Japan's ten CIs (2000) [12].

	Elec.	Gas	Water	Finance	Rail
Elec.	1.043578	0.025498	0.093584	0.0082	0.060693
Gas	0.000534	1.012813	0.001717	0.001005	0.001095
Water	0.001937	0.005211	1.105431	0.002248	0.006977
Finance	0.059927	0.029559	0.034154	1.099556	0.232122
Rail	0.002233	0.002142	0.00242	0.009354	1.003249
Logistics	0.012923	0.020586	0.011587	0.008528	0.006226
Air	0.000791	0.00063	0.000836	0.001372	0.000626
Comm.	0.012735	0.016381	0.018865	0.032934	0.017441
Gov.	0.00123	0.00131	0.001932	0.001498	0.000911
Medical	0.000007	0.000024	0.000054	0.000034	0.00003

	Logistics	Air	Comm.	Gov.	Med.
Elec.	0.011241	0.015587	0.015551	0.017824	0.02493
Gas	0.000808	0.001316	0.001071	0.001191	0.003883
Water	0.002976	0.003473	0.004135	0.004786	0.007713
Finance	0.038274	0.071628	0.046012	0.020523	0.037563
Rail	0.002407	0.002884	0.002962	0.006447	0.004207
Logistics	1.006349	0.007863	0.015381	0.010985	0.013164
Air	0.000505	1.005925	0.002804	0.001273	0.001525
Comm.	0.015884	0.021257	1.154597	0.021695	0.017611
Gov.	0.001205	0.002105	0.001109	1.00044	0.000994
Medical	0.000004	0.000006	0.000049	0.000014	1.0233

The foundation of IIM is the interdependency matrix A^* derived from the Leontief coefficients. IIM has been shown to be very effective for the *post facto* estimation of economic losses and for risk management decision making [1, 9]. The primary limitation of IIM with regard to critical infrastructure modeling is that economic dependencies rather than operational dependencies are employed. In addition, IIM, which is based on Leontief's economic model, requires a system to return to equilibrium. Since returning to the equilibrium state can take some time, IIM cannot deal with cascading latency and resilience that occur within short time periods. Moreover, most critical infrastructures are utility systems that have low economic values in input-output tables.

Table 3 presents the total requirements for the ten Japanese critical infrastructure sectors. For example, producing one unit of water (column) requires 0.093584 units of electricity (row). Note that each table value indicates the total (i.e., direct plus indirect) amounts of materials needed to produce a product (e.g., an indirect amount is the amount of material needed to produce the raw materials used to produce a product). An examination of the total requirement values reveals that the economic dependency and operational dependency are considerably different. For example, in previous operational dependency analy-

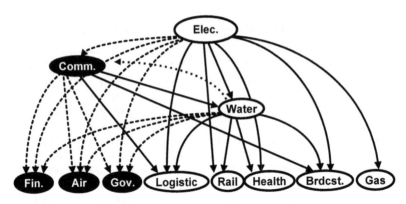

Figure 4. Dependency network for external perturbations of the electricity system.

ses conducted by the NISC Technical Committee, the financial sector was never a major contributor. However, from the economic point of view, the financial sector is clearly a major contributor to practically every critical infrastructure sector. Because of these limitations, we use a Bayesian network to model the operational dependencies existing between the ten critical infrastructure sectors and use the Bayesian network output as an external perturbation for IIM to estimate the total loss for all sectors.

4.2 Bayesian Networks

A Bayesian network is a probabilistic model that represents a set of variables and their probabilistic dependencies. The networks are quite effective and easy to maintain for a small number of nodes such as the ten critical infrastructure sectors.

Bayesian networks provide efficient representations of domain knowledge pertaining to dependencies, especially when combined with well-structured questionnaires and knowledge eliciting processes. The conditional probability values in these networks are flexible enough to express cascading latency and external interventions. However, the primary limitation of Bayesian networks is that they do not permit bilateral dependencies (e.g., the interdependency between the communications and water supply critical infrastructure sectors). Bayesian networks can express backward causal dependencies, but these are not useful for our purposes. To address the limitation, separate Bayesian networks are used for the major contributing critical infrastructure sectors. Additionally, certain adjustments have to be made in the case of interdependent systems.

Figure 4 shows the dependency network constructed from the results of the NISC Technical Committee's interdependency analysis described in Section 2.

Figure 5 shows how operational dependencies between critical infrastructures can be calculated before using IIM to estimate losses for all the critical infrastructure sectors.

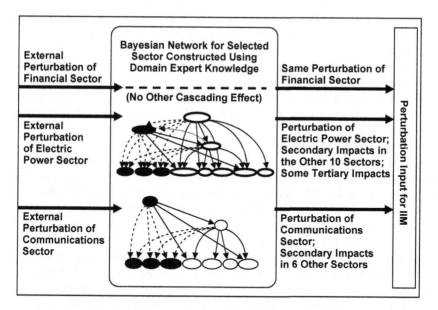

Figure 5. Calculating distributed operational impact before IIM.

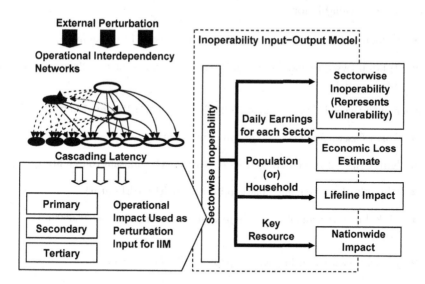

Figure 6. Modeling framework for interdependent CIs.

4.3 Modeling Framework

Figure 6 illustrates our framework for modeling critical infrastructure interdependencies. The first task is to conduct a survey to obtain information about the operational dependencies of critical infrastructure sectors and to construct Bayesian networks for three sectors – communications, electric power and water supply – that have major contributing roles. The survey questionnaires should focus on understanding the level of inoperability in each of the ten critical infrastructures caused by disruption/degradation of service in the sectors. Also, it is necessary to identify the sectors that are the major contributors to critical infrastructures with low independence (i.e., weak systems such as communication, finance, air transportation and government services). The resulting distributed impacts to the ten sectors can be used as external perturbation inputs for IIM.

National input-output tables for Japan are available from the Statistics Bureau of the Ministry of Internal Affairs and Communication [12]. The data are provided in three aggregated forms: sector tables (13 sectors); major consolidated sector tables (32 sectors); and intermediate consolidated sector tables (104 sectors). It is best to use the consolidated sector tables (104 sectors) in the interdependency and inoperability computations because they contain the information related to the ten sectors of interest.

An intra-regional coefficient matrix is used to express the inter-sector dependencies for the nine major regions in Japan. The Ministry of Economy, Trade and Industry has complied intra-regional, inter-sector input-output tables and inverse matrix coefficient tables for each of the nine regions (for the year 2000). The tables, which are provided at four levels of aggregation (12, 27, 52 and 75 sectors), are available for:

- Hokkaido (www.hkd.meti.go.jp/hoksr/h12renkan/12renkan.htm)

- Tohoku (www.tohoku.meti.go.jp/cyosa/tokei/io/io12nenn/12nenhyo_hombun. htm)

- Kanto (www.kanto.meti.go.jp/tokei/hokoku/20041214iohyo12.html)

- Tokai (www.chubu.meti.go.jp/tyosa/io7/io.htm)

- Kinki (www.kansai.meti.go.jp/1-7research/I-O/kinkisangyouren.html)

- Chugoku (www.chugoku.meti.go.jp/stat/io/h12io/h12.htm)

- Shikoku (www.shikoku.meti.go.jp/soshiki/skh_a4/4_toukei/060609io12/io12. html)

- Kyushu (www.kyushu.meti.go.jp/press/17_2/17_2_28.htm)

- Okinawa (www.pref.okinawa.jp/toukeika/io/2000/sanren_top.html)

The fundamental problem is to answer three questions given a set of external perturbations and cascading latency:

- What are the cascading inoperability and potential economic losses?

- Which critical infrastructures should be strengthened to yield optimal economic loss reduction or improvement in resilience?

- Which critical infrastructures will expose severe vulnerabilities in the event of unexpected inoperability escalation?

The combination of IIM and Bayesian networks facilitates the flexible incorporation of cascading latency and risk management intervention. The framework offers an interactive view of critical infrastructure interdependencies by providing the real-time inoperability of a critical infrastructure and a potential economic loss estimate for every adjustment (i.e., risk management decision).

4.4   Interpretation of Model Outputs

Most input-output models are used to estimate the economic losses of disasters. However, we believe that sectorwise inoperabilities can be used to obtain better assessments of disaster impact (Figure 6).

The inoperability values represent sectorwise vulnerabilities. They provide significant information about the most inoperable sectors to decision makers, which would otherwise be overlooked because of their insignificant contributions to economic impact.

The first metric is a sectorwise economic loss that can be generated from the inoperability values. This metric is widely used to assess disaster impact. It is estimated by computing the regional daily production income for each sector [1] by dividing the regional GDP of the sector by 365 (days):

$$Loss(s_i) = q_i \times (Regional\ GDP_i/365).$$

Note that $Loss(s_i)$ is the economic loss in the ith sector, q_i is the inoperability of the ith sector, and $Regional\ GDP_i$ is the regional GDP of the ith sector.

The sum of the individual sector losses yields the daily economic loss estimate for a disaster. Multidimensional metrics used to describe disaster impact can enhance risk management decision making. In complex scenarios, such as earthquakes and cyber failures, no single metric adequately measures the impact. Describing only the economic loss due to an earthquake does not reflect the stressed situation because the economic measure does not capture suffering and despair.

Therefore, a useful second metric is an "affected population" value based on the inoperability matrix. This is computed by multiplying the population of the area impacted by the disaster with the maximum value of the inoperabilities of the lifeline support critical infrastructures:

$$P_{AFF} = P_{Area} \times Max(q_0, q_1, ...q_{ci})$$

where P_{Area} is the population of the area impacted by the disaster and q_{ci} is the inoperability of the ith lifeline support critical infrastructure. The result can be presented as radar chart (Figure 7) to assist in decision making.

The third metric is the impact of a disaster on national key resources such as the Shinkansen (bullet train) network, major highways, power plants, manufacturing plants, etc. A higher concentration of these key resources in a disaster-affected region can have a significant impact on the national economy. The

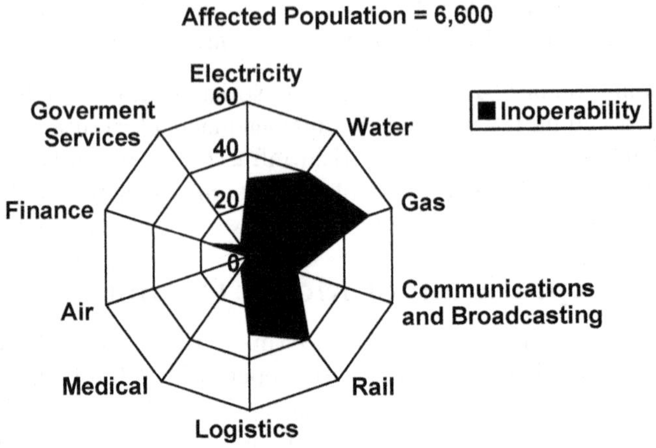

Affected Population = 6,600

Figure 7. Lifeline disruption indicator.

national key resources should be well-documented and should have a uniform weighting system to yield useful impact assessments. The multiplication of a national key resource concentration index with the inoperability of the corresponding perturbed infrastructure can provide a useful estimate of the nationwide impact.

5. Conclusions

The modeling and analysis of critical infrastructure interdependencies are important research problems. The proposed framework combining IIM and Bayesian networks facilitates the incorporation of cascading latency and risk management intervention. The framework offers an interactive view of critical infrastructure interdependencies by providing the real-time inoperability of critical infrastructures and potential economic loss estimates for adjustments made as a result of risk management decisions. Our future research will conduct detailed analyses of the application of the framework to managing risk in Japan's critical infrastructure sectors. Also, it will focus on rigorous data analysis and model adjustment strategies.

References

[1] C. Anderson, J. Santos and Y. Haimes, A risk-based input-output methodology for measuring the effects of the August 2003 Northeast Blackout, *Economic Systems Research*, vol. 19(2), pp. 183–204, 2007.

[2] Global Risk Miyamoto, 2007 Niigata Chuetsu-Oki Japan Earthquake, Reconnaissance Report, Sacramento, California (www.miyamotointernat ional.com/documents/Niigata-Chuetsu-Oki-Japan-Report.pdf), 2007.

[3] Japan News Review, Niigata earthquake death toll rises to eleven, July 23, 2007.

[4] Kyodo News, 7 killed 10 injured in Akihabara stabbing spree, *The Japan Times*, June 8, 2008.

[5] Mainichi Daily News, Tokyo Stock Exchange admits system glitch contributed to US$225 million stock glitch, December 12, 2005.

[6] W. McGill and B. Ayyub, The meaning of vulnerability in the context of critical infrastructure protection, in *Critical Infrastructure Protection: Elements of Risk*, Critical Infrastructure Protection Program, School of Law, George Mason University, Arlington, Virginia, pp. 25–48, 2007.

[7] National Information Security Center, 2007 Outputs of Interdependency Analysis, Document 5, Tokyo, Japan (www.nisc.go.jp/conference /seisaku/ciip/dai16/pdf/16siryou07.pdf), 2008.

[8] R. Olshansky, I. Nakabayashi and K. Ohnishi, Socioeconomic policy and planning aspects of the 2004 Niigata Ken Chuetsu Earthquake, *Earthquake Spectra*, vol. 22(S1), pp. S163–S175, 2006.

[9] J. Santos, Inoperability input-output modeling of disruptions to interdependent economic systems, *System Engineering*, vol. 9(1), pp. 20–34, 2006.

[10] J. Santos and Y. Haimes, Modeling the demand reduction input-output inoperability due to terrorism of interconnected infrastructures, *Risk Analysis*, vol. 24(6), 1437–1451, 2004.

[11] C. Scawthorn and E. Rathje, 2004 Niigata Ken Chuetsu, Japan, Earthquake Reconnaissance Report, Earthquake Engineering Research Institute, Oakland, California, 2006.

[12] Statistics Bureau, 2000 Input-Output Tables for Japan, Ministry of Internal Affairs and Communication, Tokyo, Japan (www.stat.go.jp/english /data/io/io00.htm), 2004.

[13] USA Today, Earthquake puts brakes on auto production in Japan, July 18, 2007.

[14] B. Wallace, Stock fiasco damages exchange's reputation, *Los Angeles Times*, December 13, 2005.

[15] P. Wiseman and K. Takahashi, Japan's nuke spill bigger than first reported, *USA Today*, July 17, 2007.

[16] Xinhuanet, IAEA to re-examine Japanese nuclear power plant, November 4, 2008.

[17] S. Yamaguchi, Current status on CIIP research in Japan, Nara Institute of Science and Technology, Ikoma City, Japan (www.doi.ics.keio.ac .jp/CIIP05/26/01-Yamaguchi.pdf), 2005.

[18] A. Zalman, Aum Shinrikyo Tokyo subway gas attack, About.com, New York (terrorism.about.com/od/originshistory/a/AumShinrikyo.htm).